INDIA
PASSPORT TO LOVE

DELIA LUCIA L. PANISSENI

ATLANTIC PUBLISHERS AND DISTRIBUTORS

Published by
ATLANTIC PUBLISHERS AND DISTRIBUTORS
B-2, Vishal Enclave, Opp. Rajouri Garden, New Delhi-27
Phones : 5413460, 5429987

Sales Office
4215/1, Ansari Road, Darya Ganj,
New Delhi-110 002
Phones : 3273880, 3285873, 3280451
Fax : 91-11-3285873
e-mail : gupta.atlantc@axcess.net.in

ISBN 81-7156-836-X

Typeset at
APD Computer Graphics, Delhi

Printed in India at
Mehra Offset Press, Delhi

DEDICATIONS

To Mr. Ricardo Enrique Panisseni, my dear husband, for the solid rock of the wholehearted love he offers me every day, where I can moor my illusions and fly from there in search of dreams.

To my wonderful friends Sajad, Ramachandra, Asif, Tanveer, Sompal, Bangladesh, Krishnamurthi, Vyjendhar, Sukbhir, and many many others, who sweetened my stay in India with the gift of their love.

THANKS TO

Mrs. Laura Castellano de Taborro, Coordinator of the "Dulce Palabra" Writing Workshop, who corrected my Spanish Version of "India, Passport to Love", and guided me with affectionate patience in the wonderful task of "Hunting the word".

Mrs. Diana Clifford (Nessie), who corrected the English Version of the book with professional interest, dedication and love. Thanks for her attention and good will.

Dr. Domar Singh Madariya, of the Ayurvedic Medical Centre of Buenos Aires. For the patient reading of my manuscript and the affection with which he pointed out some mistakes, task I had asked him because of his Hindu Birth, and the great confidence he deserves as professional and Human Being.

Mr. Majid Padar, Cultural Attachi of the India Embassy in Argentina. Also for the patience and great care in reading my manuscript, and indicating me some concepts which differed from his point of view and knowledge, of what I considered.

S.E. the Ambassador of India in Argentina, Mr. Nigam Prakash, who deigned to honour with his valued presence, the presentation of the book in my city. For his kindness, humility and love, as the worthy representative of the beloved Hindu People.

भारत का राजदूतावास
कोर्दोबा 950. बुएनोस आइरेस

EMBASSY OF INDIA
CORDOBA 950, BUENOS AIRES

सत्यमेव जयते

NO.BUE/313/1/96

April 16, 1996

Dear Mrs. Panisseni:

I'm writing to answer your letter of February 21st., requesting my opinion in relation of the manuscript of your book about India. First of all, I want you to know that I have read your manuscript with great interest. I found it trapping more than interesting. Let me congratulate you on your vivid and intimate style.

The report of your personal experiences is exceedingly honest. In spite of it, pages 11, 25, 39, 47, 55 and 61 of your manuscript attracted my attention. I send you my explanations next.

Let me repeat that the report of your personal experiences in the first person, gathers for people foreign to India's Culture, its true spirit and genius in a lucid and diaphanous style. I hope you can publish it as soon as possible.

With my warmest regards,

A. Majid Padar
Agregado Cultural

Señora Delia Lucía Lambertucci Panisseni
9 de Julio 281
(2580) Marcos Juarez
Pcia. de Córdoba

Telefax: 0472-25450

PROLOGUE

My purposes to write this book are, on the one hand, to share my experiences during a journey to India, and on the other, to clarify my own feelings, many of which arose precisely as a result of what I lived there.

The well-known thought that expresses : "Climb every mountain, cross every stream, follow the rainbow till you reach your dreams", perfectly translates the states of the soul with which I made this trip. There, people frequently asked me its exact goals, and I answered :

"I came following the rainbow". But, as everybody knows, this is an Utopia, since the rainbow has neither beginning nor end, perhaps like my dreams.

I am convinced that everything in life is a gift of God : the tree that lovingly gives its fruits or the fragrance of the flowers that open with the dew, a friendly hand on the shoulder just when we need it, the sweet singing of birds, or that other celestial music that many times and without knowing precisely the reason, springs up from the deepest of our heart. I could write a complete book just enumerating His Gifts, which may begin at the very moment I received the first blow of life.

I consider myself a really very fortunate person, whom God touches with His Hand at every moment; what's more, I feel I am a chosen person able to discover these Gifts, from the piece of bread that I take to my mouth every day, to the powerful "Friend of All", the Great Father Sun, who enlightens and fills me with energy.

Of course, the journey to India was another magnificent

gift, much more important : as if I received his caress, but not only in the body, but also in the soul; many times during this journey I felt Him so close, that I could talk with Him intimately.

If I should say in few words what was that I found in India, I would simply affirm, without hesitation, that there, I discovered God again : I saw Him specially in the one who suffers, and what's more, in the one who has the inner strength to be happy in spite of his miseries.

India is a very very broad country, almost a continent, and many times human relations can be terribly violent, specially in big cities, as well as gentle, peaceful and tolerant.

It is such a many-sided country, from its millenary philosophy to its natural and human scenery; we can expect to find not only "The One Thousand and One Nights" palaces, spiritual masters of great wisdom and holiness, or sullen hermits lost in The Himalayan caves; we can also find all the faults that accompany misery, overpopulation, hunger and religious intolerance.

If I had the gift of being able to share at least something of the much I received in this journey; if only one person reading my tales, feels in his breast the emotion I wrote them with, I believe that my aim to make my experiences known, would be largely fulfilled.

Here I introduce you, from my heart and my purest feelings, to this wonderful and fascinating country, just as I have felt it, with a total transparency, sometimes, maybe, with a lot of ingenuousness and innocence. I hope you know and share my dreams and my ideals, which are simply those of somebody who firmly believes that all Human Beings, no matter the color, race or creed, are an only and large Family.

I leave this story to your consideration, wishing that while reading it, you would remember the Little Prince's words, when he says that "the essential is not seen with the eyes", but with the heart...

DELIA L.L. PANISSENI

CONTENTS

1

CIRCUMSTANCES BEFORE THE JOURNEY

1. Bye, Elvoira...

Doctors always use the same words to announce the most terrible things :

"Sorry, we did everything possible", and behind that simple phrase of courtesy, the dead body of my mother lay.

Just a moment before, she had reluctantly eaten from my hand, while she sweetly kissed it again and again.

Can everything end this way, so simply? When doctors went away and left me alone, I couldn't believe it, and some recriminations came to my mind : "How can you die in this way! Why do you have to die like that?", I repeated to her, sobbing, time after time. "My poor Mum, always so full of life and enthusiasm, and in a few days, you faded forever; you just surrendered".

I remember that, just like a sleepwalker, I dressed her, with the help of a very understanding nurse : we dressed her in her best garment : a printed silk one she liked a lot and wore only on important occasions. We washed and combed her, while a friend of mine who was accompanying me, set off to look for my husband.

Later, we had to take her from the morgue, because the undertaking company had to arrange for the vigil, while only foolish thoughts came to my mind :

"How funny she looks, with her nice dress hanging down from her rigid body".

What followed was like an endless nightmare : she looked beautiful inside the coffin : the lines of her face became more delicate and there was a joyous sweetness in her countenance, still rose-colored.

I saw the surrounding scene like a hallucination : the room with its images, the perfume of the flowers mixed with room deodorizer, the condolences, the arrival of my elder sister, relatives, friends, neighbours; who had not received her favours sometime? : a hand for the hardest tasks, the curative herbs and vegetables from her garden, some eggs from her little hens, whom she mostly called by nicknames :

"Black, Red, Chupina, Crooked, Bald," etc....

"Chau, Elvoira", my heart told her in silence. That was the name we found funny to call her, instead of Elvira, which was her real one. How sad it was to leave her alone, there, in the cemetery, close to my father, who had preceded her more than 20 years before, and whom I'm still missing as much as the first day. I am sure that Pepoiro (instead of Pepe) would be waiting for her in that timeless Eternity, to accompany her to the Heavenly Realms.

Later, the coming back home : My God, what a desolation, how sad I felt! Memories mixed with recriminations : "What a little time I dedicated to her, poor Mum, and she had never reproached me".

I believe that not even my sister shared my feelings : she had been living abroad for so long; what could she know about the agony and despair of those last days?

How fragile we human beings are to face the death of a beloved, and go on living just like that; to fulfil the work and all the obligations we have taken in life, although we feel the pain lacerating as if the heart would break.

2. Get up Again !

...But life doesn't stop. Days and weeks went on sliding quietly; I had never thought that at scarcely four months I should face another trial : a noon, after walking the few blocks that separated the Secondary School where I gave my classes, I arrived home and found my husband lying on the floor, hemiplegic, as a consequence of what, as I knew later, had been an apoplexy or brain effusion.

Once again the siren of the ambulance drilling my ears; the Hospital where he was taken, with its routine of doctors and nurses. The nights in which I felt exhausted and got heavily asleep, stunned out of so much fatigue and fears that I refused to face, to wake up later and realize the terrible reality.

Thanks God, my faith was unbreakable : I was sure he would get ahead; but even better than my faith was his, because he was sure too. Anyway, at the beginning it was very hard; the right half of his body didn't answer to any stimulus. As days went on, only the legs acquired, or rather, recovered, a little motion; the fingers resisted, not a single millimetre, nothing at all!

Those were endless days, and nights of true anguish, in which, to make things worse, he couldn't sleep, perhaps as a result of the drugs he received just in case of a new attack. Facing such despair, all prayers that seemed forgotten came back with power, the desperate supplications to the Great Healer...

Then home again, and the real beginning of the recovery. Luckily, the physio-therapist combined her great professional ability with an extraordinary dosage of patience, sweetness and loving understanding. As a Yoga Master, I helped and supported her excellent work. Thus, we started the rehabilitation : slowly, very slowly he began to reveal some little movement, very small, which we celebrated joyfully.

My heart begged innerly to him :

> "Don't lay down your arms, fight, fight, work restlessly. Don't lose heart, and if you fall, get up again, time after time. This is Man's destiny, always ahead, always starting again, always trying again, up to the infinite..."

When we could stand him up and he gave the first little step, yet with the help of an apparatus, we both knew that the battle began to be won, thus, millimetre by millimetre. But, what an effort, my God : luckily, You were always by our side, and when we thought we didn't have any strength left, You surely raised us on your shoulders to lighten the burden!

The recovery was a real *miracle,* but a miracle of faith and work, never laying down the arms, with shouts and quarrels many times, when it was necessary.

Day after day, week after week, very slowly, fighting with every muscle that refused to answer. In a slack way, terribly little by little, the lost motion was coming back. Staggering at the beginning, and stronger each day, abilities were coming back, the physiology improved almost to normality, and in a gradual way, he was going back to work.

In such circumstances, after enduring with faith and patience a dramatic year, signed by death and despair, when it was the last thing I expected, and it was so far from my plans as travelling to the moon, I received my dear friend Giovanna's invitation to visit India!

3. Giovanna, Sister of Adventures

I had met Giovanna or Gio, as her friends call her, some years ago, at a Yoga Congress in Buenos Aires. We both attended the same seminars and travelled in the same urban bus, in which she went back from the Congress to her place downtown. Together with a friend from my city, we returned to our hotel, which was close to her flat. Smiling widely, she went towards us, sat next to me, and, I don't remember the reason, but our first casual conversation was about India, a country she had visited some years before, and the place I had always dreamt of knowing.

When we separated, we had already exchanged names, addresses and telephone numbers to share some notes about Yoga, as she, the same as me, was a teacher of this ancient science.

In this way our friendship grew when we met, every time I travelled to the Capital from my city in the interior of the country. Later, Giovanna invited me to stay at her place, because she had moved to a larger flat. During the most recent years, we met quite frequently, every time I travelled to Buenos Aires in order to take my improvement Yoga Courses.

Always, in such opportunities, before going to bed, I took a look again and again at her pictures, taken in her first visit to

India, and we talked about the possibility of making the next trip together, even though we considered it as something very remote.

In her album of India, my friend used to write some short sentences on each picture, specially referred to the feelings and emotions that certain persons and places inspired to her. I read things like "the closest to Paradise" and other thoughts of this sort. I concluded for myself that, maybe, she exaggerated a little, but after our journey I did the same with mine. Who scans my photos, perhaps will arrive at the same conclusion, though now I can assure that she didn't exaggerate at all.

Giovanna was born in Switzerland, and even though she has been living in Argentina for about 40 years, she hasn't lost (and I don't believe she will) her foreign accent yet, which, to be fair, suits her perfectly. I imagine that, in fact, she doesn't want to lose it; it's as a snobbish way.

Going back to the unusual invitation to make this journey to India, it took me by surprise; in those circumstances I was far away from any plan of this kind, and answered that unluckily, this time it would not be possible, as my husband wasn't completely recovered.

She then suggested to take his photograph to Baghavan Sri Satya Sai Baba, from Puttaparthi, and put his health in His blessed hands in order to produce the miracle of his complete recovery.

As I didn't know much about this *Avatar*, I found her suggestion a little childish, and so, everything remained suspended, and it was assumed by anticipation my impossibility to accept her unexpected invitation.

Afterwards, I told my husband about this conversation, and he asked why I wouldn't go if he was feeling well, and, besides, that journey had always been my dream, specially with my friend Giovanna. Later, I knew that, actually, he was just cheering me up outwardly.

I desperately needed something more than rewarding in my life, to charge again my exhausted batteries and to be able to take out from myself the whole burden of death and illness : to tell the truth, the brain accident wasn't only his, I suffered it too, so it is easy to understand that I did not need much pushing to take my decision.

The next day and still not believing the direction the events had taken, I phoned my friend to let her know my determination of travelling to India with her. I think she was also surprised; maybe her decision wasn't completely taken and if I hadn't made up my mind she wouldn't have set off either.

4. Getting Ready Under Stress

As soon as my obligations allowed me, I travelled to Buenos Aires to arrange the passport, to get the flight tickets and pay for them in the Travel Agency; get the vaccination[1] against the yellow fever, which was required by the Indian Government to South American travellers; in a word, to make all the previous steps for such a long journey.

Our first destination would be London, and from there, in another flight, to Bombay (India). From Argentina we contracted the Bombay-Bangalore flight, in the south, by Indian Airlines.

While the departure day was coming, the atmosphere at home was becoming tenser, with reproaches, tears and a misunderstanding and misleading environment, which were added to my logical fears before the uncertainty of what was approaching.

With this inner pulling, I travelled to Buenos Aires alone the day before the departure, and with everything in order and the consequent nerves, we boarded the plane in Ezeiza the following day. I felt so mentally upset, that I had lost all the enthusiasm for the trip, that had been my most cherished golden dream, and it took me several days to recover it.

It didn't help me the fact that just some minutes before boarding the plane, I could phone my husband, who was at home, and we couldn't avoid crying, one at each end of the line. Having so many things to say in that moment, it just came to my mind asking for Anibal, the little cat who had arrived home to stay there, only two days before. My husband answered that it had messed up the house inside, the dirty piggy!

Really, it seemed a tragicomedy : Me, ready to cross the broad world, and speaking only about the cat ! We, Human Beings, are this way, always trying to disguise or to hide our own feelings !

---

1. The Government of India doesn't require the Argentine Travellers the application of this vaccine to enter the country any more, except those who had visited yellow fever areas. (Embassy of India).

5. "Who are You, Aníbal ?"

Two or three days before travelling, a well known woman from my city, who is a seer and has medium powers, came home to ask about the possibility of going to India with us. I told her that even though I believed we were already on the date, I could give her the telephone number of the Travel Agency to find out if there was any possibility, specially if there was room in our flight or in another near ours; she already had her passport and the other documentation in order, so the only problem left was to get a seat on the plane.

We went on talking about the subject and then she, got down as if in trance, and after a short silence, began speaking very low and as to herself. She said that the journey would be excellent, the relation with my friend very good, and that in India, great emotions were waiting for us, which would made us laugh, and cry, but of happiness. She also announced that a Being from another dimension would accompany me in that land, to protect and take care of me with all his love.

After that, I interrupted her to ask if my husband would feel well; she said that he would be O.K., and would not even suffer a headache. Then she added that he also would be protected during my absence, by a very special Being named Aníbal.

That same night, or early morning, we were awaked by a cat crying outside, in front of the house, screaming loudly as if someone were cutting him up. When I went out to see what was happening, a very skinny little cat, only ears and tail, and of no more than 10 cmts. long, ran into my house. I just observed him : all black, with only the tip of the tail white.

He moved straight towards the mattress where my husband was lying down, got up to his chest, and as if it were his only goal in life, he began purring very strongly and kneading so consciously with his slender little legs, giving him all kinds of caresses

The seer's words still echoed in my ears, hence, I told my husband : "well, Aníbal has already arrived"; and this name remained for ever; really he has given my husband all his love and dedication, specially when he stayed alone, and continues that preference up to now!

6. My Baptism Flight and the "Vibhuti" Power

I had never got on a big plane, so this flight was my baptism of fire, since in the whole trip to London we, almost all the time, travelled with the safety belt fastened, due to the great turbulence that was continually shaking the machine.

In London, I made my debut of speaking English, since even though I had taught this tongue at school, I had never had the opportunity to practice it with English people. What an emotion to check that everybody understood me!

Our arrival at London was in the morning, and in the evening of that day, we would board the plane again, heading Bombay. As if we were very experienced passengers, we took the underground train in the same airport, and made our way towards Piccadilly Circus. There we went window shopping, looked over some stores and had something to eat over there.

As soon as we had arrived that morning, I called my friend Angela, whose parents are neighbours of my house in Argentina, and had sent her some messages through me. At that time she was living in the English Capital; our relation dated from some years before, since she had been one of my dearest students at Secondary School. We made an appointment downtown, in the afternoon, and we three went to a typical London Pub, to have a beer and a chat.

Soon, in this first step of the trip, I had to face some of my old and stupid fears, as climbing up escalators, which even though it may seem very childish, it always causes a strong apprehension to me. In London, in the same airport as well as at the subway stations, they were very long and exceedingly steep. I learned in my own flesh that it was not easy to put into practice the suggestion I always give others : "Fears are only overcome by facing them up!"

In time to have the new documents checked, we were back at the airport, from where we set off to downtown in the morning, and boarded the plane.

In this second stage, Western passengers became scarce, and we could closely watch the delicate features of Indian women, gracefully wearing their traditional *sarees* of rich silk and beautiful coloring. Also smart Eastern gentlemen, some of them dressed with well cut Western suits and big turbans, and others with their typical clothing, but everyone with a respectful polite attitude towards us.

The tensed moments lived the last days at home, the inexperience, the fatigue, the fears, all the repressed emotions, made me feel really very sick as soon as the plane took off.

In her handbag, my companion had some little envelopes of *vibhuti*, the sacred ash that Sai Baba materializes, still from her previous visit. She offered it to me, teaching me how to use it : the finger must be moistened with the tongue, and put then on the powder in order to stick it; later take it to the mouth, forehead and heart (moistening it again every time it was necessary), to symbolize the physical, mental and spiritual bodies respectively, to produce the healing at the three levels.

With all my faith in what I was doing and after relaxing completely, I took a receptive attitude and followed the instructions. As it was expected, the miracle happened. When I became aware of my physical body again, I felt absolutely well and so, I could enjoy the splendid vegetarian dinner (it was our choice) that we were given some moments later.

7. Bombay : My "Collision" with India

The next morning, we landed at Bombay, after advancing our watches on the basis of the official Indian time, such as the day before we had done in London. In short, we advanced 8 hours and a half.

The International Bombay Airport caused me a very bad impression : ugly, dirty, old and deteriorated. The heat was frightening and an endless queue of people were waiting for their documents and luggage to be checked, task that seemed to me, it was done reluctantly.

Appealing to all our patience we also submitted to be checked : we thought that we had enough time to rest, since not until 6 P.M. the new flight by Indian Airlines would set off; we had contracted it from Argentina, southwards to Bangalore, our first destination.

When, after numberless formalities, to change our dollars into rupees and again get our luggage back, we went outside. Then, I became aware of being in another world; immediately, a lot of ragged begging children surrounded us for some alms. When Giovanna gave them a candy bag to share, a huge fuss with punches, shouts and runs started.

From everywhere broached us taxi drivers and hotel attendants, every one wanting to take us their ways. We didn't have anything reserved, and even though my friend had written down a hotel name that somebody had suggested to her, its price was too expensive for our budget. At last, we came to an agreement with the driver of a hotel that seemed to have a fair tariff and besides, it had air conditioning in the room. After confirming the reservation by a phone call, we set off towards what we imagined would provide us a rewarding rest and the possibility to take a good bath.

We crossed the whole city through the suburbs, while watching the poor neighborhoods with their "shanty towns", as we call them here. There, in Bombay, they seemed a kind of aborigine camps, mostly made with rags, and in all the journey the landscape was equally terrifying.

We found out that, in those days, Bombay was a boiler, since several bombs had exploded in different places, because of the endless fights between Hindus and Muslims. During all the way, the driver warned us that, if somebody intercepted our route, we should not say we were Christians!

At last we arrived at the hotel, which resulted not much better than the poor buildings we had watched along our way. After registering, paying for the lodging and leaving our passports, we were taken to our room, which luckily was very clean and with a good bed.

Some Indians accompanied us to bring our bags up, and once inside the bedroom they looked at everything with great curiosity, and asked about our personal information, making us feel uncomfortable and frightened. I think that now I wouldn't react in the same way, because I recognize that their curiosity is respectful, but at that moment and having just arrived, I didn't know the way they behave with foreigners.

I wonder where I brought the courage from to ask them to leave from our room, since we wanted to rest, and without repeating, immediately they, after apologizing, left the room. O.K., I sighed in relief.

In fact, the room had the air conditioning equipment; I supposed it was the only one in the hotel that had this "luxury" : a big set with a round front part, a very old fashioned model indeed, and it worked just as a fan!

My friend and I didn't feel very safe in that place, even so when looking outwards through the window and watching all the grubby huts that surrounded us. Yet I believed that poverty was a synonym of danger!

8. The Problems Begin...and the Solutions

We could hardly rest a while staying at the Bombay Hotel. We had a bath and, very eagerly, at 4 o'clock in the afternoon, asked to be taken to the local airport (Domestic) for our flight to Bangalore. Happily we arrived there without problems, but here the first obstacle arose : all flights were suspended for an undetermined time, as a consequence of a personnel strike.

What to do? On the one hand, we didn't want to go back to that hotel, and on the other, our luggage was so bulky that it wasn't easy to move around. Luckily, the hotel driver was still there in a *Rickshaw*. Thanks God! Since he was of great help to us.

All the counters (for booking tickets) from the different airlines were crowded, with people who, just like us, wanted to travel and found this strike. Fortunately, the clerk of one of them took pity on me, and in a piece of paper, she wrote down the name of the only airway that flew to Bangalore and whose staff didn't support the measure. It was the East-West, but we discovered it worked in another airport. There we set off, always carried by the hotel rickshaw and, once there, while my friend looked after the luggage, I tried to speak to the manager.

There, the crowd was also hellish, the heat, the humidity, the uproar, the smells...At last I was attended and listened with kindness, for later hearing :

— There isn't even a single place in the six o'clock flight, but if you manage to endorse the ticket to our name, maybe, I can do something for you.

We set off again from the Domestic Airport in a race against the clock. With my humblest smile I got the endorsement, leaving once more to the other airport, to show the endorsed ticket. A clerk told us to stay there, together with the crowd that were also waiting; we did this way, with few hopes to depart really.

9. To Enjoy the Flight and the Journey Companions

After some minutes in the airport, waiting by the East West counters, which seemed centuries to us, the manager who so kindly had attended me a short time before, appeared smiling. He looked at the large number of people gathered there and stopped his eyes on mine. My breathing paralyzed when he pointed me with his forefinger, saying :

— You can.

"Holy merciful God", my heart sighed. "Thank you".

We completed the formalities, dispatched our luggage and with just half an hour of delay, finally departed to Bangalore.

Later, we remembered that, with such a haste, we had forgotten the poor hotel attendant, who was waiting outside (they aren't allowed inside the airports) just in case we needed him, and although he surely can't get to know, from here I apologize.

In this flight, westerners were very few, they could be counted with the fingers of a single hand. Not long after being in the air, it got dark. I had the seat by the window, and once calmed down of so many problems, I could enjoy my privileged place a lot.

Looking through the window, the Indian cities we flew over looked like a kaleidoscope. Their lights drew extravagant forms, as the blocks aren't square as ours, and the roads follow capricious lines, shaping circles, spirals, ovals, triangles, and every figure one can imagine.

My companion was sitting in the middle, while at the corridor side there was a smart young Hindu man, dressed in an impeccable grey suit, shirt, tie and with neatly cut hair, who politely tried to start a conversation with us. His white smile lighted up the dark and noble countenance of regular features.

For his appearance, I imagined he would be a prosperous merchant, on a business trip, or a professional; his English was quite good, not as Giovanna's, so at every moment they asked me to help as a translator.

The young man declared he was living near White Field, a village next to Bangalore, with his wife and two kids. Here, we began to know the Hindu hospitality, as he gave us his address and insisted on the honour it would be for him, to invite us to his home for lunch or dinner.

Among the varied subjects we dealt with, Giovanna told him how worried she had been about the disappearance of a couple of friends of hers, which had happened in that area of India in a flight accident, some years before. The Hindu remarked that the accident took place near the airport and his residence; and he had approached the place and could be present immediately after the disaster, where no survivors remained. The Spanish saying that the world is as small as a hanky had sense again, and this coincidence revealed once again that casualism doesn't exist, just causality !

When we arrived at Bangalore, we said good-bye to our polite new friend, who recommended us not to forget his invitation.

During the landing, we watched that all the maneuvers were guided from earth by few persons moving some little lanterns with their hands, and we could not avoid the comment :

— Super technology finished !

We went down rather far from the main building and walked towards it to pick up our luggage from the transport band. When we came outside, it was full night.

10. The Price of Inexperience

Outside Bangalore Airport and while we were looking for a taxi, somebody called my friend by her name. I imagined that he could have listened to me calling her, or, maybe, he had read her name written on the bags. His explanation was that he knew her from the former journey, and, of course, Gio couldn't avoid showing satisfaction that somebody remembered her; thus was as we met Muñhir, a chatter box, trickster and liar, the worst of all the people we dealt with in India.

With Giovanna's complacency, he took possession of our

whole plans, and even though we had written down the name of a hotel in that city, Muñhir said that it was full and insisted to take us to another one he knew, which, according to his version, was much better and besides, cheaper. We went there, but there wasn't room either. Then, our driver called an Argentine woman, who was lodged there and seemed to be his friend. After being introduced to us and the corresponding greetings took place, she invited us to share her room, which was quite spacious for herself.

The hotel attendant put two mattresses on the ground for us, and we talked till the early morning. She told us all the details and incidents that had finally brought her to that place.

The following day, she and Muñhir accompanied us to buy some Eastern clothes, in order to be more comfortable and not to feel "out of place". We acquired some metres of cloth and sarees; afterwards we took them to a tailor, who, what a coincidence !, was Muñhir's friend, to sew the garments. The following day, the clothes were all ready.

As the prices were lower than in our country, and the goods of very good quality, we didn't catch on that both, Muñhir and the Argentine "lady", were swindling us, taking advantage of our ignorance and charging everything three times, at least, its real value. Here we really paid for our inexperience.

11. Our "Oriental Look"

Muñhir, our driver, with his Argentine friend, harassed us constantly. They organized a visit of the four to White Field, about 25 kms. from Bangalore, since Sai Baba was in that little village those days, giving his *darshans* in an attractive small *ashram* : Unfortunately, we arrived there late and couldn't see him.

For this visit, both Giovanna and I had wrapped our new sarees up, according to Muñhir's instructions : first, we tied up the long piece of cloth at a side; secondly, we had to make seven folds, placing one on the other, at the front of the body; then, we turned it to the back and gathered the last piece on one shoulder. We both believed we proudly showed our "Eastern Look", even though the two fair haired, white and I, besides, blue eyed, I supposed we didn't deceive anybody.

On this first step of the journey by land, I began familiarizing with the tropical scenery, specially with the great quantity of monkeys, which wandered freely alongside the road and everywhere. I watched a lot of Indian women, with their colourful sarees, working in the quarries, breaking big blocks of stone with primitive tools. I could have enjoyed much more of the landscape and the meeting with the millenary India, but the truth is that I couldn't hide my annoyance with these persons who monopolized us completely; I'd have preferred to manage by ourselves, but Giovanna seemed so pleased with the situation...

At last, two days later we set off (the four of us !) to Puttaparthi, since we found out Sai Baba had already come back to his main ashram, Prashanti Nilayam, that means "The dwelling of Eternal Peace".

Following Muñhir's advice, more or less at halfway we turned a little aside, to visit Nandi, a hilly village, where an ancient Shiva Temple is located, one of the Gods of the Hindu Trinity, constituted by Brahma as the Creator, Vishnu as the Preserver and Shiva as the Destroyer of the Universe (to recreate). Here and to visit this old temple, we took off our shoes as the custom is. Later, we walked around and took some photographs from the top of the mountain where it is built.

According to popular tales, just from this summit Tippu Sultan threw down from the cornice the slaves who, for any reason, fell in misfortune, and the name of the place is precisely Tippu's drop (I took advantage to take a photo pushing Giovanna to the abyss).

We went on with our journey, after a stop to eat something by the road, and with the burning heat of a tropical midday, we made, at last, our way towards Puttaparthi. I was eager to arrive there, and grew impatient to be inside the ashram. I was sure that once there, I would really begin enjoying our journey.

*

2

OUR DESTINATION : PRASHANTI NILAYAM

12. At last, Puttaparthi !

About two o'clock in the afternoon and with a temperature that converted our bodies in live coal, we arrived at Puttaparthi, town born round Sai Baba Ashram, and whose name means "place of the termites", for the great quantity of these insects found there.

I wanted to lodge inside Prashanti Nilayam Ashram, to be as close as possible to this *Avatar* or Divine Sent, whose single presence summons thousands of persons approached from the most distant and remote corners of the globe.

I had already said how annoyed I felt for the endless chatter of Muñhir, our first "chauffeur", who drove us from Bangalore and didn't allow us to be just a moment alone since we had come, and organized all our tours with Giovanna's complacency, who accepted his suggestions completely. My *intuition* pointed out to me that he was a chatterbox and liar; I distrusted the sincerity of his intentions. Later, it was proved that I wasn't wrong, since he took advantage in everything he could.

Once inside the ashram and like all visitors do, we registered in the corresponding office (Registration) : we left our passports and received a card with the personal information, and the place assigned for lodging. With the heavy luggage we came in our taxi close to the place, always with Muñhir at the wheel.

Attended by the "Sevas" (God's Servants), the persons who

keep the ashram in order, we entered the so called “Sheds”, a sort of community cabin or shelter, where hundreds of people, with their mats on the naked floor, one beside the other, tried to isolate themselves the best possible, with what they had at hand : large towels, sarees, shawls or anything else to create a little intimacy. We weren’t even placed on two next seats, and for a moment, I felt lost without Gio. Trying to hide my disappointment and annoyance the best I could, I looked for her. Such a long journey just for this! I wondered.

When finally; I found my friend, I saw her weeping in despair, with several “sevas” around who tried to calm her down. My disagreement was in increase; I would say that I was almost losing my temper :

— I won’t stay here; I take the first flight back and I won’t stop until I get home — I said in a bad mood.

Together with Giovanna, who didn’t cease weeping, we went outside where we had left our taxi, and there was Muñhir, who luckily hadn’t abandoned us.

— Don’t cry, ladies, don’t cry, — he encouraged us. — If you don’t like this place, I’ll take you to a little hotel that is only some steps from the ashram, and you can come whenever you want.

We answered back :

— No, we don’t want to lodge at a hotel...We came to live here, and besides we can’t begin spending our money on hotels when we have just arrived. We came to stay here, — we obstinately repeated.

— Well, Muñhir calmed us down, and from then on, we forgot how rascal he had been. — When the room disinfection inside the ashram is over, you are going to have a place inside it, and don’t worry about the money, because here the hotels are very cheap.

Our tiredness, the burning heat, the wish to take a bath, may have convinced us more than his words. We went outside the ashram again, and were carried in the taxi to the Sai Ram Lodge, a nice little Moorish style hotel, where to tell the truth, for not much money we rented a spacious room, with a private bathroom and roof fan, a very important device, and two nice and clean beds. The furniture was completed by some shelves in front of the beds, dug in the wall, a washbasin and a rustic wooden table, on which we immediately installed the "mate"[1] equipment. Besides, a little night table between both beds.

13. "No Son Divino lo Hindúe?" (Aren't Hindus Divine?)

At the Sai Ram Lodge, we soon met who would be our attendant, a very dark young man, with nice and sweet eyes, short, bowlegged and with a white smile of even teeth, which transformed and lighted his countenance up when he smiled. As the majority of men in South India, he wore the *dhoti*, a large linen cloth opened at one side and fastened in the waist. I remember him with the typical gesture of raising the ends and tying them in front of the body, as if it were a short skirt.

During the time we stayed there, more than as a hotel attendant he behaved as our slave. Every time we asked him anything we needed, he set off like a shot to look for it, although, as he understood very little English, he brought us any other object instead.

Once we asked him to repair a leak in the basin drainage we had in the bedroom. Krishnamurthi left the room running, looking evidently for the solution. He brought a piece of sticky tape, placed it conscientiously on the leak, and smiled very satisfied to please us. Of course, the next time water flowed, the tape unstuck. My friend watched the scene, and just commented with a smile :

— No son divino lo hindúe, Dellia? (Aren´t Hindu divine, Delia?)

As time went by, we could discover that all people, even the most modest ones, have a great intuitive wisdom like our Krishnamurthi. This could be proved on an occasion when Giovanna came back to the hotel and didn't feel well (I think it could have been an insolation or heat stroke) and he immediately observed that something was wrong with her :

---

1. A popular infusion in Argentina (the same as in Uruguay and Brazil), prepared inside a special pumpkin with yerba mate and boiling water (or cold), sipped through a long narrow pipe.

— Máma isn't O.K. I am going to cure her.

He brought an *Ayurvedic* cream and began giving her wise massages on the face, arms, spine, down to the soles of her feet, by which she got better. At night, before going to sleep, he repeated the "treatment", and the following day at 4 in the morning, he was knocking on our door :

— Máaama !...

And again the "therapy". The truth is that in the second day she was already recovered and cheered up to go on enjoying...

14. Prashanti Nilayam or "The Eternal Peace Dwelling"

The day we arrived at Puttaparthi, after the vicissitudes lived, we moved into the hotel to have a bath and rest a little. Then, we returned with a better mood to Prashanti Nilayam Ashram, in order to be present at the darshan, the moment when Sai Baba leaves the temple or Mandhir, and with His naked feet, walks among the people who, with his only closeness, receive the *ananda* or blessing. When he appeared, we forgot the heat, the tiredness, the discomfort, the disappointment, to receive everything we were waiting for, and by which to have travelled to this distant place made sense.

The organization, always under the "Sevas" charge, consisted of making first an ordered queue nearly an hour before *Swami's* coming out; the first of each row got a number out of a little bag, and with this order, people went later into a kind of square that surrounded the Mandhir, whereby he walked.

Here, men and women are separated, the same as in the dining-rooms and bedrooms. The "Sevas" also check that women dress correctly, with the shoulders covered with a shawl, and without footwear inside the area.

The typical clothing is the saree, which the Indian woman has worn for thousands of years, practically without any change, and shows with a lot of grace and refinement. There is also another style, specially among young girls : the garment is called "panjavi" and consists of a costume of loose trousers and a closed tunic, more or less beneath the knees.

I could observe all this the first day, while we were sitting down enough time inside that enclosure or square, cross-legged and among a crowd of any race, easterns and westerns, waiting for His appearance in respectful silence and concentration.

There, I had also enough time to see in detail the beautiful colourful sarees on the Indian women : about six metres of cloth, nearly one metre wide, wrapped up with certain fixed rules, with the height, a more printed "compossé" end, which is fascinatingly thrown over a shoulder.

The men, inside the ashram, are generally dressed in white garments, trousers and buttoned shirts up the neck. I also noticed in the place : huge coconut palms trees, loaded with fruits, well cared tropical plants, some of them full of flowers, and beautiful entry arcades. In the middle of the square, the big temple or mandhir, painted in pink, beige and light blue, the same as all the buildings inside Prashanti Nilayam, with figures of mythological animals as the snake, the elephant and the Eagle Garuda, this last bird, considered God Vishnu's Carrier.

15. The Avatar

From the Mandhir, and preceded by a special tune that makes great flocks of black birds take off, a kind of vulture the ashram is full of, BHAGAVAN SRI SATYA SAI BABA appears like an orange cloud, and everybody remains galvanized in their places, waiting for Him to approach.

In the evening, the birds come back like dark stormy clouds and the spectacle is impressive, and when they perch on the trees again, getting ready to sleep, the fuss is deafening. According to the Hindus, the birds make this noisy disorder everywhere within the ashram, except in the trees near the Mandhir, in order not to disturb Swami's rest. The truth is they are right, since there is a great silence there.

With just looking at the persons' countenances, full of respect, of hope, of love, it is very easy to guess their feelings and expectations. Sai Baba walks slowly, barefooted on the burning pavement. The persons situated in the first rows, try to give him letters, which are not always received; sometimes he makes a bundle and throws them away, maybe knowing their message beforehand. And then, everybody else holds the breath back, fervently thinking : "Please, don't throw mine away!"

From time to time, he materializes vibhuti, the sacred ash that eager hands take to the mouth, the forehead or the heart, and sometimes, they share with the less fortunate ones. It is also a habit that the persons who are celebrating their birthdays, bring a candy tray, which Sai Baba blesses by putting his hand on it, and later he throws in handfuls among people, who receive them like something holy.

The first time I saw Him, he seemed a very old and bent man, as if he were carrying on his shoulders all the weight of Humanity. But every day I saw him different; according to Giovanna, our own moods are the ones which create those disparities.

Day after day, I was also feeling different; something was melting inside me, as if his closeness were opening the lock of my heart, and all the goodness that surely was shut in, waiting for somebody to turn the key, could be coming out from there.

Many times, tears slipped uncontrolled in his presence, as if a fountain were flowing from my eyes, but they weren't bitter tears, but liberating ones, that swept all the fears, old and recent, and left me a nice sense of peace and happiness, as if I were just born.

16. On the Way to the Ashram

The day began very early in Puttaparthi. About five in the morning and still dark, we usually set off with Giovanna, heading the ashram, which, as Muñhir had anticipated, was a few steps from our hotel, from the principal gate; but this entrance was kept for the way in and out of Sai Baba, so we had to walk along the principal road about 150 metres to have access to the Ganesha Gate, where visitors came in. We always set off early, since we wanted to arrive at the ashram before the draw of the rows, and in this way get room inside the square where Sai Baba walks through giving his darshans.

At that time, there was always great activity in the streets near the ashram : apart from the persons who were living outside, like us, and hurried up to arrive, were the flower sellers, who occupied their places in front of the gate : they tried to do their little business with devotees, which, maybe, means for them their whole family survival; they sell garlands made of little natural flowers, sewn with their own hands, sometimes right there, some flowers similar to jasmines, very tiny and scented, that were cut from big trees : there are white, yellow, orange, multicolour , and of different length, according to the use assigned. For instance, to decorate the hair, or to offer to the Gods. They also varied according to each budget.

The little carts with coconuts and other fruits also occupy their places, the same as those who sell natural fruit juices. Some wagons bring fresh greens from the market, and all kind of pulses, and the woman sellers sit crosslegged on the sidewalks, in Budha's posture, among the goods. You can see Indian women arriving with great baskets on their heads, which contain pans, glasses and other necessary utensils; they place themselves near the movement area, and begin preparing breakfast : white tea or coffee, which is made by throwing the tea or coffee inside the milk, and boiling it. After straining it, it is cooled down a little for the possible customers, with the typical gesture of passing it from a glass to another.

In other stalls, people begin kneading *chapatis* and different kinds of bread : in fact, they are like a sort of flat buns and of other shapes, made with varied kinds of flour : wheat, rice, corn, chickpeas, etc.

At some places, one can also see several sorts of fritters, always fried in the ghee or clarified butter. They seem very tempting on the *thalis*, but are uneatable to our Western palate, so hot and spicy, but Indians relish them with fruition and enjoy them enormously.

In the bazaars, usually shops of 3 or 4 metres wide, packed with goods that open to the street, many owners or their clerks live. Since very early, they begin cleaning around, with a bunch of branches of more or less 70 cmts. long, tied with strong threads, which are prepared for that purpose. You can observe both, men or women, bent down sweeping carefully, till the fronts of their shops are completely clean; then, they throw water, sometimes up to flood the place, for keeping the freshness a little longer. But thereafter, the implacable tropical sun comes again, and it is felt in its whole intensity.

17. My Dear Friends : The Beggars

In Puttaparthi, also the beggars, who arrived nobody knows where from, place themselves every morning at the same strategic spots, to wait for any charitable soul that could help them; surely they think that if persons have come to this devotion spot, their hearts must be a little tender than the rest. They are of many sorts : with the orange robe. of the *sadhus*, the renouncers who are continually walking, always in search of the Supreme Truth, with their forehead painted with ash; teethless old women who drag their rags, with hair like straw and flat and dry breasts; young women, almost girls, carrying in their scraggy arms starving babies of bulky bellies, to whom the word "future" has no meaning. And the children! ...With hopeless old people looks, that seem to hide behind their eyes, all the dread of a monsterly unfair society; people with all kinds of mutilations, without arms, without legs, whom at my footsteps cry out a breaking *Maama*. Very little children, almost babies, that scarcely walk, and when Westerners go over there, they bend their dirty heads to kiss our feet. Everybody has learnt to stretch their hands in the same gesture.

When I saw them, I couldn't avoid asking myself : "My God, why am I so fortunate? I have a home, a family, work, food, affections, and these poor beings, so human as I am, haven't got absolutely anything? Why don't we become aware that the whole Human Race, all Humanity, is a sole and great Family? Why don't we open our hearts, closed by ambition, by the materialistic competition, and learn to share with our brothers who need it so much?"

Having the luck to contribute with anything to these unhappy persons, I felt myself really a chosen being; I could only share out my bananas, something of my own food, a few rupees, but what a lot I have learned, My God! Now, I know that they exist, that they are a share of my world, exactly the same as I am, and I intend to never forget them, in order not to displace myself from my suitable space in life.

I can brightly evoke some of these beggars specially, and every time they come to my mind, something very warm also arises from my heart. For instance, I can clearly remember a young boy, without his legs and hands, only with two stumps in his arms. On the way towards the ashram and always in the same place, at the full sun, he was waiting, sitting down inside a little cart, made with a box used to carry fruits, with very coarse wooden wheels. Sometimes I left him a rupee, or something to eat, but I always smiled or mess up his dirty hair with my hands, to receive in exchange his grateful gesture of happiness. Occasionally, when he saw me coming near, he pushed his little cart to meet me, with a broad pleasant smile, to receive this only gesture. And I went on my way, with a knot in my throat, but with his tender look in my heart...

Maybe, I didn't have many material things to share out to them, but I always did it as a love gesture, with a caress, looking for their eyes which were of such humbleness, that they didn't dare look up at me, but when cheered up by my affection they did...I then received that quality of look as very few times in life I did, with the very soul placed in those eyes.

When I tell these experiences, many persons are scared, since when travelling to a country like India, there are always some "well intentioned" persons, who did the journey only as tourists, or perhaps had read about it, who warn, among other things, not to give alms and not to touch people for fear of contamination. I think that if one goes with an open and pure heart, no contamination at all can affect him, as his Inner Healer is working at full into the cells, in the own molecules of the physical body, interpenetrating it with absolute immunity.

At Puttaparthi, when I was moving from a place to another, it was usual that great bunches of children accompanied me cheerfully, holding each of my hands, at least 10 black little ones. This repeated scene, always made my friend Asif smile, who commented :

— You love Hindus and Hindus love you !

In my attitude towards the Indians there were never prevention barriers of any kind; I always behaved with an open posture, letting my own Inner Master, the wise intuition, guide each one of my gestures and conduct. At every occasion and place I proceeded in accordance with my purest feelings and I am sure that these were precisely the most beautiful things I am going to store up in life, which, I am more convinced every day, is a precious gift of God, and every moment lived in this fascinating country, is unique and irreplaceable.

18. Our Sai Ram Lodge

Even though we used to set off at about 5 in the morning, a long time before, maybe at 3 or 3.30 in the early morning, we began listening from our room, the monks and devotees' voices, who at that time made their way towards the temple, and thus, so early, they had the possibility of coming into it. They were walking as in procession, chanting *mantras* and *bhajans*, and the vibration of the OM started piercing me, and I felt I was entering another dimension, in another unreal and fantastic world.

Near our lodge, there was a several storeyed building, which was mostly occupied by Muslims, owners and clerks of the bazaars, only males, whom we also heard at night, either singing in their rooms or at a near mosque. Their tunes were heard from faraway, a mixture of moans and psalms to Allah, and everything became so mystic that, at the distance, it is difficult to describe the emotions that those sounds, harmoniously modulated and with so much feeling, arose inside me.

Generally, these Muslims, the majority very young, had arrived from Kashmir, a northern state, earlier independent, annexed[2] to the Indian Republic in spite of some of them. They are in Puttaparthi making their business around people who visit Sai Baba, or working as sellers in the bazaars. There, men are living without their families and usually several cousin-brothers and/or friends, join in order not to feel so lonely, and by the way, to share the room expenses.

Since very early, there was always so much noise around our hotel that it awakened us in the morning; men and women working as bricklayers in a building close to the hotel, an annex of it. Later, when we passed alongside, we could observe the apparently fragile women, carrying large baskets full of bricks, and other building materials on their heads. Within the hotel, there were also painters disinfecting and embellishing the rooms, who began their task early and communicated with each other shouting.

And the dogs fights? Never before had I seen dogs fighting as in India! Really, it is a struggle to death, but we can well

2. Kashmir was not "annexed " to the Indian Republic. On being India independent, Kashmir agreed from its full and free will, the access to it, by means of the so called "Accession Instrument". Since then, 11 general elections have been celebrated (Embassy of India).

imagine that if food is scarce for people[3], what can be left for the poor dogs !

Our way, that is to say, the road from the hotel up to the ashram, was like a short track with several bazaars alongside and the two hotels twisted at the back and conveyed towards the principal avenue. As soon as we left the hotel, we used to meet an old Hindu who was working all day long, bent over his table; he pressed clothes, usually washed by himself, with an old fashioned coal iron. We could see him at 5 in the morning, already inclined over the garments. At noon, at full sun and with a burning heat, as well as when we came back to our hotel in the evening, about 7.30 to 8, he was always there, tireless. One night after 9, we went with Krishna, the hotel attendant, to an old man's house, who supplied us with an ayurvedic cream, to give the "treatment" to Giovanna, who wasn't feeling well yet. There, I observed that the worn out working table had been transformed into a bed. And there was the old man sleeping, wrapped up just with a rough blanket, all his small and apparently weak body shrank and quieted in the repairing rest, to begin his task again, without pause nor haste, the following morning.

In the hotel and besides our Krishnamurthi, there were enough people engaged in different tasks, since close to the hotel a bar and restaurant work, with tables and long wooden benches, where breakfast, tea or afternoon snacks, and the most typical Hindu meals, were prepared. All these personnel slept on the floor, along the galleries that surrounded the principal body of the hotel, where the rooms were.

Quite late one night, I was reading in bed, and thought I had seen a mouse running on the floor. With a shout I woke my asleep companion up, and rushed outside the room, unlocking the several bolts of our door. "Krishna, Krishna", I shouted along the corridors frightened, and in a moment, all the personnel got up and made a fuss. The attendants tied up their dothis, since they slept dressed, and we began searching in our room; the beds and the few pieces of furniture of the room were moved, without finding the mouse, which, surely, and before such a fuss, had managed to run away!

3. There is not shortage of food but bad distribution. India produces 200 millions Tons of food grains, which is more than enough to feed its population (Embassy of India).

19. "Already Lived, Already Felt, Already Experienced"

Whenever I walked along the streets that, from our hotel, led up to the ashram, I heard the people bustle, and perceived in my nose those peculiar Indian smells, a mixture of flower scents, incense perfumes and spice fragrances, frying meal smell (and others not so pleasant), and it seemed that all those things were quite familiar, that I had already lived there before, that I was at home again, in my place, where I felt completely comfortable and happy.

Without analyzing, I experienced those feelings on many occasions, but, as I have said, without the mind taking part, and allowing myself to be only moved by my emotions, I had that sense of "already lived, already felt, already experienced". It happened to me at many opportunities, many times, in different places of India, and also with some persons, who later became my close friends. In too many circumstances I told myself : "I have already been here, I know this, it is quite familiar to me, I feel incredibly comfortable; I have loved this person from before, there is nothing new". In fact, I had never felt more at ease anywhere else.

Would it be, perhaps, the awakening of the memories of past lives? The chance of meeting very beloved people from previous reincarnations? Why was I always so interested in visiting India? Which was the reason of the attraction that this country always exerted on me, that became almost an obsession? Who am I? Who was I?

Maybe, I can never answer these questions reasonably, but I'm completely sure of the fact that this visit wasn't a casual thing, but organized by a Higher Conscience, who subtly moved all the threads and removed the obstacles one by one, for me to have my dearest dream concreted.

✱

3

MY DEAR SAJAD

20. My Muslim "Son"

On the second day of our arrival at Puttaparthi, at mid-morning, we left the hotel to walk through the surroundings; we began looking at the shop windows of the bazaars on our track, and my attention was struck by a very nice bracelet in which a snake head with little emeralds, sapphires and other precious stones, straightened up challenging : really, a very nice jewel. The serpent figure as a symbol of mistery and wisdom is common in India, and it is often found, not only in jewelry, but also in tapestry, mythological paintings, statues in temples, etc.

Whenever somebody approaches to watch a shop-window, the seller, who is usually by the door, makes with the hand the gesture of inviting to enter, while greeting you with the classical "Hello" (with stress on the "e"), which summarizes everything : Hello, how are you?, come in!, welcome!, etc.

Since I really liked the *bracelet*, we went inside to see it closer and to ask for its price. The jewel was tried on my wrist and it showed splendid, but the price was too expensive for my budget. I was a newcomer, besides, and didn't know the subtle art of bargaining yet, but later, as days were passing by, I became a specialist.

While I was admiring such a delicious piece of jewelry, another young man entered the shop too, and with great kindness, introduced himself as the seller's cousin. Really, he was only his friend, but later we got to know that it is usual among Muslims to say they are cousins. When they really are, they call themselves "cousin-brothers".

In this way I met whom would be our closest friend in India : SAJAD, a native of Kashmir. Tall, slim and charming, with long, beautiful hands and delicate manners. His features made me think more in a Persian prince than in an ordinary seller.

When we met, he was about 20 years old, although the seriousness of his manners, besides the typical beard and thin moustache that his Muslim race wears since ancient times, he seemed much older.

That first day, after leaving his "cousin's" bazaar, he took us to his own shop, which had access from the principal road, by an interior track with the fascinating name of *Samadhi* Road, what, I checked later, was really right. It was a nice interior little room, neatly tidied with good taste by himself, according to his own remarks.

His speciality, as in most of the bazaars of that area, was also the sale of silver and stone jewels, tibetan handicrafts, kashmirian carpets and shawls. The carpets, silk and wool handmade in their own origin country, of 390 knots an inch, were really first quality. He also dealt in other great variety of goods, like valuable silk paintings with scenes of the Indian mythology, cushions and embroidered tapestry, craft little bags for different uses, mashe paper objects, etc.

That first day, he left his cousin Tanveer (even younger than himself), in charge of the shop, and devoted entirely to us. We made our way visiting Sai Baba's parents' shrines, in a park nearby, the Religions Museum, and all that could be of interest in Puttaparthi for two Westerners eager to see everything, like Gio and myself.

Already in the first chat, he stated that we could rely on him for whatever we needed, and at the end of the day journey, we had become great friends, taking photos together at every propitious place, which pleased him a lot. After developing the pictures, we gave him some copies as a present, which he proudly exhibited in his bazaar.

I was absolutely happy when he asked me if I accepted to be considered as his mother, because he was very lonely and missed his own very much, whom he met only once a year, since his parents and sisters were living in Kashmir.

As I have already said, this request from such a special young man, filled me with pride : I knew that in India, when somebody asks you to be his mother, it is the greatest honour he can give you, since for them, mothers are the most sacred beings, and they are worshiped in altars beside gods. How could I refuse such a kind proposal?

I can assure that this offering wasn't just courteous words, said at a determined circumstance, but day after day he showed me his affection and devotion as a true and loving son, solving me, as well as Giovanna, all the problems, big or little, which could appear in such a distant, strange and unknown country.

21. Along Samadhi Road

For Gio and myself, it was very useful to have Sajad's shop as a meeting spot, to leave our hotel room key, when we didn't come out together, some messages, parcels, clothes, etc. He was always ready to please us in everything we needed.

Accompanying us to our hotel in the evening, became a habit. According to his words, "it wasn't right for mámas to be alone at that time". If we take Muslim women as reference, they really aren't seen anywhere, neither alone nor accompanied. Only on very few occasions and in great cities, we discovered some occasionally at full day, completely dressed in black and with the face covered with the veil.

Almost every time Sajad accompanied us, he entered our hotel room, where all things struck his attention. We usually remained talking till 9 o'clock, time at which all the lodge entries were closed with strong security bars and several latches, whereupon Sajad, reluctantly, had to go away.

It was a real pleasure to talk with our friend, extremely warm, polite and expert in almost all the subjects we were interested in, as Yoga Teachers : religions, mysticism, philosophy, mythology, Holy Books, great Masters, Eastern Literature, Poetry, etc. At the same time, he was interested in our habits, the environment in which we developed in our land, and even small matters as the prices of many articles and the daily customs.

I remember one evening when Sajad remained talking with

me in our room, while Gio was taking her bath. Suddenly, we both heard a loud noise, which came precisely from the bathroom, something like "crunch, crunch", which repeated every now and then. My "son" opened his eyes disproportionately and sent a surprised and interrogative glance towards me, while he asked :

— What is she doing there?

I don't even want to think how his imagination was flying about our extravagant Western habits. Without being able to conceal laughing, I had to point out that she was only scraping her heel hardness with the pumice stone!

Sajad declared himself as a serious and fervorous Muslim, very respectful of the habits and traditions his parents had taught him. He assured me that his main ambition in life was to become, in a far-off day, an old man whom everybody respects. The truth is that he was already respected by everyone; elder persons from other shops, consulted him at the same level, and his opinion was taken seriously into account. The same happened among his cousins and the other persons who shared the room, in the building close to ours : his word was taken literally, and nobody discussed his orders, being a true leader.

Like the majority of the Muslims, his religion was above all; 5 times a day he carried out the *namaz* : with the little praying carpet directed towards the Mecca, he worshipped his Allah; besides, he frequently visited the local mosque, where only men are allowed. In fact, throughout the whole India, the religious subject is very important : it rules all personal activities and relations with others.

Sajad's friendship and closeness became so necessary to us, as ours to him, and not a single day was spent without, in the evening, before closing, joining in his shop like a family met. If at any opportunity I hadn't appeared over there all day long, I received his reproach :

— What has happened that you have just arrived? I have been waiting for you the whole day!

On one occasion, I answered him with another question :

— Why do you wait for me?

Sajad looked at me in the eyes, and in a low voice, he seriously answered :

— To feel better.

Sometimes, he was expecting me with a nice flower in his hand, and put it lovingly in my hair; and many times, I would say everytime, when I arrived at his bazaar, he laid his best silk carpet on the floor, for me to sit down.

Since the very day we met, he wanted to lend me one of his largest carpets, the one I would choose, to use on the bed. Of course, I didn't accept. Besides, his trust to us was unconditional, leaving me alone in his shop many times, while he carried out a transaction, and offering me to take any jewel, carpet or other commodity I liked to, later, on my return to Argentina, draw him its value; but to tell the truth, to leave debts in India was never in my plans.

Usually, Sajad, as his cousins, used to wear Western fashion clothes, though very loose. Once, his mother had sent him from Kashmir, a light grey suit, made with a nice and fresh weft; the model was very Eastern : wide baggy trousers, narrow in the lower part and closed long-sleeve robe that reached to the knees. When he put it on for the first time, he looked really special. When I told him this, Sajad was very proud and happy; so, every evening he wore it to please me.

Day after day, we shared magic and wonderful moments, either absolutely silent on listening to classical Indian and Kashmiriam music, from a shop close to his, or warmly talking in front of a glass of white tea, that he always ordered from a bar nearby, as soon as I arrived, no matter the time, and he didn't accept me to *refuse* the invitation. In fact, it is habitual in India to make this invitation as a kind reception to persons who visit shops, but I, really, wasn't a customer.

Krishnamurthi, the known Hindu thinker of this century, says that with some persons it exists a deeper stage of communication, in which we meet in the same level, with the same strength, with the same passion, what he calls "communion". I am sure that from the very moment we met, there was between Sajad and me that deep communion feeling, which made that, in all circumstances, we could understand each other completely, with love and friendship, even without saying a single word. I also believe that those feelings, are quite more important than the daily communication between two human beings.

22. Great Muslim — Swiss — Argentine Party

Sometimes we invited Sajad to eat something at the only restaurant in Puttaparthi where some dishes eatable to our Western palate, not used to so many spices, were served. Generally, we were attended by Ganesha, one of the waiters who was also our friend and who, with his permanent smile, remained beside our table all the time while we had lunch. Before leaving Puttaparthi, Ganesha asked me to bring him to work in Argentina!

Sajad accepted our invitation only once or twice, but he certainly gave us a banquet when he invited us to lunch in his room. It was the week when Sai Baba had travelled to White Fields, the village near Bangalore where he has another small ashram.

Generally, when Sai Baba goes away, Prashanti Nilayam, the ashram, and all Puttaparthi, become a dead town, as most devotees follow him, as well as the businessmen, who move with their belongings to go on with the sale on that spot. As nobody knew with certainty the period he was going to be out, and it was rumored that it would be only 3 or 4 days, we, with Gio, decided to remain...and Sajad too.

Taking then advantage of the fact that only two persons stayed in the room (generally they were four), Sajad and Asif, who in that moment seemed to be his attendant, Sajad decided to formalize his invitation to lunch, which on this occasion we accepted.

They cooked a delicious meal, super abundant. Asif travelled about 50 kms. by bicycle to get some chicken pieces to overwhelm us, since in Puttaparthi no meat of any kind could be obtained.

The lunch was delicious, even though quite hot for us, and when we told them this, they were surprised, since it had been prepared very soft, just to please us.

Although both Muslims ate with his *hands*, they got cutlery for us. I noticed their ability to mix the rice with the sauce, taking small handfuls with the right hand that were neatly carried to the mouth, without touching it with the fingers. I tried to do the same, and only got to smear myself completely without being able to imitate them, and stopped the attempt at Sajad's disapproval glance, who very seriously and for all comment said :

— It is not this way.

The four of us sat down on the floor, on a very nice coloured carpet, and the menu consisted of : fried chicken with spices, salad of several kinds of vegetables as onion, cucumber, turnip, tomato, ginger and others unknown in Argentina, which Sajad sliced of the same thickness and combined the colours with a great harmony. Later, white rice and very hot tomato sauce (they called it tomato soup), bananas and papayas sectioned in little sticks, natural yoghurt and lemonade (a luxury only for us). Afterwards, a delicious lemon tea to help the digestion, prepared with threads of tea and several very tiny lemons split, squeezed out and boiled with the peeling as well.

We varied the meeting with some very interesting games, from a book that Sajad had, which, through certain drawings and codes, we could guess the past, present and future. The "party" finished after 4 in the afternoon, and the two boys made absolutely everything, without accepting our help : they prepared, cooked, then dished up and afterwards cleaned everything. They used just a little stove to cook the complete menu. The "queens", of course, always on the carpet.

Actually, this invitation to lunch has been made to us when we had recently arrived at India, but we, with so many warnings we brought, full of fears, thought :

— Won't they put any drug in the meal to rape us and rob us?

We were fools. As the friendship with them was growing, we realized they were noble and pure souls, and their love for us was true; we could absolutely trust and consider them our heart friends.

23. How to say Good-bye?

How we came to love each other with our Muslim friends, specially with Sajad, and how bitter the farewell was!

Giovanna states that, surely, these so special meetings are actually remeetings of past lives, because it is difficult for persons to cross the world to meet and love one another.

We cried a lot during our last meeting in his bazaar, when we sat alone on the beautiful carpet he always laid for me, and interchanged our presents as a ritual : he gave me a ring that he had previously assigned for me, and had worn the last two weeks before my departure, for the ring to become impregnated with his essence. It was a pity that it was so little, that I had to cut it in order to wear it some time. As I had nothing prepared to give him, I offered him my wrist watch, and Sajad asked me to write a letter mentioning that present, because on the contrary, nobody would believe him, and people would think he had stolen it.

I don't want to remember when the moment to leave Puttaparthi arrived! The other boys who shared the room, came to our hotel very early to say good-bye : one after the other, they embraced Giovanna and me, at both sides of the breast, as it is the custom. It was 5.30 in the early morning and we would leave at six.

Afterwards Sajad arrived, with the Muslim cap and his thin and long-suffering figure. He was carrying out an almost fasting from several days, because of the *Ramadan*, and all that night he had been praying in the mosque. Poor Sajad! He seemed so lonely and desolated... I wanted from the deepest of my heart and feelings, to embrace and rock him like a helpless child, as the son he had decided to be for me. In that way, maybe, I could comfort him, and also myself.

He was really very sad the day we left, and he didn't even want to shake hands, or give me a farewell embrace as the others did. How demanding his Allah is !

Only his eyes expressed all what his mouth didn't have the daring to say : that he would miss me despairingly and that right there, his heart was breaking into pieces. And I could perfectly understand him, because the same was happening to me.

Sajad, you were so young, and yet so wise that, you are going to remain inlaid in my nostalgic heart for ever, in the place of the most beautiful and magic things, to which one always comes back, even with the wings of the thoughts, as you said, "to feel better", to go on loving life, and sometimes, to be allowed reconcile with it...

✱

4

CHAITANYA DELUXE HOTEL

24. Lizards and Bats

Pamela, an Italian Sculptor very devotee of Sai Baba, came year after year from her country following the Avatar; she commented my friend about the Chaitannya Hotel, where she usually lodged, which had a great courtyard with fruit trees and a balcony all around the rooms, where one could sit for *meditation*. At that moment, the tariff was lower than in ours, besides.

For fifteen days we had lodged in the hotel Muñhir had first taken us, but in the last week Giovanna had been insisting to move to Pamela's, adducing that ours was very noisy. The truth is that I found it hard to leave the "Lodge", since in that place and surroundings, we had already made several friends. Finally, tired of her insistence and reluctantly, I consented to move; hence we hired two rickshaws, which carried our things to the new hotel.

Chaitannya Hotel was situated a little further from the ashram, always on the main road, that is the highway to Bangalore. It had really a great courtyard with big tropical trees loaded with fruits, a beautiful view of the surroundings and, the appreciated balcony where my friend would make *Japa* and meditation, besides.

As we had already done the reservation, when our rickshaws arrived, Bangladesh, the rooms attendant, was waiting for us, together with two small women, extremely thin, one middle aged and the other very young, who, he told us later, were his two wives.

Bangladesh[1] seemed about 40 years old; he was, in fact, rather older than Krishnamurthi of the other hotel, who looked about 13 or 14, but really he admitted to be 22 years of age, and whom surely we would miss very much. Of similar physiques, that is to say, both very short, very dark and with warm smiles, always ready. He mostly wore the typical dothi, gathered up as a short skirt, which discovered his short bow legs. The same as Krishna, he wore moustache, with the difference that Bangladesh's was quite dense, and the other one's only insinuated.

After exchanging some words in their language with their husband, the women loaded our huge and heavy bags on their heads and, decidedly went upstairs, towards the second floor where the chosen room was. I arrived at the conclusion that the weakness of their appearance was deceitful, since they climbed the long stairs without losing the balance nor becoming weak. Bangladesh was the last in the row, walking with a smiling face after us, but without taking absolutely anything.

As I had already remarked, I had reluctantly accepted the change of hotel, so I saw everything with bad eyes. For instance, as soon as we entered which would be our room, I discovered some pink lizards of disgusting aspect on the walls, which are plentiful in all India and revolted me, since they seemed to be peeled off.

Besides, in the bathroom ventilation hollows I sighted something alive that was moving, and imagined they were bats, which also disgusted me and I felt a great repugnance about. Bangladesh laughed at my fears, and with a large stick frightened the lizards away, which later I checked were harmless. He assured me the nests in the ventilation hollows were only of birds, for what there was nothing to be afraid of. In fact, observing them calmer, I discovered their little eyes looking trustfully at us, and in view of the reality, I managed to relax completely.

I also made my friend see that the new room was rather hotter than the previous one; a large window opened to the street, all transparently glazed and without any kind of blinds, released since midday and during all the afternoon, a lot of heat, while receiving

1. Bangladesh maybe the nickname of the person and not his name. Nevertheless, if he is coming from Bangladesh, then it would be "bangladeshi" (Embassy of India).

at full the sun rays. And this fact she did have to admit, since it was the reality.

We settled our things of normal usage, filling some shelves dug in the wall in front of our beds, and to tidy up, we covered them with a colorful broidered tapestry with flowers, birds and typical animals of India. I had bought this cover on the first days in Puttaparthi, and we had already used it for the same purpose in the other hotel. (I grew so fond of it, that I go on using it at home, hung up also in front of my bed.)

25. Bangladesh and His Two Wives

As days went by, we were becoming friends with Bangladesh, the only in the family who spoke a little English. He told us that those two women were his wives, and he had a kid with each one, a girl and a boy. Just as a joke, we asked what would happen if the situation were the wrong way round, that is to say, two men for a single woman, and very earnestly he did the gesture with one of his hands, while exclaiming :

— We cut the head!

It is the custom[2] in almost all Indian hotels we visited, that attendants clean the rooms only when the guests require the service, and somebody must always remain in the room while being done. I was who mostly stayed there. I sat down in the balcony writing my letters or having some "mates", while they were cleaning.

Bangladesh and one of his wives were in charge of the task, and I could hear that while working, they chatted in their language in a lively manner all the time, and laughed so joyfully, that I would have liked to understand their speech in order to share it.

What put my patience to test was their curiosity : they examined and touched everything they saw; continually, they asked me what was each thing they didn't know, what their usage was and their prices. Many times they even asked me for permission to see what there was inside a bag!

Their curiosity was aroused, mostly, by electronic sets, which prices they wanted to know to purchase them. Bangladesh insisted

2. Even if this was our experience in the 10 or more lodges we stayed, the Embassy of India considers that they are not hotels, but "sarai" or similar establishments.

to buy my friend's small recorder, but she didn't even vaguely think to sell it, as she had specially taken it to record bhajans during the "chanting". I suppose that really, he wanted her to give it to him as a present, since with his meagre wage of 20 or 30 dollars monthly, what could they buy !

One morning, Bangladesh came to my room while I was alone, to ask if I had clothes for washing. Generally, I washed them myself, since even though this service was very cheap, garments were much ruined, so I only made them iron (they said pressing), but outside the hotel (they were careless there). At my negative answer, Bangladesh didn't show any intention to leave; he turned over and over, as if he didn't have the courage to tell the reason that had really brought him there. He asked me if I was married; when I answered affirmatively, he wanted to know if I had children. After my negative, he inquired if I hadn't because I didn't like children. I then stated that I liked them very much, and at this stage of the conversation, Bangladesh finished offering me his little child to bring him with me to Argentina. He would give me all the documents resigning him for ever.

— Here there is neither place nor food, mámá — he argued, with the kid holding his hand innocently, looking at me with his astonished little black eyes, without understanding, luckily! what was happening.

My dear Hindus, I'd bring every helpless child, with hunger, every youth who has need of work and learning, every old person without affection, everybody, everybody, but I can only take you in my heart, and give you my unmeasurable love!

26. From the Balcony

At last, we could enjoy the famous balcony, one of the reasons in favour of the hotel change. When I got up, I sat there to have "mates", usually while my friend was asleep; then she also came closer and we watched how life bubbled underneath and around us. From very early, a lot of people were seen along the street : very erect women, who elegantly showed their colorful nice attires. For the aluminium pots and pans on their heads, surely they had a food stall near the ashram. Others carried baskets with bricks and the most heterogeneus things.

Some old dishevelled beggars stepped already towards the places where they would spend the rest of the day. Children of different ages, merrily made their way to school.

Outside, in the street, beneath our balcony, there was a little shed of no more than 2 mts. by 2 mts., from which a lot of people came out. It was difficult to think how they would pile up to sleep, since I had counted, at least, 8 persons of 3 generations, to judge by the apparent ages : grandparents, parents and sons. This place was many-sided, and the most varied activities were carried out there.

Very early morning, the oldest Hindu woman swept all around the shed, with such an enthusiasm that the raised dust blew up to our balcony. One of the teenager boys placed a small cart with coconuts and was ready to wait for the customers. When it was necessary, the place also functioned as a tyre workshop, and the two wheel carts pulled by *cows* or oxen, stopped to blow the tyres up. Auto-rickshaws, motorcycles and bikes did the same. I saw the *dhobbies* on foot beside their bikes with a cart behind loaded with great bundles of clothes, which were taken for washing to the river.

The spicy meal scents rose up to the balcony : one of the women, the middle-aged, was preparing some fritters; she took small quantities of dough with her bare hands, from a full bowl, with which she wrapped up some small red peppers, called "puta-parió" by us. She fried them in a big pan, and once ready, they seemed like doughnuts, with the little end outside, from where the Indians took them and delighfully devoured the food. When all this meal was cooked, the same as other fritters, chapatis and several kind of fried doughs, people began to meet for breakfast and taste such "delicacies".

From time to time, our hard-working neighbours also raised their eyes up towards our balcony with curiosity, and not knowing the "mate", perhaps they imagined we were drugging.

Parked at the road side, in front of the hotel, there was a kombi, from which a lot of people appeared, getting ready to work : they repaired bicycles. Not far away, a small bar with tables and benches at the front part, on which at night, the family slept, were preparing white tea and coffee, for breakfast. We were customers of this bar and every night, they kept for Giovanna a bottle of mineral water, in a little fridge, out of fashion and with visible deterioration. At her request, they put the "Bysleri" in the freezer, and on the following day, my friend bought the bottle of water converted in ice.

Sometimes, in the evening, when we came back from the ashram, we stopped to sit down on one of these benches, to drink something cold, usually a "cool drink", as the fizzy drinks are called; it was obvious that this family felt very flattered with our friendship and attended us excellently.

The week Sai Baba left towards White Field, we used to spend more time sitting down taking "mates" in our outdoor balcony. We could admire the splendid tropical scenery displayed around us towards all the cardinal points. From the hotel courtyard, the fruit trees reached up to our floor, and with just stretching the hand, we could take some papayas, coconuts, bananas or mangos; but this was not necessary since Bangladesh offered us in a tray the full ripen fruits.

Among the greenness of a magnificent park, it appeared the multicoloured dome of the Planetarium, which, unfortunately, and in spite of our interest, we couldn't visit. A little further, towards the front of us, a broad stadium with an imposing hill, at the top of which *Hanuman* is found : the monkey-headed God, who, in accordance with the Mythology helped God *Rama* in the rescue of her beloved wife from Lanka[3]. Around it, the statues of the Masters of all Religions : Jesus, Buddha, Zoroastrus, etc.

On the road, exactly opposite our hotel, there is a great arcade, in the upper side of which a shield identical to the one found inside Prashanti Nilayam can be seen, with the symbols of the principal religions in the world, besides figures of birds and other mythological animals, a *guru* teaching his *chela*, etc. All this imagery is constructed in plaster, and painted pink, ochre and light blue, that is to say, with the same colours used in all the buildings, temples and other structures inside the ashram. Coming from Bangalore and several kilometres before arriving at Puttaparthi, on the main road, we saw various arcades similar to this.

A little further on, on another hill, several imposing and attractive buildings are distinguished, like the Religions Museum,

3. It is a debatable question for the erudite ones if the present Lanka City was the Lanka quoted in the epic story "Ramayana" (Embassy of India).

which stands out with its three grey and white large domes, the Lodge for V.I.P. (Very Important Persons); (Here the President of India stays when he visits Sai Baba), the University Students Guest House, where they meet from the whole country, the beautiful University itself.

27. Visitors ! The Monkeys Arrived !

A specially hot afternoon, Giovanna and I remained to have a nap, to take advantage of the roof fan air. Suddenly, we were awakened by our neighbours' shouts and gibberish. I showed up to see the cause of such a fuss, and noticed we had visitors : a beautiful monkey family was playing in our balcony. Mother monkey with a baby stuck on her belly; very serious and erected father monkey, and two other kids a little more grown up, who didn't get tired of making all kinds of pirouettes.

One of them came closer to play with me, but I withdrew, since I didn't know if they were really dangerous. Later, people assured me that they were harmless, but I had to be careful not to smile, since showing the teeth is a challenging reason for them, and they could scratch me if they thought I was going to attack.

On another occasion, I was sitting down in the famous balcony, which faces the street, and had opened the two doors of the room, in order to air it.

When I raised my eyes from what I was reading, I noticed a grown-up monkey coming in through the courtyard side door; he crossed our room and went out very cheerfully to play where I was, making contortions among the iron bars, and he didn't stop looking at me all the time!

At night, we used to leave both room doors open, so we would have not been surprised if in the morning we found a little monkey lying in our beds. Here, anything could happen; as Gio right said to me :

— ! Estamos en India, Dellia! (we are in India, Dellia!)

We also had a dog friend, of an indefinite race which is plentiful in India : a mixture of greyhound and policial dog, average size. He followed us everywhere, inside and outside the ashram, stayed sitting down waiting for us in front of the door, and many nights he slept in our balcony.

28. "To Live, and Let Live"

Bangladesh's family, that is to say he, his two wives and the two kids, lived all together in a single room at the back of the courtyard. They cooked outside, among the rubbish of empty bottling and all kind of packing.

> — Look, Mama, this, is our kitchen-he told me once, when I approached there, pointing out the place where one of his women was neatly chopping vegetables, to prepare the family meal.

I had gone to search for an insecticide to kill ants, which in perfect formation passed through our bathroom. Bangladesh handed me a tin with powder, but in fact, the idea of killing them disgusted him. And continually, he asked me :

— Do you intend to kill them?

Even though I was not pleased by ants invading our food, since sometimes we had some fruits or other things in the room, I also had a guilty conscience. Finally, the ants followed their road quietly through our bathroom. "To live and let live" Don't I repeat it, perhaps, daily?

While Sai Baba remained absent, we could visit the Mandhir without getting up early; we stayed inside for the *bhajans* chanting, and the truth is that the vibrations were so powerful, that it wasn't difficult to join the collective ecstasy, when the music and singing reached its climax. The atmosphere created inside there was something really outstanding, and the emotions that it aroused surpassed everything known. I imagine what it would be when Swami shares this 'chanting".

Many times a day, we walked going and coming back from the hotel to the ashram, and frequently we heard, at the music shops, the same devotional tunes to Sai Baba, Sanskrit version, which lyrics, according to Giovanna, said : "Nada para ti, todo para mí" (Nothing for you, everything for me), and each of us used it at her convenience.

29. With Roberta to the Kalpattaro

My friend always reproached me the fact that people usually

"stuck" to me, and maybe she was in a way right. In fact, inside the ashram we had known a stout Italian "lady" named Roberta, whose devotion to Sai Baba was really outstanding. She had stated to us that she had already carried out several trips to Puttaparthi to be near the "santón" (Big Saint).

I don't remember the circumstances when she "stuck" to accompany us to the Kalpattaro, a hill near where the "Wishes Tree" is found, from which it is said that in his childhood, Sai Baba picked all sorts of fruits, pleasing and amusing his classmates.

The previous night, I had had a peculiar dream : during it Sajad, my Muslim "son" whom I talked about in the chapter before, was an old man, lying down at the edge of a road, with a snake basket at his side. I didn't think very much in the matter, but, on the following day, on the way to Kalpattaro, I saw exactly the scene of my dream. Logically, the old man wasn't by any means Sajad. Mere coincidence? May be...

When I told Sajad the dream, we tried to seek some symbolic meaning, and we both established that he was appointed to be "My old wise Man", as the snake represents wisdom.

Finally, we arrived, with my friend and Roberta, at that holy place on the hill, and remained there for a long while, for meditation under the "Wishes Tree". Many persons wrote their desires in a little paper, and tied them to some of the branches; thereby, looking from a certain distance, the tree seemed to be full of white birds. From that place, the whole Puttaparthi is distinguished, with the dry riverbed at its feet.

On the following days, it was difficult to get rid of Roberta, since as she was alone in India, she insisted us to accompany her everywhere, and shamed us with her vulgar behavior again and again. I remember her always bargaining in the bazaars, and when she didn't get what she wanted, she shouted from outside : "Ladri, ladri" (Thieves, thieves), "Ali Baba" (naturally referring to the "40 thieves") and things like that. If, on the other hand, the bargaining turned out well, she caught the alarmed seller's head, and stamped some resonant kisses!

Needless to say that Sajad, always so well mannered, sensitive and polite, didn't bear her even at a distance. I thought to myself : "luckily he doesn't understand what she says", since her impudent remarks would have blushed up the most shameless one. Afterwards, I realized that Sajad simulated not understanding her, since, later, on other occasions, I checked he perfectly dealt with his Italian customers.

Roberta wanted us to accompany her to Bangalore, to a Beauty Institute (she owned one in Italy), to learn the methods that were used in India, but Gio and me had other intentions, so, one fine day, without bothering to greet us, and Thanks God!, she disappeared...

30. God in a Mercedes Benz

After a long week in White Fields, finally Sai Baba came back to Puttaparthi. His arrival was a real festival : he passed in front of our hotel balcony around noon in his white and imposing Mercedes Benz. A considerable throng crowded both sides of the avenue : adult persons, his devotees, Westerners as well as Easterns, children, teenagers and youth from all the primary, secondary and university colleges.

Many persons, specially Hindus, smashed some coconuts over the pavement as he passed, what in India means the *puja* or offering that is payed to the Gods and Holy Men.

The return was about twelve, and from here on, the order was restored. His devotees came back, also the merchants who followed him, and Puttaparthi took its usual feature again.

At about 4 in the afternoon and as he has kept doing for many years, Sai Baba reappeared from the Mandhir to give his darshans. As usual, he slowly walked among people who offer him their hopes, covering without haste, barefooted, the burning pavement. Also as usual, the impressive scene of the great dark cloud that the birds make when flying away, provoked by the music anouncing His appearance.

The same spectacle and, however, it doesn't become a routine : the double orange robe (he wears the dothi underneath), leaves his nice lotus-feet bare, which all devotees from the first rows try to touch or kiss, ritual called "padha Namaskar". From closer, I could take notice of his Afro hair, the famous look which gave him such a special image, that became popular world-wide, and I saw it was beginning to become sparse.

31. The Closeness of Swami

The following morning after Sai Baba's returns, I was lucky to take number 3 and be located in the third row in front of the Mandhir, a really privileged place.

When taking my place inside the "square", I tried to find a space near Hindu women, who always showed me their affection without words, either caressing my bare-feet when, while settling, I unwillingly touched their clothes, or well with loving smiles, joining their both hands on the breast.

In the whole India, it is usual to greet raising the hands with the palms joined, and this action would replace our Western costum of shaking hands, even though its meaning is rather prettier. The gesture would mean : "My soul and yours are one", that is to say, it would point out the Spiritual Oneness of Man.

In Puttaparthi, people also made this symbolic gesture of taking hands to heart, while expressing "Om Sai Ram" (as Sai Baba invocation). Inside Prashanti Nilayam, the "sevas" use such expression to call the attention of somebody, for instance, to cover the shoulders, to take the footwear off, to advance, to move backwards, and for people coming near one another to make more room. Constantly before darshans, I heard them repeating something that sounded like "Kurcho, kurcho", to hurry up devotees who were still standing up, to sit on the floor.

Since we had arrived at Puttaparthi about 20 days before I always carried two envelopes to darshans, both containing the photos and English notes to beg Swami's help : one referred to my husband, who was recuperating from a hemiplegy he had suffered the year before, and the other had been delivered to me by a young woman of my city and was about very serious problems of her little daughter.

Every time my place allowed me, I stretched the letters, but up to that moment, unluckily, I had already changed several envelopes, which were spoiled by the heat and handling, and I had little hope he would receive them.

Actually I had had a good chance in the first day of our stay; maybe I even spoiled the so longing interview because of my inexperience. This is what happened : I was sitting near Giovanna in the first rows, and Swami slowly walked in front of us, while

I stretched my letters. Suddenly, he stopped before me, and while looking at my eyes, he asked :

— How many?

Completely confused by his near presence, and as I supposed he was asking me about the number of letters I was extending him, I answered :

— How many what?

He looked at me again and repeated the question, while my friend whispered :

— How many we are in the group.

— Seventeen, — I could hardly say, which was more or less the number of one of the argentine groups we belonged to.

He intensely looked at me again, without pronouncing a single word, while all my compatriots were paralyzed before the possibility of an interview, following the movement of my hair tail (they remarked me later with a reproaching face). Sai Baba silently continued his way, and he didn't even receive my letters. Maybe if I had answered "only two", that day the meeting would have concreted.

Even though we hadn't got it, I must point out I had Him near many times, I refer physically near, since in my heart, I felt Him close all the time...and I'm still having Him there.

One morning during darshan, on an occasion the "square" was more crowded than usual, for the closeness of God Shiva's Festival (Mahashivaratri), I allowed myself to disobey orders (I apologize) and tried to take His picture from very near, helped by the smallness of my "pocket" camera.

It was just dawning when Sai Baba appeared. When he was coming near my area, one of the first sun rays filtered through the tree branches hollows, lighting Him up, and following its way, it illuminated me too. Swami raised his eyesight to follow the ray trajectory and, among the crowd, he met my eyes (and my camera). He stopped for a moment and the picture could have been very special, but as usual, the emotion that his eyes looking at me aroused, annulled everything else, taking the strength and steadiness away from my hands, and unfortunately, the photo was a little moved.

And on another occasion, it was during our last darshan in Puttaparthi : I couldn't believe the fact to have got No. 1 in the draw. My place was in the second row in front of the temple, since the first was already occupied, maybe by some special guests or by the persons who visit the Mandhir much earlier. Sai Baba came calmly walking to my area. While approaching, I began asking for an interview :

— Swami, interview, interview please; we are leaving.

He stopped in front of me again, and with his both hands vertical, with the palms opened towards me, in the known gesture to ask for waiting, he exactly answered :

— Wait, wait.

I had already commented that His closeness left me paralyzed, and this was the reason why, when he turned one of His hands and began materializing vibhuti for me, I didn't stretch my hand to receive it. Just as well that my companion took it, and later we shared it!

When receiving His "Wait, Wait", many persons don't leave the ashram; sometimes they continue to be in Prashanti Nilayam or in Puttaparthi several months, until achieving an interview, but unfortunately, we had everything organized to set off, even though pulling out from there was a real pain in the heart.

The morning after Sai Baba's return from White Field, and as I had mentioned before, I could place myself ahead for the darshan. Once again, I stretched my letters, and fortunately, this time He received them. The two involved persons stayed in His blessed hands, and as He always says :

— WHY TO BE AFRAID IF SWAMI IS WITH YOU?
I TAKE THESE PERSONS AT MY CARE.

Actually, it was so. When I came back home, my husband told me that at a certain day, he had noticed a radical change in his health, feeling much better from then on. Later, when I phoned him relating that Sai Baba luckily had already received my letters at a determined day, he could check that it had been precisely the date of his astonishing improvement.

ISHVARA PRANIDHANA OR THY WILL BE DONE, it doesn't matter in what language we pronounce it !

✱

5

OUR RELATIONSHIP WITH THE HINDUS

32. Argentina...Maradona ?

Generally, all Indian people experienced for us, white foreigners, a great curiosity, but not morbid as if we were a rare specimen, but on the contrary, very warm and polite. Everywhere, children and adults, young and not so young, when meeting us, asked : "Where are you from?"; some of them just "From?", and almost always, when answering "Argentina", they remained bewildered, as they didn't place it. So, I usually added : "South America". Sometimes, specially younger people associated : "Argentina,...Maradona?", and they were very pleased to find out we were precisely from that place.

On some occasions, when I was at my "son" Sajad's Jewelry, or at anybody else's bazaars, with whom there was a certain familiarity, and their own friends arrived, mainly from the neighbour shops, they asked in their language, but with veiled glances at me, all the information about me. They wanted to know my complete name, origin, marital status, sons, plans, occupation, salary, etc. If their English allowed them direct communication, those questions (and many others) were dealt in a pleasant dialogue. It wasn't strange that they wanted to know if I was fond of their country, and were delighted when I answered that it seemed fascinating to me. They were specially interested about my opinion in more earnest subjects as religion, politics, etc., and even the daily things and prices, which they compared with those of their country.

I wonder if my journey had been after our President's visit to India, and they had heard his statement that Argentina was an earthly paradise, with neither inflation nor poverty and unemployment problems, the questions would have been referred to corroborate such affirmations, which must have left the innocent Hindus "haciéndose el bocho" (imagining splendid things) as we say here.

33. Snoopers!

At some opportunities we sat with my friend in a restaurant, to have lunch, dinner, or only to have a cup of coffee or tea, we observed that most Indian customers were on the watch for us.

Once, in Mysore, during a two weeks' tour we did by taxi through the South of India, we went with Ramachandra, our taxi driver, to have lunch at a restaurant we found on the way. We usually invited him, since, besides taking care of us with great loyalty, the food was very cheap for us, and Rama had a very poor salary. He never took advantage asking for expensive dishes, and even though we gave him the "menu" to choose, he always ordered the same : rice and just water to drink.

In that moment, near us there was a table with some Hindus having lunch too, and everybody turned to our side, trying to listen to the conversation. If we laughed, they did the same, and as soon the occasion appeared to insert a word, they got fully to talk with us, of course, beginning with the essential questions, and even stopped eating not to miss anything.

Another time, during a journey by train crossing the whole India from the South to the North, from Bangalore up to Delhi, we made close friends with our coach companions. As the voyage prolonged for two days and two nights, we had a lot of time to carry out bright conversations. During these chats, there was always somebody from other coaches, entering ours : silently, they got near and politely sat down just to hear in full attention, without missing a single word. When our talk finished, sometimes after some hours, they also silently, got up and left solemnly to their own coach. Always kind, prudent...and curious people.

34. Tomorrow...

Whenever we engaged people for a service, we always noticed with my friend, that Indians felt proud to have white Westerners as their customers, and they demonstrated it showing us among their equals as much as possible.

In our first week in Puttaparthi, we took a rickshaw to carry us to the Post Office, 3 or 4 kms. far away from the ashram. The story was as follows : in Prashanti Nilayam, there was also a Post Office, but during the first week of stay I had gone there every morning, without the chance to despatch my first letter home. In fact, at the opening timetable, I appeared trying to get the stamps.

The office-keeper, an old and very dark Hindu, of short height, who spoke a dreadful English, opened the modest room that was used as Post Office, cleaned it neatly from the roof down to the floor, lighted candles in a little altar in front of Sai Baba's picture, and without any haste at all, made his offerings : he began singing with a complete devotion that seemed to be never ending. He made a run all over the bhajans from a small book, did the *arati* and ended up singing the *Shanti* OM, of course by taking our participation for granted.

When, finally, he seemed to be aware of the reason of my presence there and was going to attend me, he answered my request with just a laconic : "No stamps". On asking when I could come back, he quickly answered back : "tomorrow, tomorrow". This story, day after day, mornings and afternoons. After a whole week with the same, I began losing patience and got a little angry, but the old man didn't look worried. After knowing something more about the Eastern peculiarity, I arrived at the conclusion that for them, time doesn't matter, and nobody understands our haste in trying to carry out things.

Nevertheless, when we say "tomorrow" to the Indians, the situation is rather different. Many times, along the ashram way, a child of more or less 10 years old, insistently tried to sell her flower garlands. She accompanied me all the way and, over and over, put the flowers on my hair. I had used up my refusal arguments, but she didn't give up, until a day I actually couldn't get rid of her, I said "tomorrow", and this seemed to have the desired effect, and move her away.

I forgot completely the affair, but the girl didn't, and the following morning she was smiling widely with her flowers at the very hotel gate, while remembering me :

— Máma, you promise!

And then, I had no alternative but to purchase the flowers. So, in the future, I was very careful to say "tomorrow"; I left it to the Easterns.

I come back to our journey to the other post-office, which, after the usual bargaining, we carried out with Shankar's rickshaw, a polite young boy whose customers we became later on. We agreed on some few rupees, and, letters in hand, we hopefully set off to be able, this time at last, to despatch them.

At once we realized that Shankar wanted to "put on airs" with his customers, showing us as much as he could : first, he stopped to blow the tyres, and several Hindus who were there, surrounded the rickshaw, speaking their language and looking at us without concealing, while Shankar proudly smiled. Then, he stopped at a small kiosk, and the scene repeated; at last, and as wishing that the trip would last as much as possible, he stopped again at a side of the road, went down the scooter, and, with a cloth, began to polish the rickshaw, with us on it, waiting! Finally, I had to tell him, with my best smile, that we were in a hurry, if not we would still be along the post office way...

When at last, we arrived at the Post Office, we saw a mountain of letters on the floor, with the Hindus sitting around classifying them. As an attention to us, they stamped ours too, since with so many stops, we were just at closing time.

While we took some photos in the surroundings, of course, with Shankar, his rickshaw, besides several children who got near to "pose", we saw the correspondence set off inside some dirty postal sacks, which were carried by some clerks, by bicycle!, to the next town. Gio discovered the scene and, pointing with her forefinger, she exclaimed :

— There our letters go! What a long time they would take to arrive!

Well, they took more than a month to reach their destination, but, luckily, not a single piece was lost.

35. Bargaining and Hospitality

During the three months I stayed in India on my first journey, I observed that the most westerners who visit this wonderful country (that is to say Sai Baba's devotees in Puttaparthi, as in whatever place of .the North, South, Centre, East and West as well), on their pilgrimage or visits to the Masters, or for tourism, or only for business, don't pay much attention to the Indians; each one is in his own affair, and treats them like inferior persons, or ignore them completely, specially the low social class. They don't know what they are losing, indeed! There is a great majority of very poor Indians, but neither dirty nor opportunist as somebody thinks when speaking about bargaining. This matter is an ancient custom in the whole east; I guess it doesn't mean they want to swindle us; my opinion is that everybody tries to get the maximum for what they sell, either goods or services, and when the transaction is over, after hours of bargaining sometimes, they fulfil the agreement accurately. They also use the same method among their equals, besides.

Everybody in India gave me the change scrupulously, without taking advantage of my inexperience with the rupees, and if anytime I left something forgotten, they ran to give it back to me.

As it is the custom, at the temple entrances and almost everywhere, the footwear is left outside; when I tell this in my country, without exception, people ask me :

— And weren't they stolen? Did you always find them at the exit?

Yes, I always found them when leaving, and to tell the truth, I have never known of anyone who had them missing.

I repeat that their curiosity about Westerners is exceedingly polite and respectful, and indeed I am proud of the affection that Indians offered me at full heart : the same Hindus, Muslims, Sikhs as any other races who are living together in the Indian Sub-Continent. I don't think that in my own country we are able to give that special kind of friendship and humble hospitality to foreigners. And what can I say about Europeans, at least in the few countries I got to know, a foreigner is absolutely anonymous!

And if speaking about hospitality, I can't forget the attendants of the hotel we stayed in New Delhi. In fact, when I remained there some days alone, the elder of the three men who kept our floor, invited me many times with insistence; to move to his home. His wife and children would take care of me, Vyjendhar assured me over and over all day long.

Although I didn't accept the invitation since others were my plans, he made me promise that, before my return, I would drop in to his place, for his family to meet me.

Guided by Sompal, the youngest of the attendants, we turned a little aside the taxi route driving us to the airport, and intended to greet Vyjendhar and his family, as he had asked.

How pleasant my surprise was when I arrived! His nice and sweet wife, and his three sons, the elder a teenager, were outside waiting for me, with their hands joined at the front and a very warm and polite : "Namaste, Namaste". Then, we all entered the house, and shared a white tea and biscuits with this family. There, I could observe that he only had a single room for everybody : the couple and the three kids, and a little place outside, where his wife cooked on the ground, at the Hindu custom. And this home they had, which for them was so much, they wanted to share with me. How is it possible not to take them in my heart for ever!

36. Compliments...the Muslim Way

We had already been in Puttaparthi for a month, enjoying Sai Baba's closeness and blessing; twice a day we shared his darshans, and sometimes we also saw Him during the "chanting" of bhajans. We were so at ease that it was hard just to think of going away.

Besides Sajad, we had other several friends near the hotel, who greeted us with the "Ssshau", knew our names and smiled at us when passing by.

Whenever I visited Sajad's shop in the evening, some young boys who kept other bazaars in the surroundings, went there in order to look over and make friends.

One of them, specially, asked me to teach him some Spanish phrases. His interest was to learn how to say : "eres hermosa; me gustas mucho" (You are beautiful, I like you a lot) and things like that. But when the boy repeated them, even after many attempts, it sounded something like : "eresh hermusha; mi gushtash musho".

He said it in a very mischievous way, pointing to me with the look and gesture.

I was very amused by the comic pronunciation, but the one who didn't smile at all was Sajad; such jokes got him annoyed and he couldn't conceal his displeasure. Thus, to make his friends' visits over, he took a duster manufactured by himself with narrow cloth stripes tied to a stick, and began shaking his carpets vigorously. A lot of dust blew up, but he didn't stop, until the "gallants", obviously uncomfortable, chose going away...

37. Sorry for being Nasty-minded

As I daily walked along Samadhi Road towards Sajad's Bazaar, I sometimes talked with neighbour businessmen. For instance, with a nice Muslim trader, who was usually waiting for me at his door, to ask about some special *asanas* for his cervical problem. Once we had had a chat and, of course, among other information, he wanted to know my occupation, I had stated that I was a Yoga Master.

Sajad was rather jealous of my other friends, and as soon he heard my voice in the surroundings, he immediately came to "rescue" me, and very earnestly led me to his shop.

It was precisely as a result of this man's attitude that a misunderstanding had arisen. With Giovanna, we had seen him several times, walking hand in hand with another man more or less of his same age (he looked about 40).

Very suspiciously, my friend had commented :

— De eshto hay en todo lado (Of this kind there are everywhere).

She was referring, no doubt, to homosexual couples. As I haven't got any kind of prejudices, I didn't pay much attention, until another day I found one of Sajad's cousin, walking together with an elder man, lovingly embraced by the waist.

With what I intended to be as tactful as possible, I asked Sajad about his cousin, in the sense if he was the kind of man who is attracted by those of his same sex, telling later what I had seen. My "son" looked at me very annoyed, as if he had seen perversion itself; he seriously pointed out that that man was his uncle, and, besides, this behaviour between very loved persons of the same sex, either relatives or just friends, was a Muslim custom.

Afterwards, they didn't attract our attention any more, since observing better the persons' conduct, we saw a lot of young men, and not so young, in the same attitude. Sorry for being nasty-minded!

38. Our Plans for the South

With my friend, we intended to travel a little through the country, to make a tour across South India to meet some Masters, Holy Men and Women, to visit certain Yoga Ashrams, and later, to make our way towards the North, to the *Himalayas*, to try to lodge at "The Divine Life Society", the Ashram that the renowned Yogi Swami Sivananda had founded at the beginning of this Century in Rishikesh.

Every day, Giovanna told me :

— I want to have an interview with Sai Baba for him
to materialize me a ring; then we can leave calmly
to go on with our planned tour.

But I felt so at ease at Puttaparthi, that every time that Swami was approaching, I begged with the mind :

— Please Swami, don't give us interview yet, because
I don't want to go still away from here, — and I am
sure that He received my message.

There, the days were sweetly slipping, without important novelties. After a month's stay, I began to get the route to follow ready. With my friend, we overhauled the places we intended to visit and with this itinerary in hand, I consulted some Tourism Agencies, better to say Taxi Agencies, to compare the prices.

At the end, we chose the budget that better fitted our finances and seemed the best, because of the car to rent as well as of the apparent reliability of the Agency, and with a real sorrow in our hearts, we settled on the departure day.

Since the night before, the taxi appointed to carry us to Bangalore, where the tour began indeed, with its driver sleeping inside, stayed under the balcony of our hotel room.

Very early in the morning, we loaded up our luggage into the taxi, with loyal Bangladesh's help, and warmly seen off by all our Muslim friends, who were already there at 5 o'clock in the morning, we set off...

✸

6

ON RAMACHANDRA'S HANDS, THE TIGER OF THE ROUTE

39. Goddess *Kali* at work

For the section from Puttaparthi to Bangalore, the Taxi-Agency had designated a driver, who, afterwards, in Bangalore, would be changed for the definite one, who would drive us through the whole run. This first driver was asthmatic and made strange sounds at breathing, as it cost him a great effort.

To make things worse, he got quite nervous, since, just when we set off, still in the early morning, we faced up the first and more unusual obstacle : several women, most of them old dishevelled ones, had blocked the road throwing big pieces of concrete on the pavement. The whole group was dancing, making odd rites and even stranger dances. They seemed a witches' group more than normal beings.

Our taxi had to stop, since it was impossible to cross, and at once, I stepped out of the car and approached, trying to convince the women to change their attitude. I guess they didn't understand English at all, since they just went on making the universal gesture of asking for money.

Endowed with a great courage (or irresponsibility), I turned a deaf ear to my friend's and driver's shouts, who very frightened, begged me to come back to the car. And there I continued negotiating, when the police arrived, cleared the road of stones and we could go on with our journey without any other trouble.

After the scare, we laughed a lot at remembering the incident, which, luckily, didn't go further. Giovanna assured that so angry, I seemed Goddess Kali, moving her several arms, who, indeed!, looks actually terrible.

Thus, among laughters, we arrived at Bangalore, where, in one of the great hotels, the Taxi Agency we had contracted in the Puttaparthi Branch, had its headquarter.

There, we had breakfast, rested for a while, paid half the fees and handed in the itinerary with the places we wanted to visit.

The most important matter : we got rid of the huge bags we carried, which were always our nightmare. From here on, every time we could leave the luggage in the safe-deposit, we felt a great relief, to have "taken out a weight from ourselves". It was thus in all the word sense, since they were so heavy that we couldn't even drag them.

In Puttaparthi, the bags had cracked several times because they were filled up, but up to that moment, we relied on my "son" Sajad's help, who had managed to take them to be repaired but from then on, unfortunately, we had to solve the problems that arose, by ourselves...

At this office, we could do all the arrangement related to the tour, and they kindly offered to try to get the train tickets, since at our returning, we would set off again northwards, more exactly to New Delhi, the Capital of the Country, crossing along the whole India, from South to North.

40. Our Driver, Ramachandra

At the Taxi Agency Office, in Bangalore, we met Ramachandra, who would be our driver in all the tour run : a very young boy, of about 24, a slim handsome Hindu, of nice and regular features, as black "as the night", with shining hair and a well cut moustache.

His dark and brilliant eyes sparkled threatening when he got angry (we could check it later), of clever appearance and humble attitude. Like the majority of his race, his white and even teeth made his face flash when smiling.

But, what attracted my attention indeed, was the slow sideward of his head, a doubtful gesture for us, but for the Hindus it means : yes, all right, O.K., it is that way, I agree, etc.

And his hands...! Very seldom in my life have I seen a person who better expressed himself with the single movement of his hands : Ramachandra's hands were like birds, sometimes flying, free and light, opened and raised, as waiting for the Grace of Heaven to descend over them; others in harmonious stillness, abandoned and absent; sometimes closed, gripped by impotence. All the subtle inflections, all the shades when wanting to express something were summed up with the attitude of them. And, if at the distance, I try now to evoke him, the first things that spring up in my mind are his eyes and his hands.

With Ramachandra, we shared two wonderful weeks travelling through South India, and he became one of our great friends, always reliable, polite, obliging, and with the humility that is distinctive of almost all Indians, in their relationship with foreigners.

In general, at the office of the Taxi Agency, all the car drivers are sitting down on the floor, around their boss's desk, and customers can choose among them, the one they like best. As we didn't know anybody, it was the people of the Agency who selected Ramachandra. I think that for such occasion they looked for somebody who could manage fairly well with the languages and dialects of the different states we were going to travel through, as well as the English, and the fact is that we didn't have any trouble of that kind in the whole journey.

Our first destination, with Ramachandra already at the wheel : Ramana *Maharshee* Ashram, in Tiruṇvannamalai; we set off towards there, with many illusions and expectations.

While crossing through Bangalore City, very clean and peaceful, with broad and tree-lined avenues, we passed by a great stadium, and noticed the contrast of a huge turmoil outside, with the police uselessly trying to put some order by fair club blows. The matter was a cricket match, quite a popular sport in India, more specifically, of India high class, which remained as British inheritance.

The problem was that a lot of young boys, who surely didn't have the means to pay for the tickets, were climbing "like spiders" by the high barred fabric fence, trying, of course, to gatecrash.

In the prevailing chaos, an absent-minded boy who was passing by on his bicycle, observing also the scene, collided against our car. At once, Ramachandra stopped the taxi, got down very angry with his eyes sparkling, and reprimanded the boy, giving him also some quick slaps. Then, he came back very resolute, evaluated the damage and surely considered the risk his job would run if the vehicle was broken; with an expert glance he estimated that the damage was minimum. He got back to the taxi, started the engine again and went on with the journey, while we watched his grave countenance in the mirror. Very pleased, my friend just commented :

— Me gusta porque éshte é un gayito. (I like him because he is as brave as a little rooster).

Since the departure, we could appreciate how well he drove the wheel : quick to react, careful, wise and a lynx-eyed to avoid any obstacles, and the fact is that these good reflexes are more than necessary to travel in India.

41. The South Landscape

The journey was wonderful; the landscape astonishing. While crossing the South, from the Centre Eastwards, we went through a lot of villages, always crowded with very poor people. They lived at the road side, in straw roof shacks, a kind of closed sheds, many times sharing the places with their animals, specially cows and goats.

I consider that for this humble families, their animals are something very esteemed, since, from them they get the milk, a help in the farming tasks, and even the dung for fuel. They are so valuablé, that even at some political demonstrations we saw, some Hindus were taking their cows, perhaps because of the risk of being stolen in their absence.

We saw large cultivated rice fields, in different steps : paddy areas, where the little plants were put by hand, others in varied sizes of growing, from a few centimetres up to ready to be reaped.

Sometimes, they were at full harvesting and from afar, the spectacle was outstanding indeed. They seemed multicolored little marks, scattered all over the field, as if a great printed piece of cloth was spread. When approaching, we saw they were hundreds of Indian women, who were performing their farm task, working with the rice as they have been doing for thousands of years, with their ancient sarees waving at the wind : red, yellow, green, blue, white, golden, silver, etc.

The groups who were already harvesting the rice, did it as in the Middle Ages, striking the dried plants with their seeds against the pavement, for the grains to fall off. Sometimes and with the same aim, they made cows or oxen turn over the heap of dried plants.

Every time we came across these "stoppers", our driver stopped the taxi completely, until it was possible to go on. If there was any chance, they were eluded by one side; otherwise, if people made signs to him, encouraging him in that sense, Rama drove slowly and carefully the taxi over it.

Frequently, at nightfall, when the sun set, proud little women went back home, very straight and self-satisfied : on their heads a rice bag, perhaps the payment of the hard working day, with which would secure, at least for a time, the family food.

We also came across some wagons, so loaded with rice straw, that the cart had disappeared under the cargo, and there was no room even for the driver. They travelled step by step along the crowded road, letting the tame cows or oxen give the rhythm to the run, without neither hastening nor punishing them. They were led by thin and ragged Hindus, with a hollow in the belly, but with such dignity in their black countenances, that instead of pity, only a great admiration arose on me.

All the luxuriant tropical vegetation file past our eyes; also a large variety of animals : large number of monkeys, some elephants which were moved for hard forestal works, crossed the road from time to time; exotic birds of bright plumage, which aren't afraid of men, since in India life is honoured.

Most Indians respect the *Ahimsa* or no hurt, so popularized by the beloved Mahatma Gandhi, the precept which refers not only to human beings, but also to all our travelling mates like trees, animals, and the environment. It includes in the same way ideas, plans, illusions; no killing, no stealing, no seizing up the others' works or dreams.

Always a constant feature : mountains in the distance, great coconut palms, extensive banana trees and other tropical thick plants, filled with beautiful flowers, or tasty fruits and inhabited by huge and multi-colored birds.

By this area, the road wasn't very good; sometimes it only had one way and others it didn't exist actually. All the time we came across some deviations because it was in construction, or it was being repaired. There, we also saw a great number of women who worked dressed in their ancient sarees, which seemed to be very comfortable even for these hard duties.

We travelled through many Indian areas, and it was usual to find people engaged in repairing or building roads, with very rudimentary machinery. For instance, we observed that in some places, they didn't use the heavy roller as in our country, but they rolled a kind of cylinder, pushed by hand over the tar, absolutely barefooted!

We came through villages where Indians were only dressed with loincloth, and I imagine they were the so called "wind-dressed", whose religion assign them this manner to be nude.

42. A Bathroom, Please!

In the first step of the journey with Ramachandra, luckily, we didn't have any other incident, and we could go on with the trip without problems, except for what happened to my friend : since for some days, she had been victim of what in India causes real worry : diarrhoea ! I imagined it was as a result of the disorders on her diet she had made at Puttaparthi. As if it were funny, she ate the very hot Hindu meals which our stomachs weren't used to, and drank frozen drinks.

This diarrhoea problem had been annoying her for several days. We had already consulted at Prashanti Nilayam an earnest homeopathic doctor who assisted his patients inside the Ashram, who prescribed, and also provided her with some medicines. But Giovanna, eager to be well as soon as possible, mixed them with other allopathic ones that Nives, an Italian friend, had given her, other ayurvedic pills bought at a kiosk, besides my phytotropic drops against diarrhoea (that luckily I never needed), and the result was that she got worse every day.

While we were in Puttaparthi, I took care of her, and the Muslim boys boiled rice every day to counteract it, but during the trip it wasn't so easy to follow the right diet.

Even though the landscape was fascinating indeed, my friend couldn't enjoy it much, since others were her urgencies. By the South, we travelled mostly through villages, thus it wasn't easy to get a bathroom.

Once, we stopped at a little and modest bar, to eat something and, by the way, to use the bathroom, since they had told us they possessed this "luxury". It was, actually, a plain stall on the sidewalk, a very common modality in India. The food, a variety of fried doughnuts, were heaped on a rough table in the open air, where the flies weren't lacking, fluttering around or enjoying the "banquet".

After several hours travelling, the hunger was felt : I bought something similar to a tiny pasty, with half a spoon of sweet stuffing and a lot of spices, and two fritters opened like little books. In my honor, this singular "menu" was served on a piece of newspaper of doubtful cleaning. I plucked up courage and ate it up, and it wasn't so bad as I had thought.

About the bathroom, which was the most pressing need, it was a little room in the house, absolutely empty, without door or a curtain to be used instead. Around it, there were at least 30 Hindu observers, looking at the scene with total curiosity. Failed attempt! We had to go on travelling and see if we had better luck in the following village.

It had been more than five hours since our departure from Bangalore. From time to time, Ramachandra stopped the taxi and pointed towards the field :

— Open space, *Ma'am*!

My friend hurried to answer "No, No", since truly, the place was never absolutely deserted. One could always see a cross-legged Hindu, sitting down under a tree, very quiet, maybe meditating. Besides, Giovanna dreaded snakes (and me too), which could be found in the pasture-land, or coiled round at any shrubbery. Thus, we had to endure (specially her) until we arrived at Ramana Maharshee's Ashram, in the evening.

43. The Sacred Fire Hill

In a beautiful Eastern evening splendor, we arrived at our

destination at Tirunvannamalai, and I'm going to quote Paul Brunton[1] to describe this sublime moment :

> "The sun was going to lie down in the night bed and the lovely spreading of bright colors imprisoned the heart. The blazing fire ball made its travelling downwards, to later sink itself in the jungle. It adopted orange shades, as a prelude of its quick disappearance of the light blue vault. Around it, the sky took all the spectrum colors, giving our eyes a present, with a feast no painter could ever produce.
>
> There was an ecstasy calm. The birds trill were not heard any more. The monkeys chat had ceased. The giant red circle disappeared in another dimension. Its panorama of snaked fire tongues sunk in the darkness. The calm pierced my thoughts and its beauty reached me up to the soul."[1]

Thus, in a wonderful Eastern sunset, we arrived at Ramana Maharshee's Ashram, placed a few kilometers from Tirunvannamalai Village. The Maharshee was a great sage, holy man and well known yogi, who had died some years before. From an early age, he felt God's call, and the Arunachala Mountain or "The Sacred Fire Hill" exerted a strange fascination over him.

This mountain straightens up lonely very near the ashram, and it is the place in whose caves the Rishee used to meditate. Today, a great number of pilgrims and Spiritual Seekers turn there.

Ramana's mortal remains are buried in what today is the Meditation Hall or Maha *Samadhi*, together with his cow, and several times a day, the persons who visit it, meet there for meditation or the chanting of bhajans.

When we arrived, after introducing ourselves to the monks in charge of the ashram, and showing them a letter in which they had accepted our request to stay there for some days, we were lodged in a tidy apartment. We noticed that it had two bathrooms : one, turkish style, with the hollow on the ground, and the second one for bathing, with the known pail and jug to pour water, as it is the habit in most of the Indian bathrooms.

1. Brunton, Paul. "The Secret India" (Chapter IX, in his "The Sacred Fire Hill", page 161) — Buenos Aires — Editorial KIER — 10th Edition 1992).

Our place was opposite the main ashram building, just crossing the road : rather quiet, clean, with big and beautiful trees and a lot of monkeys and birds, specially a great number of peacocks with showy tails like giant fans, which were seen appearing on the roofs, or flying freely throughout the whole ashram, as if it were the Paradise, with their splendid iridescent plumage.

After enduring the long journey without being able to empty her intestines, my friend didn't feel very spirited; so, as soon as we settled, she lied down and slept about 18 running hours, in order to recuperate her strength.

The first evening I set off to the dining-room alone, ready to do the same as the others, since actually it was my debut of ashram life. When I arrived there, I observed there were Eastern and Western persons, already arranged; everybody sitting down on the floor waiting for their meals, and I did the same.

A kind of round shaped tray, made with several neatly sewn leaves, was placed in front of me. On it, the monks served the meal, which was brought in great buckets; the rice, yellow with spices, and some green and pulse stew, put into bowls. Everybody mixed the rice and sauces with their hands, with the typical gesture of stirring it and then, taking the food into the mouth neatly in little handfuls, which I couldn't manage very well.

Between the strong spices and the hot sauces, I was unacustomed to, my stomach was feeling a little upset, and I was already sicken even at the sight of the pails. Luckily, the menu included milk and bananas, and when the Swami saw I couldn't swallow the rice, he kindly brought me another glass of milk and two extra bananas, so I fed myself very well anyway.

In the morning, breakfast was also a glass of milk, and a kind of bread prepared with rice flour and cooked in steam, which could be rubbed with golden date sugar, always flavoured with spices, that were a little more eatable this way.

Appearing through all the barred windows that opened to the courtyard, monkeys were sitting down waiting for the scraps.

At breakfast ending I approached with my tray, to share my rice bread with them, which, despite my good will, I couldn't swallow, neither alone nor with the sugar, but before even making the gesture of taking the bread with my hand in order to deliver it to them, they had already, quick and delicately taken it across the bars, including the tray and everything.

In the dining-room, I felt very proud of myself and thought I was behaving perfectly right, when another person sitting next to me, furtively touched my shoulder and whispered :

— With the right hand...

She was alluding to the ancient Indian custom to take food only with that hand, since the left one is used for other ends.

At our service, we had a very nice and polite young boy, who was always attentive to our smallest needs, and slept in front of our apartment; he became Ramachandra's close friend, who during the two weeks' tour, always slept inside the taxi. Car and driver stayed within the ashram courtyard, very near our door, so we didn't have any reason to be afraid of, and always felt very well protected.

Practically, my friend didn't take too much part in the ashram activities, except for some visits at the Meditation Room; she didn't feel willing to be present at the Dining Room either, so in the morning I asked breakfast for her and she had it in our room. Later, she was in a better mood, and we set off with the taxi to visit some ancient temples, which are several kilometres straight ahead.

44. "Wherever You Go, Do What You See"

At Tirunvannamalai Village, we visited some of these ancient temples which, in accordance with people's remark, were more than a thousand years old.

> "Their facade are covered with sculptures, of statues with legend subjects, Hindu Gods at meditation or loving embrace, mythologic animals and birds imagery."[2]

I asked some Indians who had built those wonderful masterpieces, and in a very innocent way, they answered : "The Gods", and if they affirm it, why would I doubt it!

Such pyramid shaped temples, with a truncated end, are very

2. 3. 4. Brunton, Paul—"The Secret India" (Chapter IX, in his "The Sacred Fire Hill" — Pages 157, 158, 159) — Bs. Aires — Edit. Kier — 10th Edition 1992.

popular in the whole India. Their deities are found inside a small chamber, without any ornaments, "sinister shrines of dark misteries"[3]. Only priests may enter there, who are considered like the Gods' servants : they act as intermediaries between Gods and devotees, besides washing, dressing, taking them to bed and getting them up again when the moment arrives.

My friend and I crossed deserted galleries, where the abandonment atmosphere was interrupted only by the monkeys' shouts. We went through gloomy cloisters which shut hundred of carved stone pillars in, always with mythological figures, and entered a large hall, from where the piercing scent of burnt incense reached us.

Already from outside, it was heard "the rhythmic and monotonous beating of the drums, the singing of religious hymns on the side of the priests, the shell trumpet and the melancholy and rough notes of the cymbals"[4], that came from inside the cloisters.

When we approached where the devotees were, a priest painted us the two horizontal ash lines on our foreheads, Shivaist or Shiva worshipers' symbol, God's aspect that in the Hindu Trinity is considered as the Universe destroyer, to create again, in an eternal cosmic dance.

We took part of the *Arati* or fire offering, and made our "puja" by placing half a coconut and some rupees on a tray. The priest who might enter the sanctuary where "the Gods dwell", carried the offerings there, made the *ritual* and then brought it back, blessed.

The devotees, with their hands, made the gesture as if they were pushing to attract those blessings towards their bodies, in a very soft and delicate manner. Of course, we also made the same ("Wherever you go, do what you see"). O.K.

We walked through several of these ancient temples and took nice pictures, some of them with Ramachandra, who happily agreed, or kindly offered to take some to us.

45. The Sadhu's Goddess

It was inside one of the cloisters of these ancient temples in Tirunvannamalai, where we had a meeting with an old sadhu. In our ashram gateway, we could usually find some of these renouncers, completely absent minded in the reading of Holy Books, or singing Veda Hymns to Gods'honour.

It is very easy to find many of these singular persons walking along the roads in total abstraction, and also on the pilgrimage spots. They are considered India spiritual keepers and there are millions of them scattered through the whole country, from South to North and from East to West. The rest of the population, mostly feel proud of them; they revere and help them. People are also a little afraid, since they are considered as personages with special powers.

Sadhus are real ascetics, renouncers looking for the Supreme Truth. They abandon family, home and all personal properties, bringing the walking stick or trident as their only treasure and a bowl to beg rice. Some of them, belong to very wealthy families, or of a socially high *caste*.

Every three years they gather at great religious festivals called the "Kumba Melha", which are carried out in turns, in four holy cities. During them, all gurus, sadhus, and other spiritual masters, and also devotees, pilgrims and spiritual seekers, come together to these places to chant and perform "pujas" to the Gods and other religious rites.

Someone defined the sadhus as "the Gods' friends" and "misunderstood among men", the ones who "follow the wind way". This description is very suitable to them; it is usual to meet them with their ochre robes beside the roads sides, around temples and at the ashrams gateways, where monks give them some food, and they don't remain at the same spot, to avoid *attachment*.

On looking through in one of these millenary temple cloisters, I met two feverish eyes, maybe by so much fasting, in a tall and lean body. The ocher robe very spoiled, nearly frayed, over a long linen in the same condition, tied at the waist, which covered his thin legs.

I was moved by the silent pleading of his look, so I took some rupees out of my pocket, handed them to him, while taking his skinny hands between mines. Not believing that somebody could deign to touch him, at one he bent down to the ground and kissed my feet.

This gesture touched me deeply, since it is a worship sign towards Gods and Saints, or else to the person who one chooses as his Master, the Guru "who dispel the darkness and takes you to the light".

Later, this Sadhu himself accepted to take a photo with us, taking off for that aim the upper part of his ragged attire. Then, we could see such a lean chest, that the ribs pushed the skin, and I deduced that if somebody had wanted to make him a thorax study, he would have not even needed to use X-Rays.

46. "Good Morning Máam, Set off ?"

The next morning, very early, we got ready to leave Tirunvannamalai and set out again. It was usual that my friend loaf around in bed up to the last moment, and usually, I awakened her with my "mates".

The taxi looked clean and shining, the same as Ramachandra, our driver, who smiling widely put his black head out :

— Good morning, Máams, O.K.?

In the tape recorder of the car, Indian music; the scent of perfumed incense : a very promising environment.

We left every place with nostalgia in our heart. In spite of the early time, the view along the road was always more or less the same, with very few variations : we went through many small towns of twisted streets, with our taxi at man's pace, zigzagging among people going on foot, riding bicycles, auto-rickshaws, pigs, goats, cows, travelling sellers offering their goods with much insistence, rough shops and stalls on streets and sidewalks, of exotic fruits, roasted seeds, greens, etc.

It was in the highway where the contrast between the ancient and the modern vehicles were mainly noticed : the Middle Ages and the Twentieth Century living harmoniously together : it could be seen from modern cars, buses and lorries, up to old wagons pulled by oxen.

Each vehicle made its horn sound as loud and sharp as possible. At the back of each one the same inscription could be read, which was like an invitation : "Sound Horn". Everybody, without exception, obeyed the suggestion, our Ramachandra included, making a hellish fuss!

And I don't say this as criticism, since somebody may think that this row bothered me; on the contrary. It seemed that I'd never seen life boiling as in this fascinating country, in this real human tide I happily integrated myself.

And thus, we carried our way on to Pondicherri city, to the meeting of *Sri* Aurobindo Ashram, where we already imagined that warm and moving experiences would be waiting for us, in which, with no doubt, our hearts would be entirely involved.

✷

7

SRI AUROBINDO ASHRAM

47. On the Bengal Gulf

It was about noon when, after some investigations, we arrived with the taxi driven by Ramachandra, at the Park Guest House of Sri Aurobindo Ashram. It was a coquette building of several storeys, Moorish style, where the green colour prevails in the front part, and very well cared, outside as well as inside, which lay down absolutely on the sea, on the Bengal Bay.

After finding out all our antecedents and being accepted, we were registered, and later led to which would be our room on the ground-floor : just metres from a shining blue sea, that extended before our sight in its whole splendor.

In front of the building, a well cared park, with the grass recently mowed, and so green, that in the mornings the dew drops seemed tiny gems scattered on its surface.

Everywhere flower plants, not only in bordered areas and nurseries, but also in profusion of all sizes pots, harmoniously spread over. From hanging creepers, the jasmines offered their exquisite perfume.

Exactly in front of our room, the gateway park was fenced in and was guarded by two artistic stucco elephants, which figure has an important significance in India, and it is repeated in museums, gardens, parks, squares, temples : always the peaceful figures of nice elephants decorate these places.

Already inside the room, we were received by the deep looks, so holy and sweet, from huge pictures in white and black, of two spiritual giants : Sri Aurobindo Ghose and his companion, Mira Alfassa, named *Mother* by him, who was his collaborator in the Ashram's tasks.

These big pictures were hung one beside the other, against the wall in front of our beds : Sri Aurobindo, of delicate features and in the prime of life. Mother, also in her youth : a French woman of dazzling beauty, who had arrived from her country to establish next to this great yogi and political man, who fought for the Independence of his country, the beloved India.

About Mother, who seconded and continued Aurobindo's works, it is said she liked to be surrounded by beautiful, refined, coquette and of great luxury things, leaving her particular seal of delicate good taste in the several Pondicherri Ashrams, as well as in Delhi Branch, in the Capital of the Country.

Every morning when I woke up, the first things I felt over me, were those deep and beautiful eyes, from Aurobindo and Mother, and their looks remained the whole day in my mind and my heart. What a message these two pure souls would bring from immortality! Two spiritually realized beings, whom I had always admired, and whose teachings constitute the basis of the Integral Yoga Philosophy, which I was seizing as time went by!

In the evening, sitting outside, in the balcony, in front of the room, a gentle and mild breeze that came from the sea, seemed to caress me quietly. I could hear the wave rumor breaking on the beach. Among the silhouettes of slender palm trees, I could distinguish the white lace of its foam. Everything was absolutely perfect...

48. The "European" Pondicherry

During our first day in Pondicherry, we visited the house where they lived, and now their sacred mortal remains rest : the tombs of these two beloved personages : Sri Aurobindo and the Mother, who survived him for more than 20 years.

Many people, like us, visit this spot with a real devotion; we saw several ones in a meditative attitude, kneeled down around their shrines, with concentration and worship. The place's background is very holy, and the powerful vibrations of these two souls are felt in a special way.

In the adjacent gardens, there was a great variety of colourful flowers and plants, and over the marbles of the tombs, devotees had drawn hearts, sacred symbols like the *OM* and other figures, with petals of natural flowers. Some of them in only one color : white, pink, yellow, lilac, orange, red, and others multicolour, in perfect harmony and beauty.

This decoration was not just on the flat of the marbles, but also all around, flowing down on all sides as exquisite water falls. The scent was transporting, and a peace and sanctity silence was breathed everywhere : I felt those places were blessed and would go on radiating a divinity aura, left by these holy and wise persons, and that the powerful influences of these yogis would follow reaching their disciples, who, like me, try to carry out their wonderful teachings.

My greatest admiration towards Sri Aurobindo, is based in his universal vision about religions, and the certainty that every person, no matter the race or creed, may realize God in his heart, following any of the *Paths*.

Generally at noon, sometimes also in the evening, we had lunch or dinner in another Aurobindo Ashram, in which we saw this loved Master's dream come true : thousands of persons, from India as well as from near or far away spots of the world, shared with pleasure the food that kind hands had prepared and served everybody with the same sweetness.

Even though the dining rooms, as it occurs in almost all Indian ashrams, are silence areas, the same we could note the brotherhood and solidarity prevailing, either when keeping a place at the table, or sharing their chapatis, reaching us a glass of water, or only receiving their good will gesture when looking or just smiling at us, with the hands joined over the heart.

Pondicherry City is of a considerable importance; I do not know whether to call it a tourist or a holy city. By its square blocks, it seems more an European city, with wide tree-lined streets and avenues. This style so common in the West, is rarely found in the South of the country nor in the rest of India. There, usually, the streets become twisted and take unexpected shapes and directions; they rise, go down, widen, get as narrow as a corridor; they coil or spring again, interrupted by some buildings, in a thousand capricious shapes and without any studied symmetry.

Besides, there, in Pondicherry, the pattern building is seen very European and modern in style, and they are mostly painted white. By the fact it had been for a long time a French Colony, the prevailing language is French, in addition to its local idiom.

As my friend Giovanna speaks French perfectly, she was ready to show her abilities in Pondicherri, but this wasn't necessary, since inside the ashram where we stayed as well as in the whole city, there weren't problems to manage in English.

49. "The City of Dawn"

It was impossible to remain in Pondicherry City and not to visit Auroville ("The City of Dawn"), very few kilometres from the first, the wonderful spot which somebody called "An Utopia in action".

It was founded in 1968 by five thousand persons from 114 countries and 23 Indian States. It is, in fact, the place dreamt by Sri Aurobindo and accomplished by Mother, for persons all over the world, without race or religious creed differences, could live harmoniously together. On the opening day, in the emission that during the inauguration Radio India transmitted, to make this event without precedent known, these words were heard :

> "There should be a place on earth that no nation would demand as her own, where all good will Human Beings with a true aspiration, could live freely as world citizens, obeying only one authority : that of the Supreme Truth. A place of peace, agreement and harmony, where all man's fighting instincts might be used exclusively to conquer the causes of their miseries and sufferings, to overcome their weaknesses and ignorance and to triumph over their limitations and incapacities; a place where spiritual needs and the anxiety to progress, would precede the satisfaction of wishes and passions, and the search for pleasures and material interests.
>
> In this place, children could grow up and develop integrally, without losing touch with their souls, and education would be given not to pass examinations

or to get certificates and job places, but to enrich existing faculties in each one and bring to light other new ones.

In this place, titles and positions would be replaced by opportunities to serve and organize. The material needs of each one, would be fairly covered and the intellectual, moral and spiritual superiority, would find the way to express themselves in the general organization, by means of a rise in the duties and responsibilities, and not in the power and personal satisfactions.

The artistic beauty in all its expressions : painting, sculpture, music, literature would be equally at everybody's reach, and the possibility to share the happiness that this produces, would only be limited to the single capacity and not to the social and financial position. Since in this ideal place, money wouldn't be the sovereign God; individual values would have much more importance than material wealth and social position.

Work wouldn't be the means to earn one's living, but the way to express and develop one's own capacity and possibilities, at the same time it would be giving a service to the whole community, which would provide each one with the necessary things for its living and a space for action.

To sum up, a place where the individual relations, which are almost exclusively based on competition and rivalry, would be replaced by relations of collaboration, emulation to realization of the good, and to a real brotherhood."[1]

At the moment of its foundation 30 years ago, this city-community was only a desert of reddish ground, with only one

1. Sri Aurobindo Ashram Publications — Delhi Branch, printed at Taj Services Ltd. E-100-103, Sector 6, for Sri Aurobindo Ashrams, and "Un Sueño...", "Yoga, Art and Life Science — Bs. Aires — No. 30-year 7, 7/8/95 ("Auroville...").

aspiration : "The Unity in the Diversity". Some few pioneers began consolidating the project, just a handful of dreamers in a world without borders, with steel muscles and spirited hearts, impregnated by Aurobindo's words : "The development of the Divine *Consciousness* will be the last sense of evolution on earth".

Today, within an area of about 25 kms., there are, without counting visitors, more than 1000 inhabitants, and in spite of speaking so many strange and different languages (more than 55), everybody understands Auroville's message.

A huge Indian fig tree marks the geographical centre of the place. At the shadow of this big tree, Mother used to sit down to meditate, and it is said that it was precisely there, where she had the vision of this great project.

From the fig tree as the centre, twelve gardens stretch today, surrounded by lotus shaped urns, which contain soil from the 124 founder countries, as a symbol of the Human Oneness.

The road from Pondicherri (or Pondicherry) to Auroville extends along alleys with a lot of traffic, always heterogeneous. On passing through with the taxi, I noticed straw circular shacks, built inside dense coconut palm and cashewnut tree woods, and those pictures called forth to me the presence of African tribes, instead of Indian population.

A small faded sign, so unclear that we almost surpassed it, reminded us that we were already at Auroville, approaching the other triangle vertex, where the building of what represents the core, the soul of Auroville is being finished : the Matri-Mandhir, "House of the Creator Strength" or "The Pavilion of the Divine Love", started in 1971 and almost finished.

Mother called it "The Babel Tower the wrong way round", surely alluding at God's purpose to punish man's arrogance wanting to reach Heaven, by diversifying the languages to create disorder and confusion, while in this version the contrary is attempted, that is to say, the Oneness of Human Being.

Matri Mandhir is an spherical figure of about 36 mts. diameter, covered outside with big golden lotus flowers (this ornamentation is not finished yet). Steel and concrete ramps lead to its inner chamber, circular shaped also, where it can be reached by a long spiral staircase.

To get into this chamber, we left all our ownership outside, and they gave us clean and disinfected socks. When I got used to the half light reigning in that moment, I could observe the large room with a conic roof and plenty of columns; the walls as well as the floor and pillars, were completely covered with pure white marble.

From the top of its dome, a ray of light pierced and was reflected in a crystal sphere placed on the floor, and then all the enclosure went slowly changing its tone, and at some moments it was getting as clear as a bright sunny day, to fade at once in a crepuscular half-light.

In this absolutely empty, white and silent space, all the people were sitting in a meditative and respectful attitude. I watched my friend, completely absent-minded, and Ramachandra, our driver, very earnestly sitting down by my side, and I said to myself that this was the way I would like people to gather, as in The Divine Love Pavilion, in this place of real inner calm, of quietness, of meeting with oneself without rituals or *ceremonies*.

The external noises, such as the breeze flowing through the trees, caused strange resonances, and I felt I was in another unreal and fantastic world. In my mind, Mother's words went on echoing : "I invite you to the Great Adventure".

Some persons in charge of the project commented to me that in such a place, it was necessary neither police nor army or institutional authorities; just a 12 persons' council, which, together with a secretariat, take charge of the administrative and financial work, with weekly meetings where anybody may freely participate.

The organization is flexible and it fits to the community needs. Auroville is self-sufficient, and there are workshops where, in a craftsman way, all kinds of goods are manufactured : clothes, footwear, wooden furniture, printing, jewels, candles, incense sticks, etc.

They also receive donations, not only from their own inhabitants, but from visitors, and from the national and foreign governments as well. About properties, they are neither bought nor sold, so private property doesn't exist.

A very green Auroville receives travellers today, and the more than two million trees planted in its beginning, are now full of flowers, fruits, birds, multi-coloured butterflies.

Crafts and sciences are not absent either, and persons that nowadays are living there, not only plant, build and educate; they also make handicrafts, write poems, investigate and create.

This is a dream that is becoming reality : the dream of two "colossus", who imagined a world where the whole Human Race was a single and Great Family. I am sure that Sri Aurobindo and Mother, from their places beyond, together with angels and saints, would be pleased, smiling, to see their projects realizing, and this Great Family of the Human Beings, joined in love, instead of divided by religions.

50. The Mark of Aurobindo

A well organized tour took us through all Aurobindo Foundation's Ashrams, which gives occupation, roof and food to a great number of Indians. We could see them working, each one in his-speciality : rice paper, that is worked by hand and in a very peculiar way, stamping later piece after piece; the handicraft incense sticks, perfumed with exquisite natural fragrances : rose, jasmine, musk, parijal, mattipal, sandal, etc. Some of them very rare, typical of those Indian regions.

Besides, the dyeing Batik technique, performed with patience and devotion by skilled and loving Hindu hands; the cotton fabrics and clothes, manufactured with simple and primitive mills, which monotonous sound maintains an established beating. I also noticed the block printing technique.

A coquette boutique next to the Matri-Mandhir shows and sells all the goods manufactured in the different ashrams : there, you can get nice slippers crochet plaited, suggestive perfumes, scented incense sticks, books edited in their printers, cotton T-shirts, hand printed bags, post-cards, table cloths, free stones and also mounted in delicate jewels, bijouterie, strong thread hammocks, embroidered and painted cushions, candles, etc. As usual, the lack of space in our bags restrained the enthusiasm before so many beautiful crafts.

Ramachandra, our driver, also looked over everything, and sometimes he called our attention about an article he had discovered and considered exceptionally special, and, really, it was of a very good taste.

Close to the "cottage" we three, sat down for a drink, at a

nice bar, where some natural juices and tempting cakes were served. I remember that canteen specially, since it was decorated in a particular way, with "collages" in bright colour cloth, harmoniously combined, with predominance of turquoise and yellow colours, in its different shades. They were symmetrically placed from the lamps to the roof, and the spot looked singularly beautiful.

Everywhere one crosses through, the whole Pondicherry and its surroundings, carry the mark of Aurobindo's step : this great poet, philosopher, writer, hero of India's Independence and above all, Grand Yogi and Spiritual Master, who was born in Calcutta in 1872. At some opportunities he was under arrest by the British, as a consequence of the spirited nationalist statements he made in the magazines of his Publishing House, of course, against the usurpers.

It was just during a stay in jail that he had a transcendental vision and realized that for the best achievement of his aims, he had to go on the Spiritual Path.

Likewise, he decided to settle down in Pondicherri, at that time a French Colony, moving away from the English clutches. There, he devoted himself to Yoga experiences; he wrote several books, which, as time passed, became the "Catechism" of Integral Yoga, such as "Synthesis of Yoga", "The Ideal of Human Oneness", "The Divine Life", "Letters on Yoga", and many others, while the Mother, already at that time his collaborator, stayed mostly in charge of the Ashram, guiding the Education activities.

This precious dream of the Human Oneness, may not be an isolated fact. It was also already said by Mother :

> "It is impossible to have a change in a lonely place on earth, without involving the whole terrestrial consciousness in the change. It is inevitable : everything is tightly interwoven, and a vibration at one place, will necessarily have repercussion in the whole planet."

Personally, I think, with no doubt, that in a non far future, every person of good will on earth, will be also able to live in this manner.

51. The Ayurvedic Powders at Work

During our trip through the different Aurobindo's Ashrams, in

Pondicherri, we specially visited the Ayurvedic Section, where two kind doctors of this ancient science, attended the patients free. Besides, and with the help of local personnel, they prepared all the medicines with absolutely natural products from the vegetable, animal and mineral reigns.

This real Holistic Medicine, Yoga's sister, is also based on the Vedas Teaching, the most ancient sacred books Humanity knows of. The word "Ayurveda" means literally "Long Life Science" and it respects all the healing methods, from a drug to a hand on the shoulder, on the basis of the principle that "Everything that heals is Medicine".

Keeping in mind the whole aspects of Human Being, that is to say physical, mental and spiritual, it advises to control the negative emotions like anger, jealousy, envy, fear, cruelty, pride, lust, etc., cultivating on the other hand the noble feelings of love, humility, good will, forgiveness, etc., to enable persons to discover the inexhaustible spring of happiness they carry on within.

In India, two ancient doctors, who systematized this science, after the arrival of the writing, are very revered : Sri Sushruta (600 years B.D.) and Sri Charak (800 years B.D.). The first of them, defined Health State thus :

> "The sound person is the one in which the Bio-energy, the humors and the metabolism are in balance; the excretion of bodily waste is regular and the senses, the mind and the soul keep calm."[2]

It was precisely one of these ayurvedic powders, that Ashram's Doctors prescribed my friend Giovanna, with which, luckily, and after more than 10 days of discomfort and worries, she could control her annoying diarrhoea with just one ingestion.

These preparations don't practically have expiry, since for more than a year, they keep its complete power and afterwards, get weakening gradually, but without becoming toxic. Besides being cheap, I could check at several occasions that they are effective indeed : from India I despatched a parcel by air-mail, with some brain tonics for my husband in Argentina, and the result was spectacular.

---

2. Dr. Domar Singh Madariya (An Ideal Medical Science — Integral Yoga Magazine. Buenos Aires, Year 4, No 26 — Pages 34; 1992).

As I had already said, Ayurveda is a Holistic Science, and one must not find strange that, generally, the medical inquiry starts with this simple (or not so simple) question :

ARE YOU A HAPPY PERSON ?

52. Let's Enjoy the Beach !

Bordering our Guest House, the sea was fenced in with big stones, so there wasn't much beach itself left to enjoy.

Besides, the seas are holy places where the Hindus don't bathe for the only pleasure of amusing themselves and playing, as we Westerners do, but only when they think it is necessary, they go into the water absolutely dressed to give themselves ablutions to purify in body and soul.

Women are seen specially fascinating with their sarees on, which languidly float on the sea surface, and it gives the impression that a long figure subtly chases the physical body.

We had decided with my friend, to take a rest day, not to make any visit nor to go out, but just rest and tan at the beach. Very early we told Rama that we wouldn't need him and suggested our driver to take also a free day, and go for a drive downtown to "see the girls".

Usually, Ramachandra came with his taxi inside the ashram, and stayed in front of our room, but in this place and for the first time since we set off, it was not allowed this way. The same, Rama was always around the ashram, as near as possible, and very attentive to our needs.

On this occasion, at the suggestion to take a free day, he answered smiling : "O.K., O.K. Máam", slowly shaking his head from left to right, as a sign of agreement.

We calmly got dressed : we put on the swimsuit under our tunic, up to the feet long, and came down walking slowly to the beach. Of course, dressed this way we entered the water, that was nicely lukewarm. Later, we walked a little by the shore to dry the clothes, and we noticed that almost nobody was seen by the surroundings.

As I said, almost nobody, since, sitting down on one of the huge stones was Ramachandra, who didn't take his eyes away from us! Naturally, and in spite of his "O.K., O.K.", actually he had never thought of moving away and letting us alone, even though we had asked him expressly. He felt that his obligation was to look after us and then he stayed there, not leaving even for a minute to fulfil his "duty", as Rama said.

This place over the Bengala Gulf, is absolutely charming, and we felt wonderfully at ease inside the Guest House as well as in all the places we visited and that carries Aurobindo's mark. Besides, the weather accompanied us with some splendid days, of pleasant temperature, with a totally clear and shining sky, of an incredible blue; the sea breeze frolicked with our skin, touching it lightly when passing, and at nights, it cooled the atmosphere enough. We could have stayed at this spot *Ad infinitum*. But our route to carry out, didn't let us change much of what we had planned.

With the Ayurvedic powders, Gio had improved and felt wonderfully, even though she had lost some kilos, and I annoyed her telling she seemed our friend the sadhu.

We had planned to go on southwards and visit Swami Premananda's Ashram, our dear Mataji Indra Devi's Guru, from which the only thing we knew, was that it was situated near Trichi or Tiruchirapally City.

We also wanted to visit the summer retreat of Sai Baba at Kodaykanal, taking the southward route again to Cape Comorin, the most Southern spot of India, where Kanyakumari town is situated, and it is the meeting place of the three Oceans : Indian Ocean, Arabian Sea and Bengala Bay.

During the few days of stay in Pondicherri, I felt greatly surprised since I had not seen almost any beggars in this zone, but on setting off early towards our next destination, the terrible reality again : long avenues with their side walks full up of persons sleeping out in the open, and I had to face again the sad situation of such a many-sided country.

✱

8

THE GURU OF MATAJI INDRA DEVI

53. Premananda Ashram?

Tiruchirapally or Trichi, is a big and crowded city, and Giovanna just knew that Swami Premananda's Ashram was nearby, but the truth was that we didn't have the exact or close address, but we would not give up visiting him. If it is said that "asking one reaches Rome", how weren't we going to meet Premananda?

With the car plate 7733, the noble vehicle which was our taxi, its driver Ramachandra in charge, we turned over and over by the surroundings. From time to time, Rama put his black head out, to ask any passer-by who inspired him more confidence:

— Premananda Ashram?

Without exception and before answering, all the looks slid towards the back seat, to observe with no dissimulation the two white foreigners that attracted their curiosity. At once, surely several persons surrounded the taxi to exchange their impressions about the place, discussing among them the different possibilities, always with oblique, or sometimes direct looks towards our place. The one who offered himself to accompany us to the Ashram was never absent, waiting, of course, for the rupees he could receive as a tip for his "services".

In spite of having set off, as usual, very early, to avoid the hottest hours, and being the distance rather short, with this searching for the place it was almost noon.

In those moments, in the middle of March, the thermometer

didn't drop the 48 or 50°, and during the day, the heat was really unbearable.

54. Sabhina, the Sweet

After so many inquiries, we finally arrived at our aim : a little, very clean and neat ashram, with cared gardens full of multi-coloured flowers, with the impression of being still under construction.

We were received very kindly by Sabhina, an European lady gracefully dressed in the Eastern fashion, with a beautiful red silk saree that suited her wonderfully. Young and very pretty, she told us later that she had been living in the ashram close to her Master, for a long time, may be about 4 years (I don't remember exactly). I imagine she was residing there as a *Sanyasin* or renouncer, what means a removal from the world, and a life as a nun, in search of the spiritual realization.

Sabhina acted as a secretary and messenger of the Swami. She stated that she knew our Mataji Indra Devi, the "First Yoga Lady" in Argentina, who visits her Guru every time she travels to India. I have known that there, she is received, revered and honored as a queen, or a goddess, it is all the same.

Our idea was to meet the Hindu Master and then, go on our journey, but, as I have already said, in India, and specially within an ashram, time is measured by other parameters.

In fact, Sabhina didn't give us many hopes about the possibility to have an interview with her Guru. In the meantime, she invited us to the Meditation Room, where several persons had already gathered singing bhajans. Likewise, she stated that it was actually difficult that Swami would come out at noon, but with the attempt we wouldn't miss anything.

55. Waiting for the Master

Not very hopeful for Sabhina's words, we settled next to the others, in the Meditation Room. I observed that the enclosure was modest but very clean, and it was adorned with plenty of flowers, which exhaled exquisite fragrances.

Sitting cross-legged on the floor, there were a lot of Indian persons, besides a good number of Westerners, men and women, young ones and not so young.

After this analysis, I tried to concentrate myself in the "chanting" or bhajans singing, but my always anxious mind was already thinking of all the time we had "wasted" to reach to that place, and was elapsing with such a long journey still ahead; not only for the distance in kilometres, but for the material time it takes in India to travel sometimes through relatively short distances, due to the varied mixture that also drive on the road : people on foot with great bundles on their heads, the two wheel carts pulled by oxen, that walk at little steps from one village to the other; bicycles, motorbikes, cars, buses, lorries, elephants, monkeys, goats, and once, I even saw the road occupied by a "posse" of nice ducks, which in a perfect parade were urged on by her owner, and it gave the impression that she managed them by a rope tied to each one!

I had already remarked that our Ramachandra was a true genius to elude all the obstacles without losing, apparently, his Eastern calm. He smiled very pleased before my remarks that he was "the tiger of the roads", as I told him. And, of course, he was : over and over he surpassed as an arrow all the "stoppers"; he made his way through at clean horn blowing and on the left, as it is still done in India, as an inheritance of the British dominion.

56. Swami Premananda in Person !

In this and other worries I was pondering, when everybody kept silent inside the Meditation Room, before the surprise to see Swami Premananda, in person, coming into the large enclosure and ascending to his "throne". This was a big arm-chair with a high back, constructed in dark wood, almost black, and all beautifully carved in delicate filigree; it was upholstered in purple velvet and placed at one side, very close to the altar.

His presence filled with happiness all the countenances of the people present. He himself radiated a great joy, with his nice eyes, shining and deep, which on smiling, lighted up all his olive skin face. His hair was also very dark and abundant.

I could observe him from near : vital, stout and quite young; I guess he was about 40 years old. Dressed in a very showy way, with a dark red satin dhoti, and a large shawl of the same color and cloth, on his strong and solid shoulders. Native of Sri Lanka, this Swami Premananda was a very cheerful man indeed, full of life and energy.

Never losing the smile, he started singing a bhajan, a merry devotional tune, "a cappella". The persons present accompanied him clapping hands, to make the rhythm. Later he made some funny remarks about a pair of clogs that were brought to him from Holland by a devotee, which he wore and tried to walk with, keeping his balance on them, what caused a lot of laughter for the grotesque figure he offered, while he continually asked : "Are they worn this way?"

I don't know if it lasted minutes or hours, but everyone was caught up by his joy, and it didn't matter to anybody how much or little time was already elapsing. Then, he answered some questions made by the people present, in his own dialect (from Indians) and others in English, posed by Westerners.

At the end, he asked if there was anybody ready to leave, and, incredible thing!, the lovely Sabhina appointed us for a personal and private interview.

We went into the Audience Room with the heart in our hands. We couldn't believe the luck we had had! Swami was waiting for us dressed just with the dhoti and the upper part of his body naked, with the same smile that had accompanied him since he had appeared, and a frank and nice attitude.

57. The interview and the Miracle

Now, I think that in those incredible moments during the interview with Swami Premananda, someone else was speaking instead of me, while I couldn't release myself from his ardent eyes. I remember having mentioned Mataji Indra Devi as whom we had heard talking about him, and he showed very pleased for this statement.

I also explained him that we were travelling through India, and our wish was to know his Holy Men, and if he would be so kind to bless us for going on our trip.

With the smile always in his lips, he placed his hands over our heads, whispering some words we didn't understand; then, he made circles in the air around us, and other rituals, while assuring that everything would be going on very well, and we would not have any problems at all.

While talking, the Swami caressed along my hand, and when he withdrew it, I observed he had materialized scented sandal powder there, which I took a little to my mouth and the rest to my breast.

I knew that to some persons, he had created "from nothing", rose petals and also little statues of Hindu Deities on their hands, but I didn't even imagine that I would be the one chosen for his miracles.

Afterwards I withdrew my hand, guessing that the interview had finished, but the Swami took it again and went on caressing it in the same way, while looking in my eyes, he stated :

— Don't worry; don't worry.

I felt a kind of fear to know what was happening in my hand. I was unable even to explain my own sensations rationally, when I caught a glimpse of something golden in the middle of my palm.

Scarcely can I now remember to have thanked him. What I do know is that I went out of the place like a sleepwalker, and I didn't have even the absolute certainty if I had indeed been the one who had the experience, or if everything happened to another person, and I was simply a spectator, as somebody who is only looking at the other actors of a film movie.

But the small *Ganesha* statue (the Hindu God with an elephant head) which I was still squeezing in my hand, with fear even to open it, brought me to the fact of his miracle, of his prodigious power to change energy into matter.

I was still walking in the air, unable or without wanting to recover, when Sabhina turned us to reality : she invited us to lunch in the ashram (she said she transmitted Swami's wishes in that sense).

Giovanna and I were very pleased by such a kind invitation, but we didn't see any canteen nearby where our driver could have lunch.

In fact, Sabhina had also invited him, but Rama refused firmly again and again. Before such an emphatic and reiterated refusal,

Sabhina pointed him a place very close to the ashram, where he could have lunch if that was his wish.

This attitude of Ramachandra annoyed us a little : how could he be so rude and refuse such a kind invitation! but Sabhina, who knew the Hindus better than us, commented:

— Poor man; what happens is that he is not used to be treated by white people like a Human Being! — and I guess she was right.

About Giovanna and I, we didn't want to refuse that charming request and listening to our stomachs which were claiming NOISILY for something to eat, resolutely approached the Dining Room and shared with all the other fellow guests, who sincerely congratulated us for the interview and envied our luck. Some of them told us that they had been living in the ashram for more than 15 days, and could not even see the Swami closely.

The menu, was always the typical of India, specially inside the ashrams : white rice with hot vegetables and pulse stews, very fresh natural yoghurt, and bananas. I suppose there were *chapatis* also, as they can not be lacking in Indian tables.

When we finally set off, we were so happy that we had even forgotten the heat. With Ramachandra's taxi, we came back to the road and went towards the interior of the country, bound for Kodaykanal City, the Summer residence of Sai Baba.

We had the certainty that moments of great happiness will be waiting for us there, even more now that we had the blessing of dear Mataji Indra Devi's Guru, the beloved Swami Premananda.

✷

9

TOWARDS THE LAND'S END

58. Red Bananas and Sweet Jack Fruits

After leaving Trichi and still shocked and moved by the materializations of Swami Premananda, we went on the journey to Kodaykanal, an incredible place situated in the middle of the mountain. We travelled for several hours admiring a spectacular scenery; we went up and down the cliffs and avoided hundreds of curves and precipices. From time to time, a crystalline waterfall cheered up the great landscape even more.

In many stretches, the road was flanked, in both sides, by tropical trees like the jack fruit, a huge sort similar to our great eucalyptus, full up with yellowish green fruits hanging from their branches, and as big as giant watermelons. They have a wrinkled and rough skin, full of little balls, and inside, the eatable part is a great quantity of small parcels like green medium-sized capsicums, clearer, tender and very very sweet, with a big seed in the interior.

My friend and I loved eating these delicious fruits, the same as the exquisite bananas, red outside and very creamy inside, really sweet, which are cropped in this area. Often, we demanded the taxi to stop, to get such splendid and exotic fruits, so that, together with the admiration of the scenery, we savored these delights.

Finally, we arrived at Kodaykanal, which seemed to us more similar to a town of the Swiss Canton than to a Southern Indian village : among mountains, jumping waterfalls of pure water, cool and pleasant weather.

We lodged when the sun had set, at a pretty hotel on the hillside, where we could rest after all the emotions of the day.

Very early the next morning, we went off to admire the surroundings : from the hotel and downwards to a lake, there were balconies with trees, flower pots, tables and benches to sit from time to time to enjoy the scenery or take something, with very carefully paved tracks and skillfully scattered lights.

These paths and balconies, descended to a very clear lake, from the banks of which, lots of tropical fishes of varied shapes, sizes and colours could be appreciated. The spectacle was a festival for the eyes, but much more for the heart and feelings when observing people, and specially children, admiring rejoiced such beauty, but respecting life and without trying to trap them, as surely we would see in the West.

The same happened with flowers and plants. Then, I reflected on how Indians, marvelously carry out the Yogic precept of Ahimsa or No Hurting, and so they can enjoy everything the Grand God gave us in his infinite kindness, but without ruining or taking advantage of it. That respect for animals and environment, that is in short no more than respect for life, seemed to me it was the most beautiful, the most intelligent philosophy of a country, that to our Western eyes, are still living in the Middle Ages and in the most terrifying poverty on material things, may teach their own children and the whole world.

There, in Kodaykanal, we visited Sai Baba's Summer's Shelter, which he uses when the Southern Summer shows all its torridness and the temperatures are so high that life gets difficult, until the Monsoon arrives and refreshes a little the atmosphere.

The two storeyed house is situated in the outskirts of the city. The persons who were in charge of it, allowed us the entrance, and we could notice it was really very large and pretty, outside the same as inside.

We came into a spacious room, with great pictures of Sai Baba and other Hinduism deities, something like a temple, sanctuary or Meditation Room. The keepers gave us also, as a present, some little parcels of *vibhuti*, and then, we went on our journey, taking some pictures from very beautiful sceneries.

I specially remember a place where the peaks of the mountains emerged among a sea of fog, and the sight was spectacular. We also admired the zone's handicraft and got some presents, like the slight little angels made with thin straw and embroidered with sequins, which with its wings open, looked very pretty at home, hanging in the Christmas Tree.

On the next day, in the first early hours, we went on our journey southwards, going back through the picturesque cliff roads among the hill flanks; we enjoyed the landscape again,...and its delicious fruits.

Even though the mileage is not so long, we travelled all day long again, since, as I have said on other occasions, in most Indian roads one must avoid implausible quantities of specimen that also use the roads to move around, besides the normal traffic of vehicles, which they are already stuffed with, and the constant hellish noise of the horns.

59. The Lighthouse of the Land's End

It got dark again when we arrived at our destination : Comorin Cape, the most Southern Indian spot, where, as I have already said, meet the Arabian Sea, the Indian Ocean and the Bengal Bay. There, the Land's End lighthouse is situated, and really it is the end of the earth, since southwards there is only open sea.

As it could not be different, it is a holy place and here the natives also get into the water dressed to perform their ablutions, to be purified physical, mental and spiritually. On the following day, Giovanna and I did the same, as it can be supposed.

We got to lodge in a hotel that belonged to the Government of that Tamil Nadu State, very comfortable, with air conditioning and literally on the beach, with a broad balcony open to the sea. There, we used to sit down and, while delighting in the magic marine scenery, we wrote our letters or cards, or had "mates", which we accompanied with some fruits like dates, raisins, bananas, and all kinds of oily seeds : almond , brown chestnut, walnut, peanut, etc. which were sold in the street stalls, everywhere.

An early morning and while I was still in the bathroom, my friend went out to sit at the balcony to enjoy the marine breeze. As soon as she put her head out, she began to call me, shouting :

— "Dellia, Dellia, veni, asomate, hay tiburones en el

mar" (Dellia, Dellia, come here, show up, there are sharks in the sea!).

I didn't take her seriously, since I knew how exaggerated she was. So, I calmly went out to see what was happening : actually, there was nothing to worry about, since the terrible "sharks" were only the black silhouettes of some little fishing boats, which in great quantities had gone to sea, just in front of our hotel. The truth is that they did seem to be sharks, with their fins outside the water.

Walking through this Kanyakumari village, was an unforgettable experience; we went along the red sand beach, and arrived at the memorial of the immortal Mahatma Gandhi. It is the place where the urn containing his ashes was originally put, and from where they were submerged into the sea, on the 12th February, 1948.

In that spot, every 12th of October of each year, the day of his birth, at 12 o'clock sharp, the time he was born at, a light ray enters from the dome, colliding against a diamond that is in a small sphere in a pedestal on the floor, and all the place, usually in half-light, illuminates. Thus, one can clearly read some very beautiful words of this Holy Father, well known as "The Light of India", that he wrote in relation to the virgin Southern seas.

We continued wandering among the hundred bazaars near the beach, even though we tried to be more than careful with our money and documents, since we had read a sign that prevented : "Be careful with the thieves". Also, and as it is imagined, our Ramachandra looked after us closely, not losing sight of us even for an instant.

60. Dark and Mystic : Goddess Kanya's Temple

In Kanyakumari, the bazaars or sale stalls were mostly of shells and ornamental goods, exquisitely made with them. With Giovanna, we bought a sort of carrousels, similar to large lanterns, made with thousands of shells of different sizes, worked as a handicraft in the combination of their colours and dimensions.

There, it was possible to get very exotic kinds of shells, as some very rare specimen pyramid shaped, which are a real beauty. Also, there was a great variety of golden printed sarees, exclusive of this Tamil Nadu region.

The Temple to Goddess Kanya, a manifestation of Parvati, that gives the place its name, seemed to me a little dark, more appropriated for secret sacrifice ceremonies. To the Hindus, surely, it didn't cause the same impression, since it was always crowded.

Between the piercing incense scent and the frenzy of the religious tunes that accompanied the rhythmic beating of the *tampuras*, which increased its intensity to reach a climax, we began feeling ourselves a little asphyxiated and had to go out.

According to the Mythology, this Goddess was making penances to win Lord Shiva's hand, and in her mortifying spot, on a rock inside the sea, her footprint remained stamped. In that original place, offshore, a temple had been built, which was worshipped up to a short time ago, but with the water advance, the place had to be abandoned and was later erected in the present spot, inland.

Even though the temple has its front part eastwards, that is to say, towards the sea, the main gates facing the ocean are opened only five times a year. The local belief is that the dazzling sparkle of the gem of the nose ring that adorns the Goddess, sometimes attracts the ships, which find their ruin when they collide against the rocks. Usually, the access to the temple is by the westward door, while the Eastern ones are kept closed.

An aura of holiness summons sages and devotees to this place, who purify themselves bathing with complete reverence where the three oceans meet.

The Mythology tells that God Hanuman, the monkey headed deity so popular in India, dropped some lumps of soil over Kanyakumari, while crossing towards Lanka to help God *Rama* in the rescue of his wife, victim of the demons. For this reason, the herbs that are found in some of the surrounding mountains, are reputed to possess exceptional medicinal value.

61. Towards the Rock Memorial

Staying in Kanyakumari, it is an obligation to visit the Rock Memorial, built in honor of Swami Vivekananda, which is found in the sea, some minutes away by ferry, and whose imposing silhouette is distinguished from the shore.

It is said that this great saint, patriot and yogi, used to meditate on that sacred place, about his mission in life, which he had foreseen was linked with the rescue of his people, from the clutches of poverty, ignorance and slavery.

For three consecutive days and nights, he was sitting down, meditating in that place, until it was revealed to him the timeless *Upanishads*, about the true worship to God through the unselfish service to Humanity, what is known with the name of *Karma* Yoga.

He clearly understood the reason why India had fallen from such a glorious height, and realized the way it could be restored to that preeminence again, recapturing the national ideals of renouncing and unselfish service. Unluckily, in that same place he left his physical body in a Maha Samadhi, at the early age of 39 years old.

Swami Vivekananda had pointed out that the lack of an adequate education among the masses, was the rootcause of all the misfortunes that afflicted the Indian Society. He also spoke about the uselessness of preaching *Vedanta* to empty stomachs. I agree completely with this philosophy...

For several days, my friend and I were travelling through South India, and we observed that the more we moved away in that direction, the fewer Western people we met, in such a way that in this place, we hadn't found a single white person yet.

During the ferry journey to visit Swami Vivekananda's Memorial, we shared the boat with some 300 or more black people, specially with several school pupils. The children were brought by their teachers and at every moment kept an admirable behavior. Chinese, Hindu-Chinese persons, from Sri Lanka and other Asiatic States were also travelling; some of them, we had met in other places, and they already smiled at us, greeted and even exchanged remarks and opinions (one of these persons precisely, suggested me the preparation of this book). Everyone, without exception, children and adults, made this pilgrimage or visit with the most absolute reverence.

The trip was really delicious, among the raising of our ship to the waves' crests, and then the descent, with that special sense of emptiness that everybody enjoyed and each person showed with different pleasure exclamations.

At a certain moment I became aware and told my friend : all the passengers' looks converged on us, all the little eyes were addressed towards our place. As usual, they were tender, affectionate, respectful glances, even though not exempt from curiosity.

When we reached our destination, all the children wanted to shake our hands or only touch us, as if we were something they had never seen before. I thought that perhaps, many of them had seen very few whites, or none at all, in their whole life.

Once on the rock where the Memorial was built, there were long accesses upwards, marked with large and showy arrows, following the right route. Inside such a special complex, the children as well as the adults, went on behaving calmly and respectfully; we were amazed to see the children sitting down cross-legged at the Meditation Room.

To have access to the Rock Memorial, the same as everywhere, we had to leave our sandals outside, and the camera as well (Always the unpleasant "Not allowed").

Through some booklets and books we bought inside the place, we found out that the mentioned construction was inaugurated on September 2nd, 1970, by the *Ramakrishna* Mission's President, and also by, at that time, India's President. That date commemorated the 77th anniversary of the Historical Message that Swami Vivekananda directed at the World Religions Parliament in Chicago, celebrated in 1893.

Later, in 1972, at the 110th Anniversary of his birthday, the committee in charge of this work, began the second phase. They organized service activities in all the social spheres and established a lay order (not monastic), for training life workers. This organization is today known with the name of Vivekananda Kendra, and its missionaries aspire to serve in the whole country. They have the general headquarters in a "campus" or camp of 100 acres, where one can reach by bus or train, from Kanyakumari.

Several buildings form the Memorial, which, as we were informed, was built in Tamil style of the Chola Period Architecture, with sculpted stone pillars, open platforms and great domes. Such monuments receive the name of Mandapam, and besides the Temple, Meditation Hall, the Swami Samadhi *Shrine* with a large bronze statue, it has a bookshop, a great library with the work of this grand yogi, etc. Two big stone elephants are keeping the main entrance.

From the South side of the Memorial, there is a wonderful view of the three Oceans meeting, thus people visit this place not only for its holiness, but also for its majestic beauty : specially in the early morning and in the evening, when the sweet music of the waves invited us to sit down there in silence, to meditate about the high ideals of patriotism and love for his country, that this saint left to posterity.

62. Surya Namaskar (The Sun Salutation)

In the evening, we came from the Rock Memorial back to Kanyakumari city, just at the moment when thousands of pilgrims gathered on the beach in absolute silence, to salute the setting sun. Some of them lifted their arms up to the sky in front of the "King Star", in the reverent ritual called Surya Namaskar (Sun Salutation), in the standing posture, with the palms-of the hands in front, and the arms raised over the head, to receive its energy. The thumbs of both hands hooked, shape the Trimurti Symbol, which in the Hinduism means the three aspects (the triangle figure) that constitute the One : Brahma, Vishnu and Shiva.

The spectacle of the shining red sphere that sank in the horizon, and with its reflection tinged the three seas of golden, was magnificent; the persons performing their worship ceremonies to God Surya (the Sun), while surely, from the depths of their minds and hearts repeated the invocation *mantras* : "OM, Mitraya Namaha"...(I salute the Friend of All).

There, everything conjugated to create a decidedly magic atmosphere, from which it was very difficult to be taken away : the subtle cloth sarees waved by the breeze; the scents, a mixture of incense and spices; the divine music of the *ragas* that was heard as a background and showed the virtue of their best players : Ravi Shankar, Santoor, Chaurasia... And in such a particular place, it came back again the same feeling of "already lived, already experienced", which I had felt in previous situations, as well as later on.

Mixed with this atmosphere of magic spell, the aromas of meals were added, which were offered on improvised stalls in the open air, served on rustic and blackened wooden planks, which separated the cook from the customer, with coarse long benches of the same material, outside, where the public sat to enjoy the "banquet".

The scents were tempting and we were hungry, so we familiarly sat on one of those benches, together with the Hindus, and savoured some very delicious omelettes, cooked in front of us, and that were, really good!

63. Motorized Sadhus

When we came back with Ramachandra, walking to our hotel along the shore, we observed some buses on the marine avenue, apparently very old fashioned, loaded up to the roof with all kinds of belongings, like pans, frying pans and other receptacles.

On both sides, in front, at the back and even under these vehicles, I saw many persons lying down resting on the sand, just protected with a blanket or rag cloth; others were trying to light the fire with thin dried tree branches, poking it with strong blows, to get flame instead of smoke; some of them were sitting cross-legged on the sand, kneading consciously inside a receptacle, what surely would later become chapatis.

We saw some adults, many seemingly very elder, whom we name "Third Age", with that bad habit we have to label people. According to our driver's remarks, they were groups that were constantly travelling to pilgrimage spots, a sort of "motorized sadhus", while performing all the tasks necessary for their survival.

I had read that from this place of Kanyakumari and up to Calcutta, in the North, pilgrimages that last a whole year are carried out, called Bharat Parikrama. They cover about 22,000 kms., with stops in 187 cities and villages. Its aim is the recreation of a new conscience of the country's unity, in a great effort of national integration.

Along these extensive journeys, a lot of programmes are fulfilled, and young men and women are specially motivated by Swami Vivekananda's messages, in order to inspire them in the ancient spiritual Indian Inheritance.

This spot on Comorin Cape is, truly, very special in many senses. In accordance with the Vivekananda Kendra's information, it is the only place in the world where, by its geographic position, you can simultaneously see two suns, one rising and the other setting! Personally, I think that, perhaps, it is some optic illusion, since I believe that such statement doesn't resist a scientific analysis.

64. Vivekananda Kendra

The organization that functions in Kanyakumari, called the Vivekananda Kendra, quoted before, besides the maintenance of the Rock Memorial and the spread of the Swami's teachings and ideals, it carries out many other activities, like the ones I detail next, among others :

Maintenance of an Ashram in Kashmir, besides carrying out a chain of service activities through its many branches.

Education Activities by means of 14 residential schools in Arunachala Pradesh, 3 schools in Assam, one school in Port Blair and one in Kanyakumari itself.

Sanitary activities with dispensary, a Holistic Health Home with Yoga Therapies, also with residence, for various psychosomatic diseases, besides Magneto Therapy and Homeopathy.

Thirty Rural Medical Centres in seven districts.

Eye Hospital in these same districts, with free cataract operations and supply of spectacles, also free.

A Medical Centre in Bihar, a Hospital in Nagaland, a Children Hospital in Calcutta and a well organized Yoga Therapy Centre at Bangalore.

Man Making Mission Area : Yoga camps in Kanyakumari, Kashmir and in Maharastra, besides Spiritual Retreats in the two first mentioned.

Rural Development : 78 centres in Tamil Nadu and five in Kerala, with nutrition programmes for children and other more than 500 centres covering more than 1500 children.

Frequent cultural competitions for school and college students.

Residential camps for men, women and children, where they are trained in youth leadership, environmental awareness, development of the eco-system, etc.

Provision of drinking water facilities in water scarcity areas, specially affected by droughts.

A lot of other centers scattered all over the country, for adult education, tailoring centres, carpentry centres, etc.

Journals, books and booklets are published, to spread the message of the life and teachings of the Master, as well as of the diverse activities of the Centres, the aim of which is always to kindle the interest in the glorious Indian heritage, as in the unchangeable life values.

All this information was given to me in one of those Centres; besides, the Vivekananda Kendra's activities are published in a small booklet in English, edited by this Centre, entitled "The Land's End — Kanyakumari", printed in Tamil Nadu, India, 1991.

I think it is very important for the world to know this information, and for the reader to learn that while most persons' goal is the competition and the fight for money and power, there are others who unselfishly work TO HAVE A BETTER WORLD.

65. The Glorious Indian Heritage

Swami Vivekananda was the great disciple of Sri Ramakrishna. He was born in Calcutta in 1863 and carried the spiritual truths, which were taught by the ancient holy and wise Indian Sages, to a lot of European and Far Eastern countries. His writings and lectures in his scarce 10 years of active life, add up more than four thousand pages, and, as I have commented before, he achieved Maha Samadhi and left his physical body at the age of 39.

All those who led the Movement for India's Liberation after this saint and patriot, have been directly or indirectly influenced by him : Tilak, Gandhi, Aurobindo, Nehru, etc.; each one of these leaders, extremist or moderate nationalists, including the humblest and most insignificant soldiers for this country's freedom, were all inspired absolute and definitively by Swami Vivekananda, by his calls to action and by his blessings.

He served his dear India as a first order patriot more than as a monk, as a conscience waker, more than a prophet of the nationalist service...

I let myself remember and transcript Vivekananda's own words :

> "I will also sacrifice my life; everyone of you, should do the same. All these words are only the beginning. Believe me, from the coward shedding of your life-blood will arise gigantic, heroic workers and warriors of God, who will revolutionize the whole world.
>
> You can be rich businessmen, well paid administrators, flourishing doctors, prosperous farmers and highly-paid workers in any sphere. But use your positions of vantage to serve the masses, to uplift them, to raise them to the full level of human dignity. You needn't be sanyasins with the ochre robe. You can be Sanyasins in spirit, dedicating your lives and all your activities to the altar of Motherland, by making yourselves Servants of the People of India, worshippers of that God who, by the ignorant, is called Man."[1]

In the personal way, I seized on many of his inspired thoughts, for instance when he says :·

> "THROUGH THE HEART COMES INSPIRATION. LOVE OPENS THE MOST IMPOSING GATES. LOVE IS THE GATE TO ALL THE SECRETS OF THE UNIVERSE".

✷

---

1. Swami Vivekananda (in his "Swami Vivekananda on Modern Youth"). A Publication of the Vivekananda Kendra, Pages 29-30; Printed on India; 2nd. Edition 1991, summed up by the author.

10

THE EARTHLY PARADISE

66. Burials with Music and Feast

The night before our leaving from Kanyakumari, Ramachandra, who as usual slept inside his car in the back courtyard of the hotel, next to our room, moved the taxi to the front for our better comfort in the morning.

His respectful, humble and protective closeness, made us feel always safe and cared. We also had Swami Premananda's blessing for the rest of the trip. What other things did we need asking? Absolutely nothing, only to be grateful for such a lot of gifts.

With this attitude, we went back to the main road, and travelled a short distance of about 100 kms., now northbound, by the West coast of India. At mid morning we reached Trivandrum City, which we had to cross to arrive to our destination, Kovalam Beach.

Precisely while we were going through this crowded city, we noticed a beautifully adorned cart, with a lot of natural flowers in delicate garlands, which was preceded by a band of many musicians on foot, playing what seemed cheerful tunes. A great number of people were coming after this cart, also walking, and one could observe a festive air, as if it were an important celebration.

We had already seen a similar scene in another city we had travelled through, and then we noticed that inside the cart, a person whom we didn't pay much attention to, was lying quietly.

I had consulted Ramachandra about it, who had laconically answered something like "beri". I repeated the question and he answered exactly the same, this second time with a little impatient tone.

I deduced it would be a special celebration called this way, and didn't go on with the interrogation, nor to bother him (Rama used to lose his temper sometimes). Your strange habits and rituals are your business, I said to myself...

This time, a similar spectacle : again a greater cart, ornamented in a still more luxurious way. The carriage passed by our side, always with the band and the entourage, and we had to stop our vehicle not be in the way.

Then, I looked inside it, and saw a middle aged very pale person, seemingly a Muslim for his black beard. In this occasion he was straight and quietly sitting down inside the wagon, on a high chair.

I could observe him closely and told myself that he was looking really... cadaverous. And there, I caught on that he was a corpse really, and all the procession wasn't more than a...*burial*. Here, I associated what Rama had wanted to tell me was "burial".

I thought it would be a Muslim indeed, or a person belonging to any other religion which buries the dead, and don't cremate them as the Hindus do.

This second time and after deducing it was a "burial", I remarked to our driver that in my opinion, it didn't seem appropriate neither the music band nor so much noisy gaiety, when surely his widow and the rest of the family would be distressingly crying. Very gravely Rama answered that they would cry for ten minutes and then would win through. As I didn't agree, he came to lengthen the period : "Let's suppose that it is twenty minutes", he answered back, making myself understand that I didn't know much about his people's behavior, and that just to catch even a glimpse of their mentality, I had to live in India at least for five years.

I imagine he was referring to the Hindu belief in the reincarnation doctrine, which makes them not fear death. This can be seen in many Eastern countries, where this step of leaving the physical body is just like to discard an old and worn out dress, to put on an absolutely new other one later.

67. "The Earthly Eden"

After leaving the crowded city of Trivandrum behind, in a

few minutes we arrived at the paradisiacal beaches of Kovalam. If up to that moment many of the places we had visited seemed to us the most similar to Paradise, this spot was, no doubt, the Earthly Eden.

A great bay of amazing beaches, very fine white and black sands, and a sea of lukewarm and transparent water of a deep turquoise color, from which the peaks of some mountains appeared.

On their shores, slender palm trees were scarcely waved by the breeze, and at the bay beginning, the high shape of a lighthouse as a silent watchtower of such dazzling beauty. At the end, the fishermen's barges, which came back from the sea in the evening with their precious cargo, while the last sun rays reflected their golden light on the water, and dyed the whole bay, as far as the sight reached, of a warm golden colour.

The fruit sellers walked along the shore with large baskets on their heads, offering their goods with insistence : juicy pineapples, very sweet papayas, delicious jack fruits, bananas, coconuts, etc., picked from the big tropical trees of the zone.

All around the bay semicircle, typical restaurants with fascinating names lined up; we use to go to a specially nice one, the *Kaylasa*, which had tight threads of shells as curtains, skilfully hung in doors and other openings.

There were also a lot of bazaars, attended by young Muslims, who, the same as in other places, invited from their doors with the classical : "Héllow", pronounced with the stress on the "e", and in a very particular way, mixture of greeting and invitation to come in. They offered Tibetan handicrafts, Kashmirian carpets handmade in wool and silk, paintings, jewels and many other very pretty goods, that is to say, the kind of articles there are everywhere.

On that beach, a great selection of clothes were similarly offered to be sold, like shawls, dresses, skirts, tunics, slippers, long and loose shirts, etc., besides pictures, tapestry, blankets, etc., manufactured and tinged as handicrafts with the "batik" technique.

As it happens all over India, the sellers may follow their potential customers, day after day, and every time and place, trying to sell their goods, and the bargaining becomes a skilled competence, almost a refined art, between seller and customer.

68. The Ayurvedic Massage : the Pleasure (with Capital Letters)

At Kovalam Beach, the Ayurvedic Massage is very popular. All along the shore and in the interior of the little village, we could read some posters promoting these services, with their respective prices. Some of them were performed by doctors of this ancient science in specialized institutions, and others vied with lower prices, and were practised by expert massagists not physicians.

As I was very interested to receive these massages, and after studying all the offered possibilities, I made an appointment with a couple of Ayurvedic doctors. I got one at six o'clock, in the morning of our leaving day.

Still at night and half asleep, I went to the place, up the narrow street in front of our hotel. The Hindu doctor had already opened the surgery and she was waiting for me with everything ready.

A great quantity of scented essential oils were poured on my naked body, from a full jug placed close to my stretcher before beginning. Really skilled hands made a professional and conscious work.

She began from the feet, followed at the front of the body up to the head; then went on at the back part, again from feet to head. Not a single centimeter of my body remained without being looked over, while all the *chakras* or energy centers were activated, which I have knowledge of as a Yoga Master.

During a profitable hour, the pleasant Hindu doctor restlessly worked, and to tell the truth, after the session I felt like a new one, with an energy that sprang from each one of my skin pores.

The little jug with essential oil that she had prepared first, was already completely empty, and every one of its drops had been absorbed by my body with pleasure, helped by those hands that, slowly and lovingly, had carried out their task perfectly.

69. Sea, Moon, Palm Trees, Quietness...

Walking along the beach of Kovalam in the evening, was a paradisiac experience : relatively few foreigners gather in those places, and as the natives only take their purifying ablutions, actually very few persons were walking along the bay.

What artist, what painter, would be able to capture these magic instants? Who else could give us ever a present like this one, but the Supreme Painter? While Surya, the gigantic fire disk, hid quietly in the horizon, the waters received its last image : the whole bay seemed to catch fire with its blazing golden tone.

Also the shore restaurants added up to the spectacle : their tables were laid outside, on the sand, placing lanterns with candles on each one of them. When it began getting dark, the scenery was of such an extraordinary stillness and beauty, that my words could hardly express it with justice.

With my friend, we had got a little hotel, modest but very pretty and according to our budget, with a comfortable balcony over the beach; just sitting there, we could see among the palm tree silhouettes, the filigree that the foam drew when the waves broke gracefully against the shore sand. Also the mountains that surrounded the place...and our Ramachandra, with his taxi located in the hotel garden, just in front of our balcony, among leafy and green banana trees.

On some occasions, I used to sit down in the balcony to have "mates" or to write, and big birds perched around me, waiting for some crumbs to eat, and that confidence of animals, that as nobody bothers them, they don't know the fear to men, made me feel with my heart in peace.

Generally, breakfast and afternoon snack (sometimes also lunch and dinner), consisted of tasty "mates", which equipment had been taken from my home (yerba mate and herbs from my courtyard) in Argentina; besides fruits and seeds like papayas, bananas, dates, chestnuts, raisins, etc., from India.

Every time that, from the balcony, I dropped my sight to the garden, I met the warm and shining smile of Ramachandra, as if he wanted to assure me :

> — Here I am, don't worry, I take care of you, — and this humble and respectful closeness infused me, really, a lot of confidence.

70. In Absolute Communion with the Creator

An early morning of our short stay in this glorious place of Kovalam Beach, I woke up from a peaceful and deep dream, and thought it was already full day, since outside, among the palm trees, a great brightness was perceived. During the whole journey, my friend and I slept with the doors and windows open, since we had always felt very safe.

I got up from the bed and walked to the veranda, to find out if it had already dawned actually, and checked it was just the moon in its fullness, shining so intensely as if it were a sun.

From my place, I saw it letting itself down among palm tree silhouettes and, trembling, reflected on the sea. The spectacle was so magnificent, so fascinating that, as if I were hypnotized, I came down the hotel stairs and, walking, I went close to the sea.

Only a dog followed me, which I didn't know where he appeared from, and accompanied me, with his wet snout touching my hand, and later lying down lovingly at my feet.

Dressed in just a light nightdress, and a shawl over the shoulders, I sat down on a big stone on the shore, and there I lost notion of the time and space; I don't know if I was there two, three or more hours, in absolute communion with the Creator and in harmony with His wonderful masterpiece; I felt as never before, I took part in this universe, ruled by the same powers that govern it.

That glorious sensation of Oneness that I experienced from the depth of my heart, brought about such an indescribable feeling of joy, such an intense and powerful happiness and bliss, that I could only free through tears, which began flowing from my eyes in an uncontrollable way. I remember that, from the deepest and purest of my soul, it sprang like a prayer : "Thank you, God, for such wonderful works, and thank You also, for choosing me to enjoy them".

When I came back to physical consciousness, it was already full day and the sea breeze was rather cool. Some Muslims were coming back from praying and chanting in their mosque (it was still Ramadan month), and started cleaning their shops.

During the days we stayed in this dream place, we made friends with one of the boys, also native of Kashmir and that, by chance?, knew my "son" Sajad. This young boy had his bazaar at the end of our alley, on the shore. That morning, we exchanged some smiles and occasional remarks. I suppose he thought :

— How eccentric these Westerners are, going to the beach in the early morning, just with sleeping clothes!

Every evening, more exactly from twilight, we sat with my friend at one of the little tables on the shore, of course, with the lantern lit. If our wish was to eat some fish, we might even choose the cut preferred, from a stall where several specimen were exhibited, which had been recently brought by the fishermen. Almost always, we invited Rama to have lunch with us, but he, as usually, only asked for rice, very hot of course!

The only thing that put our patience to the test, was that we had to wait (not less than two hours) for our menu to be ready. As the meals were made at the very moment, they were always very fresh.

Besides, in that spot, restaurants in general, have only one gas heater, or a portable stove with only one burner, many times just a coarse brick spit, and with such a precarious equipment, they cooked really delicious food.

We said : "Why hurrying...We are in India!". Waiting with such an edenic spectacle was all a gift from God. How could we even think of growing impatient? Sea, moon, palm-trees, silence, stillness, little lights twinkling at each table : it is very difficult to describe so much beauty, so much harmony, so much peace!...

71. The Discordant Note

The beach of Kovalam is considered a tourist spot by foreigners, and there some Westerners are found, mostly Europeans. The women, shamelessly, are tanning in the sun top-less, in spite of a great poster that forbids this modality. The truth is that Hindus look at them to laugh, and the other Westerners don't pay the slightest attention. Personally, it seems to me impolite to visit a country where people are so respectful of their customs, and behave in this way. Of course, we, Westerners, come from a "civilized" world.

Anyway and according to my philosophy : Who am I to judge others? Sometimes, I joked with Giovanna about top-less : "If we let our tops drop, things would be rather different", since both have been very well endowed by Mother Nature in the upper part.

Sometimes, when my friend set off alone to the beach, she received my advice :

— Be careful with men! Remember that Muslims fast all month long, so don't waste time showing yourself top-less!

This was, of course, a joke, since luckily, and as the seer had forecast, our relation during the trip was very good in all senses.

I realized that in India, the foreigner is considered a separate cast, but Indians decide if he is worth of respect or not, in accordance with his behavior. I had, and go on having, the full certainty that, both Gio and me, would honor in all the word's sense, the customs and philosophy of this wonderful country, whose inhabitants, from one or the other race, distinguished us with their friendship, their trust, their hospitality, always offering everything, even their own hearts.

For this reason, in each place we were leaving behind, a piece of us remained, which came out from the heart and the feelings. Each of the experiences we had, will be remembered with a real longing, specially the days enjoyed in this authentic earthly paradise.

But we had a programme, more or less tight, to follow, and time was always short, so to get the bags ready again to go on the journey. So many times did we pack and unpack, that we would have to be experts and perform the work in a jiffy, but it is also true that in each place there were new temptations to purchase, that certainly the problem was space. And it was better not even to remember the monstruous bags that were waiting for us in the Left-Luggage office in Bangalore!

72. "Your Plans are My Business, Máma!"

In this fantastic beach, there was actually one single thing that bothered me, and it was the police's attitude, who as soon as they saw a Hindu approaching Western persons, immediately came near to scare him with earnest threats to take him as prisoner. According to the police, white people complained about being annoyed by Indians!

I may understand that tourism can be favored but, how can it be that precisely the house owners, are bothered by the police? Besides, Hindus, even though very insistent offering their goods or services, are in that way earning their livings, and they behave in the same way throughout India.

Of what they can get, perhaps, depends their own survival and that of the whole family; they are not saving money to spend on Video Games or to acquire the last C.D. (compact disc). If Western people are bothered by such an insistence, such an Indian attitude, why don't they better stay in their own country! Or well just concern themselves with visiting only "civilized" countries!

Sincerely, I had never observed neither a confidential nor a shameless posture on the Indians' behalf, but always, although insistent, they kept an attitude of great respect and humility. And I bring to my mind an occasion in which several rickshaw drivers went to meet me, at the hotel exit, and came close to offer their services. One of them advanced and asked me :

— Máma, which are your plans for today?

— And what do my plans matter to you? — I answered amused.

He, without turning a hair, went on walking beside me, and earnestly answered back :

— Your plans are my business, Máma.

And how could I get angry, or even annoyed, if he was absolutely right!

73. These Blessed Hindus!

Another episode that also happened at the Beach of Kovalam, paints the Hindus at their full size. This time, it was about a fruit seller : every day while we remained in this paradisiac place, a friendly Hindu woman appeared, very thin and with an advanced pregnancy, to judge by her prominent belly.

She offered me her pineapples, which were carried in a large basket over the head. To tell the truth, her appearance was more of a gypsy than of a Hindu, and I called her "the pineapples' thin woman".

From the first day, a flowing of liking was established between us, and we had already made friends, so I usually purchased her those fruits, which she delivered quick and skilfully peeled with a long knife, that she used with such a swiftness as if it were just a potato-peeler.

The "Thin woman" searched for me and found me wherever I was; in the beach, tanning in the sun, bathing in the sea, or having lunch at a restaurant, or just "snooping" about the bazaars; but the fact is that I could never bargain with her. In attempting a price reduction, she put my hand over her belly, arguing :

— Máma, you are very friendly and I love you very much, but I can't lower this price to you. What I assure you, Máma, is that my fruits are very very good, — and she made a gesture twisting her hand at the side of her face. Then she added :

— And for you, Máma, I am going to choose the best!.

She always won, since I let her convince me. On one occasion that, as she usually did, she appeared, I had had lunch late, a good dessert included, and I was not willing to eat the pineapple. Thus, I told her, but she didn't even turn a hair :

— You eat it later, — she simply said.

As she couldn't convince me, she added, placing my hand on her belly :

— Look Máma, I came on foot from my village several kilometres from here, with this heat, the great basket and my belly, and until I sell everything, I can't go back home.

— I have nothing to peel it either, — I argued defending myself.

— When you decide to eat it, my mother will peel it, — she answered back.

I didn't see anybody in the surroundings who could be her mother, and supposed it was a tale to convince me. Besides, I was tired of discussing and wanted to be alone, sunbathing.

A little annoyed by such insistence, but not wishing to be rude or offend her either, I reluctantly took out my rupees, and handed them over to her in silence, with a long and exaggerated sigh. She put the money over her forehead as a sign of gratitude, and set off with her basket on the head, very straight and pleased to do her will.

I left the fruit aside, covered with a towel, and went on tanning in the sun, forgetting the promise completely. Some time later (I had already taken several baths), I sat down again on the sand, to get ready for reading.

I then remembered I had the pineapple and took it in my hands, thinking how I could peel it, when an old thin and toothless woman, who didn't speak a single word in English, and I didn't even know where she had appeared from, approached, took the fruit with her skinny hands, and with a long and sharp knife, in a jiffy, neatly peeled it and handed it to me with a friendly smile. Ah, these blessed Hindus !

✸

11

THE "GARDEN CITY" AND THE PEACEFUL BANGALORE

74. The "Living Incense Stick"

After enjoying the delicious Ayurvedic Massage, we set off from the enchanted beaches of Kovalam, with Ramachandra's taxi, bound for Mysore, "The Garden City" of India.

The skilled Ayurvedic Doctor had recommended not bathing before, at least, several hours, to boost the massotheraphy effects, so I sensed all my skin very smooth and lubricated. I exhaled a piercing but pleasant scent of Eastern essences, for what our driver laughed and joked, assuring that I had become a real "living incense stick".

We travelled all day long, always very hot, and the spectacular tropical landscape spread again before our sight : huge trees, flowers, rare and multicoloured birds, slender butterflies, enormous and colorful, intrepid monkeys, tame elephants, pigs, goats, persons on foot with big bundles over their heads, who occupied half-way, very crowded towns, where the taxi could just circulate at man pace...

As the sight was repeated, we didn't even pay attention to it, and it seemed the most natural thing to travel in this way. As I had commented, all the vehicles invited to blow the hooter because of the "Sound Horn" written at the back part, and nobody, included Ramachandra, skimped its usage on the roads, so the hellish bustle was also constant.

In this run, as well as in all the journeys we did, I always observed a lot of persons, women and men of all ages, with impressive bundles over their heads, who moved on foot along the roads, and who, besides slowing down the traffic, usually very crowded, also ran risk of their own safety.

On this matter, I consulted our driver, who plainly explained :

— To move from one village to the other, rich people go by bicycle, cart or motorcycle, but poor people must go on foot, Máam!

75. A "Visit" in the Bathroom

Luckily, and thanks to the Ayurvedic powder, my friend was no more in a hurry to get a bathroom on the road, so we could travel with more calmness. Only at noon we stopped to have lunch at a modest stall we found at a side of the road, just in front of a humble school, where I observed the children taking their classes in the courtyard, sitting down cross-legged under the tree shadows.

Then, I couldn't but remember the concepts of the exquisite Indian poet Rabindranath Tagore, about this custom :

> "Under the shady trees and the glories of the sky, a child is in his natural setting amidst the flowers and the song-birds; there he may more easily express the hidden wealth of his individual endowment. True *education* is not pumped and crammed in from outward sources, but aids in bringing to the surface the infinite hoard of wisdom within."[1]

As soon as our taxi stopped, the school children stood up with a jump, and I imagine, with their teacher's permission, they ran to where we were, surrounding us to "pose".

An old Hindu woman, who was passing by, did the same; she strongly embraced me, and proposed me to change her saree for my dress, to have it as a souvenir. All the time we remained there, she stayed very close observing everything, and when I had to say

1. Paramahansa Yogananda : "Autobiography of a Yogi" — Chapter XXIX. In his "Rabindranath Tagore and me Compare Systems of Teaching", Page 262, Bombay (India) by Jaico Publishing House — authorized of Yogoda Satsanga Society of India-Self Realization Fellowship — (Copyright 1946) 10th impression 1992.

her good-bye to set off, she also begged me to take her to my country!

Once settled in the improvised restaurant, we sat down on large and coarse wooden benches, at a rustic and not very clean table; we imitated Rama, who neatly washed, with a little water from his glass, the piece of banana leaf put for each of us as a dish. The day menu? Rice! What else could it be?

A beautiful Hindu woman attended to us with the meal. While she was getting it ready, I consulted her if there was a bathroom, and she proudly answered affirmatively. Very politely she accompanied me up to the end of the "dining-room", a kind of veranda all opened at the front part, and whose floor was only the ground, well swept and watered. She pointed at the place where the bathroom was placed, in the courtyard.

It was, in fact, half a little room (I wouldn't know what other name to give it), more or less of 1.50 mts. diameter, with only three walls not taller than my waist. A semi-transparent cloth functioned as a door, perhaps an old saree, or rags of a sheet.

The floor, only the sandy ground, completely flattened and clean, without any hole or anything that denoted its usage. In this sense, I have not inhibitions, so I calmly bent down to perform what I was going to do.

Soon, as the most natural thing, the cloth door raised, and a friendly goat got inside to accompany me. With a total confidence, she rubbed tamely her head against my body. I only opted for smiling while I caressed her. As my friend Giovanna well says, there is nothing to be amazed at : "Te das cuenta, Dellia? Estamos en India!" (Do you realize, Delia? We are in India!)

76. The Temple at Chamudi Hill and the "One Thousand and One Nights" Palace

Finally, we arrived at Mysore, the famous "Garden City", really charming. We lodged at a nice hotel, and, as it was early, we set off again towards the Durga Goddess Temple, placed over a mountain called Chamudi Hill. Half way along the road, while we were climbing it up : Nandi statue, a great bull of more than 5 Mts. high, considered Shiva's vehicle, made of dark material, nearly black, and very ornamented. Most people in their ascent up to the temple, stopped there to leave an offer, and we did the same, to take some pictures.

The temple in question is very ancient, with the classical shape of a truncated pyramid, as most of the Hinduistic temples. We were informed that it dated from the beginning of this second millennium. Its outside, as Paul Brunton describes and I have quoted before, is completely covered with sculptures of subjects of the Mythology, birds and animals, as well as Hindu Deities in "meditative postures or of close embrace".

We also visited palaces of "One Thousand and One Nights", as the Mysore Palace, where the *maharajas* lived since the 16th century. The present palace is the rebuilding of the original one, made of wood, which was destroyed almost completely because of a fire.

The most renowned of the Sultans who inhabited it, was, no doubt, Tippu Sultan, considered a National Hero since he fought against the British, immolating his life for India's freedom. In the 17th Century he governed that little feudal kingdom called "The Mysore Dynasty", which was founded in 1399 and had 24 sultans until the year 1947, when the Indian Republic was established.

This monumental palace, of grey granite, is an amazing baroque building, Moorish and Hindu style. It consists of a three storeyed building with towers that rise up to five storeys, crowned by imposing domes standing out in the middle of the construction, some huge golden ones. Local and foreign artists took part in its construction and decoration and, of course, fire-proof materials were used, mostly from that area.

In front of the structure, one can observe slender carved wooden pillars and great arcades that open to the large hall entrance. Besides, a roomy open veranda where the Sultan showed himself to his people on important occasions, sitting down in his golden throne.

This throne is placed in the palace, today a museum, and it consists of a main armchair, with a little staircase that leads to it, and a sunshade, all artistically worked in gold, with Sanskrit golden inscriptions concerning his God : Lord Krishna. This real masterpiece belonged to the Royal Family of Mysore for many generations, and its story is really exciting, the same as the symbolism of its decoration.

One of the most imposing halls in this palace is, no doubt, the so called Ambavilasa, which is upstairs. With a size of 65 square feet and 10 feet high, magnificently decorated with paintings on walls and ceiling, which main subjects consist of peacocks, zodiac signs, the Hindu Trilogy, the ten Vishnu's incarnations, etc., and the same ornamentation is repeated on its splendid floors.

The doors, some of them engraved in silver and ivory, others carved in rose wood; the decorative lamps of Japanese porcelain, the exquisite and dazzling vitraux, its pillars and arcades covered with green jade, the marble statues...! It is impossible to describe coherently such ostentation and beauty!

In this Ambavilasa Room, the European visitors were received to make transactions, specially the "British Friends", and I think that the expression "Asiatic luxury" doesn't even make justice to all that display.

The apartments of the Harem women, also rivalled in refinement and good taste, each one of them decorated in different colours and details, I suppose, in accordance with the personality of his numerous wives, or, perhaps, according to the Sultan's preference for every one of his "ladies".

Our attention was attracted by the pavilion of dolls, manufactured with varied materials and models. They were exhibited during the Dasara (or of the 10 days) festivities that culminated in a procession led by the Maharaja, who in such occasion utilized another arm-chair, also made of gold, in which more than 80 Kgs. of this noble metal were used. About the doll worship, it is still a tradition nowadays in Mysore, for certain festivities.

We visited a central lounge with hunting trophies of Wadiyar, one of the latest Maharajas, consisting of tigers, bisons, leopards, elephant's heads, rhinoceros, etc., likewise buffalos, zebras and giraffes of African origin, given to Wadiyar as a present, during a safari he had been on in that country.

All the animals were embalmed by the taxidermist Van Ingen, one of the most internationally famous. Later, and perhaps for conscience trouble, this Maharaja left hunting and became the President of the World Association to protect the Wild Life.

The hunting pavilion isn't usually open to the public, but seldom, the same as the Weapons Room. This Militar Museum consists of a great collection of all sorts, which are of interest not only from the historical point of view, but also as art masterpieces. It is supposed that each one of them, from the simplest knife to the most queer rifle, would have a large story to tell, in general very interesting, which sometimes are reminded through an inscription.

In another of the monumental halls, we could observe a great picture of Ganesha, the elephant-headed God, whose devotion is greatly preferred in the whole India, and it is found in most Indian homes as the one who "attracts good luck"; sometimes the worship reaches such a point, that people build for him a small temple or niche over the same roof of the house, which is very usual to observe when travelling through the country.

That Ganesha statue in the Mysore Palace, is said to have remained intact when the fire destroyed the old wooden palace, for what it was later integrated to the rebuilt palace. According to our guide, the figure is made of stucco, with 450 sacred black stones, collected and carried from 300 different holy India spots.

Marble staircases, beautifully polished, take us from one pavilion to the other; archs with precious and semi-precious stones inlaid, like lapislazuli, jade, amethyst, ruby, coral and many others, create a wonderful harmony in the shape of flowers, borders, animals, birds, gods, etc., all a poem in form and colour, that it could difficultly be translated in a plain description.

From one of the halls, the visitor may have a panoramic sight of the fountains and temples of the neighborhood, as well as of the gate or monumental entrance through which one accesses to such a great palace. A little further on, others can be distinguished, as Lalit Mahal, and even Chamudi Hill, the mountain where it is the known temple to Durga Goddess, we had visited before.

Vast open spaces in front of the Mysore Palace, are presided by two great bronze tigers, and very well kept gardens with slender lighting columns added charm and majesty to the complex.

Sometimes during the festivities, the entire palace is illuminated with light garlands that follow the whole building outlines, which makes it shine as a heavenly pavilion built with star powder and sprang from the infinite space, and from which it seems that at any moment angels and cherubs could appear to soar in the sky. Then, one believes to be already in Paradise, and imagines that the dream of a palace just built of light has become truth.

The spectacle is so amazing that many visitors, who know the beauties of the whole world, consider that the Mysore Palace can not be compared with anything they had seen in all their lives.

In the evening, we left this fabulous palace, which contrasted greatly with the poverty of the surroundings, and although I was still dazzled by such wealth and opulence, I wondered how many persons could be fed all their lives, just with the value of one of the pieces exhibited there, and the truth was that such a contrast faded out the impact that all the luxury had caused on me.

77. A Feast for the Senses

When we were leaving the Mysore Palace, the sellers of incense sticks and other goods made with scented sandal wood, didn't give us a moment's respite; I can remember even the voice tone of their convincing arguments, while walking by our side all the way to the taxi;

— Máma, this is the best sandal wood, only thirty rupees, Máma, specially for you.

They stressed "specially for you" with their tone, with a humble and begging glance at our eyes. As we had become experts in the delicate bargaining art, we got some little wooden handicrafts at very good price, of course, "specially for us"

Just 18 kms. from Mysore and with the first lights of the nightfall, we visited the Gardens or Brindavan, in the dam and reservoir of Krishnarajanagar (King Krishna's lake), built in the Kauvery River. At that time, the light, sound and colour spectacle was really hallucinating.

Actually, they are large gardens raised on the other side of the dam walls, at whose interior one enters by crossing through a great arch or gate. It is usual in India to have the entrance to all the important places, presided by one of these gates.

We began getting inside the Brindavan : we walked through beautifully built gardens, which shaped harmonic avenues and tracks, at the sides of water channels about two or three metres wide.

As we were advancing, and always with a magnificent sight towards the four ways, we observed the great quantity, variety and colouring of the flowers, that completely filled the gardens, like stains of shades, exquisitely sprinkled, among stairs that rose and went down because of the unevenness of the ground.

After a short distance, the water of the channels, before still, began rising in little dancing fountains, which were changing their shapes according to the music variations, coming down or up, every time the "ragas" descended in the music scale, or went "in crescendo"

The more we entered the Brindavan, the more springs of different shapes and colours appeared at our eyes, which couldn't embrace such wonders.

We had to advance with speed among a lot of people, since the stretch was long, and we didn't want to be too late for coming back at our hotel. Actually, and as a prudence rule, we always tried not to travel at night, to avoid troubles, in this far-off and mysterious country.

As I have already said, our eyes were unable to manage between admiring the Brindavan beauties without missing anything, and not losing track of Ramachandra, who was preceding us, and whom we were afraid of losing among the crowd.

The figures constantly varied, the further we got in : high lighted up springs were surrounded by other smaller ones, which danced around as making rounds. High and slender coloured jet water drew different sized arcades, for later joining together, shaping a sort of dome.

Here and there they sprang like ears that rose to the sky, which emerged from big and round crowns, accompanied in its turn by other smaller and concentric ones.

Ahead, a great lake, in the center of which, what is known as the "Russian Fountain" arose : a sort of large carrousel all of light, from where the waters, as if were long fringes, fell downwards to the lake.

When we arrived at the end of the run, it was already impossible for the mind to register and analyse such beauty : the waters, that in perfect symmetry flowed at different levels, built like a huge cathedral, which also transmuted its shape, size and colour, in accordance with the different musical levels : white, yellow, pink, deep orange, blue, fuchsia, violet...; they grew upwards, blew up hollowing, lay languidly down, to emerge later again in very high rows.

To admire such a spectacle, people sat down on long tiers, surrounding the front of the "cathedral", as if it were an amphitheater, whose actors were those impressing dancing waters, a real joy for the eyes, the ears and the heart.

To go back, we retraced the same way; the eyes tried to withhold such beauty to record it for ever in the retina, although it exceeded the human capacity. It was a pity we couldn't capture with the camera or the movie-camera such valuable and precious pictures. Also there, the hateful chart "not allowed", so I can just take advantage of my memory and my feelings, to recreate these fantastic and incredible images!

What a lot of harmony, what a lot of beauty in shapes and colours! A silent thank to the artist who imagined and planned, the same to the workers who built this Brindavan, for the intimate glory of our senses.

78. "Live and Enjoy Your Freedom"

In Mysore, a refreshing rest at our hotel, after such a lot of emotions. The following day, very early in the morning, we set out to undertake the last section of the South India tour, always with the taxi driven by who had been our chauffeur, and already was our great friend, Ramachandra.

While making our way towards the road, we went through downtown. As by chance, Rama asked us if we wanted to visit the "CHU" (it sounded so). Without knowing what was he speaking about, I asked him back, and he just cleared up : "animals". I then enquired if he was referring to a rare animal with that name, but he, in his bad English, answered that it wasn't one, but a lot, making great gestures with his hands.

"Stung" by curiosity and without finding out yet what he meant (nor did I feel encouraged to go on asking), we accepted to go, and what wouldn't be our surprise when he parked his car in front of the Zoo!

Once inside it, my friend set off to the great monkeys cages, since she had heard they knew how to sing the OM and other rites. Rama neatly walked through the whole zoo, without missing anything at all. He only stopped and turned his head towards me, to glance with an obvious disgust, when seeing I had delayed a moment with some University Students of another Indian state. They had kindly asked me to take some shots together, to which I agreed; very politely they would leave me their names and addresses, and also requested mine, for sending the copies.

To tell the truth, I don't like Zoologics at all, although Mysore's looked better than others I had seen in my country, since the animals had quite a big space and their habitat relatively well imitated; for instance, I observed that birds were in spacious cages, with natural trees inside.

Some showy peacocks attracted my attention : of a pure whiteness, without a single feather of another colour; with the large opened out fan of their tails, they looked spectacular. I noticed that at some places, the feathers shaped as satin rings, which stood out brighter than the rest.

I walked through without a fixed route, and didn't follow any order. I had just lost sight of both, Giovanna and Ramachandra. I stepped through the Aquarium, with very rare species of tropical fishes, and, in a bend of the way, the lions compartments appeared.

When I approached, a splendid specimen tamely raised its head and eyes towards me, and as hypnotized, I came closer to its cage, without being able to get rid of that stare, which I felt as a mixture of message and begging.

Without realizing what was happening, I began weeping, at first in silence : I only noticed the tears that got my face wet. Then, and as if they came from an inexhaustible fountain, I experienced my heart overflowed; it flowed compassionate feelings, of justice, of freedom, for these poor beings to which men believes with the right to enslave. The weeping became so irrepressible that the sobs shook my whole body, so I had to go out, to try to calm down.

On one occasion, I told this experience to George, a German friend whom I had met at Aurobindo Ashram, Delhi Branch, and he tried to calm me down about the meaning of this lion look.

According to George, the noble animal just wanted to tell me :

— Don't worry; everything is all right. There are many jailed men as well, although they don't realize it; live and enjoy your freedom, but don't forget me.

AND OF COURSE I AM NOT GOING TO FORGET YOU, MY DEAR COMPANION ON THE WAY OF THE LIFE!

79. "Music, Music"

When a while later, Giovanna and Rama went out of the Zoo, I was already calmed down. In the meantime, I had bought a little musical instrument, from a very black Hindu seller, of small body and great charm, who managed to take out wonderful sounds from such a precarious apparatus.

The "instrument" looked as a little and rustic violin. It was assembled with half a coconut shell, covered with a leather patch, from which a round handle stick appeared, as thick as a broom, more or less of about 40 cmts. long.

At the end of it, two small wooden pieces of rather less diameter, put one opposite the other, acted as a peg. Two ropes of thin wire stretched by means of them, with a tiny piece of wood put underneath that kept the ropes even tauter.

A minute bow made with a thin wooden bent stick, in the ends of which a thin but strong fiber thread, used for making it sound, was tied up.

The Hindu followed me everywhere playing his instrument. Smilingly, he tried to convince me with his extraordinary musical ability. As besides, the price was quite accessible (and I am very "tender", my husband says), of course, after the known bargaining, in the end he won, and I had no choice but to purchase it.

Right there he gave me some musical lessons, while I was waiting for my friends to come out. The Hindu assured me that if I practised during a week, I'd make it sound as well as he did.

While we were going on with the taxi journey, bound for Bangalore, I martyred my companions' ears, trying to get a pleasant sound, as the seller did wonderfully. I went on practicing with the great amusement of Rama, who cheered me up asking "Music, Music!", and Giovanna covering her ears with her hands...

80. "Believing is Seeing"

After the spoiled visit (for me) to the Zoo, and accompanied by the new instrument, we set off going to Bangalore. In this stretch of the journey, my friend remembered that, in the surroundings, another "Santón" (as the Italians says) lived. About him, we had heard a really interesting story : it seemed to be that on a certain occasion, a known thief was reprimanded by Sai Baba, who reproached him his behaviour, to what the man stated he was acting that way, since he needed to feed his family.

It is said that Sai Baba was moved and understanding such a hard situation, handed him two little medals, one with his image and the other with Sai Baba Shirdi's, a well known Muslim sage, who is considered his previous incarnation. He also gave him as a present, huge pictures of both, assuring him that from there on, people would visit his place and *miracles* would come about. With the donations he received, he could very well feed his children and therefore, he wouldn't need to go on breaking the law.

In fact, the two great pictures of these holy men, started to exhale vibhuti, and people began approaching to witness such wonders. As Sai Baba had anticipated, with those means he supports not only his own family, but also an orphanage he himself built, in which he offers shelter and food (and love) to a lot of homeless children, or belonging to very poor families.

Always asking, we arrived at the place, where we were kindly received by the very person. After greeting him and introducing ourselves, he invited us to come to a kind of temple, where the two saints pictures that breathed out vibhuti were. There, we sat down on the floor in front of him; he placed Sai Baba's medal in Giovanna's hand, and in mine, he put Sai Baba Shirdi's. Before my astonishment, it began flowing from my hand, in the place where the little medal was, a honeyed liquid called *Amrita* or sacred nectar.

The Swami collected it with a big spoon three times and gave it to me to drink, while all the time it went on slipping away through my fingers. Something similar happened also to my friend.

In accordance with his statements, that flowing depended on the person's good karma. The truth is that in India, such exceptional events happened to us, that they were becoming common, and one even stops amazing, as if it were the most natural thing.

Just when I was moving away from such deeds, the thought of which would be the sortileges, which strengths or powers would produce these miracles, surprised me, and I reverted the reflection of "seeing is believing" by "believing is seeing".

Our tour throughout the South of India was coming to an end. Already before arriving at Bangalore, where the itinerary really was over, we realized that another step of the journey had been fulfilled, leaving us such an extraordinary balance of personal experiences, that, although nothing to wonder at remained ahead, the objective was already absolutely fulfilled.

The plan with my friend was to rest a day at Bangalore, and find out if Sai Baba was in White Fields, in order to take another darshan. Besides there, in Bangalore, we would have to take over our "nightmare" again : the monstruous bags that were waiting for us in the "Left-Luggage" of the Taxi Agency, to go on travelling northwards, first to Delhi, the Country Capital and later, and from there, to the Himalayas.

What most saddened us was to become aware of our separation from Ramachandra, who, during the two weeks' tour, had been much more than an engaged taxi driver, but the best of the friends, reliable, faithful adviser, good companion and guardian angel : humble, polite, respectful, and always unconditionally at our disposition. Of course, we were going to notice his absence enormously, and the truth is we missed him a lot.

81. What happened with the Magic?

When the tour through South India came to an end and as I have already commented, we had decided with my friend to travel northwards by train, crossing over the whole country. In this way, we would have more opportunities to see the landscape, the Geography, and to live experiences different from the ones of the plane journey.

I have also already explained that our next destination would be New Delhi, the Country Capital. From there, we would move to know more or less near places as Agra and Jaipur, to go on travelling then bound for The Himalayas.

The last objective would be "The Divine Life Society's Ashram", founded by Swami Shivananda at Rishikesh, on the first hills of this imposing range and next to the holy Ganges River.

The same Taxi Agency we contracted for our South Tour, and was in charge of getting the train tickets, advised us the Second "A" category, since we wanted it to be air-conditioned, and in spite of being the Second Class, it was the only with this comfort.

Although the passages were booked with more than 15 days of anticipation, that is to say, before setting off from Bangalore, they remarked that it was not at all easy to get them, since in India all the means of transport are always crowded.

On our way back in Ramachandra's taxi and, in accordance with our plans, we rested one day in Bangalore and took advantage of the occasion to come close to White Field, about 25 kms. away. We had been told that, indeed, in those days Sai Baba was in his coquette ashram in that little village, and we didn't want to lose the very last darshan (for us).

Besides, we experienced a great happiness before the idea of meeting our dear Muslim friends again, specially Sajad, my "son", who certainly would move there, as almost all the commerce from Puttaparthi did. Likewise, we anticipated the joy to greet other Swami's devotees, whom we had made friends with in Prashanti Nilayam Ashram, who invariably followed Sai Baba.

Still in Ramachandra's taxi, which we contracted for one day more, we arrived at White Fields just on time to share the darshan, but, unluckily, and I didn't know why, we waited together with the other devotees for a long time inside the enclosure, but Sai Baba didn't appear.

About our Muslim friends, we heard they had also moved there, since when we arrived, we had met Sajad's cousins who commented us they had rented a small place, just in front of the Ashram entrance.

After the frustrated darshan, I made my way towards the appointed place, while my friend delayed herself shopping and greeting several friends.

I met Sajad very lonely and taciturn; as the Ramadan was still going on, he looked even more weakened by the partial fast he was still keeping, which wasn't only about food, but also of gestures, words and even emotions.

He looked really sick, broken physical and morally, as if he didn't want to be affected by the love we mutually experienced, he kept his feelings at a distance and under control.

The sorrow and sadness of the separation just 15 days ago, he let me guess at Puttaparthi, was only a silent reproach in his lovely and large eyes. He seemed a thrashed dog, that does not even dare approach to receive a caress, for the fear of being ill-treated again.

At Puttaparthi, the code we used to speak to one another had always functioned : he called me "cat's eyes", and I told him "my wise old man".. But at that moment, Sajad had built a wall of silence between us, and I believe that no secret code was able to knock it down.

Unfortunately, there was no privacy in that ugly place they occupied there, all open in the front part and with people coming and going.

As I usually did in Puttaparthi, I sat down on the floor, hoping to recover that tenderness flow we had enjoyed together so many times.

Sajad sat down on the furthest corner of the small room, his dark eyes very low, looking on the floor, almost closed by the black and silky eyelashes.

His long, beautiful and sensitive hands, which always had for me an affectionate love gesture, were fallen down on his lap, motionless and emptied of caresses, as if life had run away from them.

I needed more than ever to have some moments of warm approach with him, since I was almost ready to go away. How many things my heart told him, but his silence made the words remained strangled in my throat, "My Sweet Old Wise Man"! The minutes sorrowfully crawled, and in that emptiness without neither gestures nor words, the suffering, the anguish and the desperation occupied its place.

When the leaving time arrived and Ramachandra fetched me, just then Sajad raised his feverish eyes towards me, but let me go away, always in silence, not even getting up from his corner...

82. At the Holy Mother's Feet

When we left White Field, I felt a knot in my throat. To think that I had arrived with so many hopes that morning! I tried to overcome that grief, but I knew that from then on, the sadness would accompany me for a long while.

With those feelings, we began searching the Holy Mother, a very well known Swami Sivananda's disciple, who, according to some indications, had her ashram near White Field.

As usual, we started to find out where this Holy Mother was located, since, as it couldn't be otherwise, we didn't have the exact address. About midday we managed to find her, being received by her *Chela*, who kindly invited us to come in, stating that his Master would attend us in a minute.

In the meantime, we observed the place : small, humble, but absolutely clean and cheerful; everywhere in the garden, flowers and trees with appetizing fruits.

Inside the room where we were led to, a large arm-chair with a high back, a plain table, some wooden benches and several shelves full of books, adhered to the walls, constituted the whole furniture.

The "Holy Mother" didn't take a long time to appear : a sweet old lady, who seemed to be more than 80 years of age, of a kind countenance and very nice manners. My friend and I sat down modestly at her feet, one at each side of the big seat where the woman sat.

First of all, we asked for her blessing, which she warmly conceded, putting her hands over our heads. Later, she remained completely still and with her little eyes raised to Heaven, as if in a trance state.

Very often since I knew my friend, she had commented her worry about the fate of a couple of friends of hers, who had travelled to India six or seven years before. Seemingly, they had a flight accident and never came back to Argentina.

Giovanna had planned to travel with them on such occasion, but before it, she had a premonitory dream in which she saw the plane fall. Impressed by what she thought was an announcement, and also for other private reasons, she decided not to accompany them. Her friends didn't take it seriously and set off anyway, but unfortunately, the premonition came true and they never returned.

By chance, or better by causality, the young Hindu who was sitting at our side in the flight from Bombay to Bangalore, at our arrival, had been present at the accident that had happened next to his residence, precisely there in White Field.

Giovana's anxiety was in the sense that her friends could be alive, perhaps mutilated or shocked with loss of their memory, at any remote Indian hospital. We had thought of investigating about it, and were looking where to start from.

The scarcely understandable babbling of the Holy Mother brought us to reality. She spoke to my friend, telling her not to worry for those persons, that they were in another dimension, absolutely well, and that with such an anguish and anxiety, she was bothering them in their evolution.

Later, she was returning little by little to awareness, and in a clearer and straighter way, repeated the same. My friend couldn't stop weeping, and Holy Mother recriminated her again :

— Please, stop weeping because you go on disturbing them with such grief; let them be quiet to develop in peace.

Once those first moments of great emotion went by, she talked friendly with us; among other subjects, we spoke about the need or not to have a Guru or Master for the Spiritual Growing. My friend insisted that, for her, it was essential, while I stated that there was not such a necessity for me.

The Holy Mother agreed to have one if he is required, to be later set aside to listen and accept the own interior master orders, our wise and holy *intuition*.

Once more the Hindus hospitality! The old sweet lady insisted us to stay for lunch, suggesting her diligent chela to lay the table for us : of course always the same menu with rice as the main dish, vegetables and pulse stews, the greens grown at her orchard, among which cucumber and turnips could be seen.

She even put cutlery for us! For dessert, very sweet papayas, recently picked from a big tree that adorned her garden, becoming the known Hindu proverb true : "The Guest is God".

Besides, some books were given to us, as a present, whose author was the Holy Mother, and finally we left, running out of words to express our thanks, since she didn't accept a single rupee.

Giovanna and I insisted to pay even for the books, but the Mother, mischievously declared :

— The price is on the first page.

We looked where she had pointed, and could just read : "Price : Divine Love".

83. Farewell in the "Tandoori" Fashion

Still moved by the experiences with the Holy Mother, we came back to our taxi, that was patiently waiting for us outside the ashram, and returned early to Bangalore. The following day we would set off from there, in the Karnataka Express, bound for the North.

In that afternoon and evening we rested a little and put our things in order, and the next morning, that is to say, the last day, we visited the commercial area of Bangalore. The same as when we had arrived, the city looked modern and very quiet, with its broad tree-lined avenues and pleasant weather.

We had thought of going shopping there, specially to buy a present for Ramachandra, our loyal driver, as gratitude for all the kindness and dedication he had offered us during the tour, although, at every moment, he said he was only carrying out his "duty".

As a farewell, we invited Rama to lunch with us, at a restaurant which speciality was "Tandoory Chicken". We had really known this place since our arrival at Bangalore, for we had discovered it in our going trip, with its rustic tables placed in the courtyard, under the big trees shadow, and the very good food.

In fact, "tandoori" is a big barrel where fire is prepared, and then the chicken is cooked after being introduced in several sauces of different colours. They are prepared with yoghurt and a variety of spices, from which chili (or chilly) is, of course, always present.

From the courtyard, we could observe how they put the chicken to be cooked; first, all red coloured. At half roasting, it was removed with the toasted seasoning, to put it again back in the tandoori green coloured with other spices; later orange, next dark-brown, etc. That process was repeated for more than an hour and half. All the spices as curry, garam masala, turmeric, chili, etc., "paraded".

When finally! It was ready, it was a delicious dish, even though very hot, in spite of the recommendation we always made before lunch : "Please, not hot", and they assured, also as usual : "O.K., O.K.", shaking their heads sidewards.

I remember to have perfectly scraped it outside with a knife; I would say I nearly peeled it completely to remove the seasoning remainder, but anyway and by such "hotness", my lips got hurt.

Despite this, I can say we enjoyed the dish, the same as the dessert : fruit salad with ice cream, a blessing to calm such a "fire".

When the lunch was over, they brought little bowls with lukewarm water and lemon juice, to wash our hands, since the three of us had eaten with our natural cutlery : the fingers. Besides, another small plate with aniseed for a good digestion. Usually, this is the habit at every restaurant in South India, and we tried to chew the hard seeds the better we could. We asked them to wrap the rest of the seeds in a napkin, to take them home, to be later added to the other herbs when having in our "mates".

As an exception for being the farewell, and due to our insistence, Rama asked also for a piece of chicken to eat with the rice. He seemed very pleased when he received the shirt we had given him as a present, besides some copies of the pictures we had taken together along the tour, and a tip in rupees. I am sure his greatest happiness was the photos, since he was always delighted to "pose" with us.

84. The Handsome Sikh from Punjab

The owner or keeper of the Tandoori Restaurant, was a young and very attractive Sikh, of lovely features and warm smile. He wore the typical turban that distinguishes that race native of Punjab, who practise the Guru Nanak's teachings.

The same as the first time, he came in person to greet us at our table, declaring it would be really a great honor for him, to invite us specially the next opportunity we visited Bangalore.

He asked us about our next destination : we informed him that that very afternoon we would set off to New Delhi, and took advantage of him to ask if he knew in the Country's Capital a hotel to recommend to us. Immediately, he wrote down on a piece of paper, the name and address of one where he usually lodged in his trips. When we arrived at New Delhi, in fact, we went precisely to stay there, which was very comfortable, perfectly situated and of a fair tariff.

After thanking for this information and greeting the handsome Sikh, we set off towards the hotel in Ramachandra's taxi, to complete the preparations and take over the "nightmare", the huge bags we had left at the Left-Luggage Office : this time we couldn't run away; they had to set off with us on the train !

The Karnataka Express would leave the Train Terminal Station of Bangalore at 4 o'clock in the afternoon; in time, Rama carried us there. Our train was already at its platform : it would take us two days and two nights towards the next destination : New Delhi.

The train would be our home on rails, which moved us away from all the known beings : from the persons who looked after us and became our closest friends, and from the Holy Masters at whose feet we had confided all our hopes and illusions.

From there on, new persons, new places and experiences spread before us. Even though the uncertainty of the unknown things got us a little anxious, we were absolutely sure that new and wonderful experiences would be waiting for us, and the Grace would go on flowing over our heads.

*

12

KARNATAKA EXPRESS

85. Dispute with the *Coolies*

Along and across India, at every train or bus station, groups of "coolies" (porters) concerned with the baggage, are always present, who are recognized by their typical red turbans.

Of course, they couldn't be missing there either, at the Train Terminal of Bangalore Station, who seemed to be led by one of fierce features and not worthy of confidence at all. He turned out to be as he looked : quite shameless; to raise our bags to the carriage, from the platform in front of the door, he tried to charge 300 rupees (10 Dollars), tariff which was exorbitant in India.

Naturally, Goddess Kali (me) had to discuss heatedly. Nobody else took part; the others were just observing at a careful distance, watching how the matter would finish.

In accordance with Gio's opinion, I looked very angry, shaking my "many arms". I reproached him for being so rascal; that he made a mistake thinking that for being foreigners we were millionaires, that it was very wrong of him to take advantage of people in such a way. Always in a hot manner I threw to his face that we had travelled to India looking for Holy Persons, and instead we met thieves; I told him everything the anger brought to my mind..., and I could translate into English.

The very rough man laid down his hostility. I could observe, in spite of my annoyance, that his countenance was transforming before such a warm defense. Finally, we reached an understanding at a reasonable price, and UP!, with the applause of everybody else.

With a great emotion we said good-bye to Ramachandra, who embraced us at both sides of the bosom, as it is the custom. With the help of the, now smiling coolies, we arranged all the luggage in the little carriage, the seats of which we had already booked, and would share with other people. Luckily, everything was at the reach of our sight, very well ordered, so we had nothing to worry about.

From the platform, the train looked rather dirty, but once placed inside, we noted that at least our section was very comfortable and immaculately clean. Unusual fact in India, it set off with a moderate accuracy, remaining Ramachandra's image in our retinas, greeting us from the platform, with his hands like birds that waved in farewell, and his black eyes wet of emotion, the same as ours.

86. Our Carriage and the Travelling Mates

At the beginning, in front of our place, a young couple with a very nice small girl sat down. The child, with her astonished eyes outlined with kajal, and the plait tied up with an exquisite bun, looked as a typical black doll.

At the side of the coach, there was another seat, occupied by a middle-aged Sikh gentleman with a great black turban who, as soon as we set off, made friend with the Hindu sitting in front of us; they talked warmly and went everywhere together, I think, looking for a place in another carriage to be nearer each other.

After about two hours, I suppose they got it, since they inter changed their places with two young men who were travelling together, of more or less 30 years of age. These youngsters were located at the bench situated on the right side (for us) of the wagon, on the corridor. The vacant double seat in front of us, was later taken by a Hindu lady, very friendly, named Manju, who, to open the chat, told us she lived in Delhi and worked as a journalist in a newspaper.

Each one of the three seats had the size of a single bed, and was calculated for two persons, so they were roomy and comfortable. At night, the backings were raised to become two couchettes. In short, the carriage was distributed thus : two long seats one in front of the other, for two persons each, four in total (we were only three), and one at a side, for other two persons.

All the carriages were mixed, for men and women. To close the compartment at night, from the corridor side, there were two beautiful and close-woven curtains, made in satin brocade, shining turquoise, printed with big bright golden roses, which completely isolated passengers from outside. Those curtains were in set with the seats upholstery, also made in blue turquoise colour.

Our companions were all kind and friendly, apart from peaceful and silent. The boys were dressed in Western style, with trousers and shirt, although they wore comfortable Indian sandals.

In spite of being Catholics, according to their words, they spent a long time on still meditation, attitude which is more common among Eastern people. By the way, they commented us that in many places of the world, the Catholic Church was adopting the classic Yoga asanas or postures to do its rituals.

At sleeping time, Manju only dropped her head and stretched her legs, practically without changing the position. I would say that she didn't move during all night long, since when she woke up, in the morning, she kept the same posture; she had not even folded her showy panjavi, composed of very loose fuchsia trousers that narrowed downwards and a striped golden yellow and fuchsia tunic.

She used the *bindhu* on the forehead, her race distinctive, which she showed off with a great coquetry and touched it from time to time. As a contrast, we woke up with our clothes all folded, and what can I say about it, after the second night!

The two boys worked together in Bangalore, I think at the Finance Treasury Ministry Department; one of them, called Iraju, was married, and told us that his wife was expecting a baby. Cecil, the other, was single, and during the trip became Manju's very close friend, with whom he seemed to feel rather at ease : he asked for her address and telephone number in Delhi, to arrange future meetings. Of course, we all interchanged our addresses and telephones numbers.

87. A Long Night with an Empty Stomach

At the Karnataka Express, I late found out that there wasn't a Dining Carriage, but quite before meal time, a waiter passed through to take the orders. In the morning, and from very early, the breakfast : individual thermos with white coffee or tea, spicy omelets or other fritters like doughnuts, always very seasoned. Lunch and supper, Hindu typical meals : the rice was, of course, present, with hot stews of vegetables and pulses, yoghurt and chapatis.

Once, the waiter realized I wasn't pleased with the menu, and brought me a great plastic pack with noodles instead, a very thin kind of them, with dried assorted vegetables also chopped very little. They were of instant preparation, having to add only boiling water, and the change was welcomed by my stomach.

The first night of the journey, among the delicious tandoori chicken, the icy dessert and the last moment haste, my appetite was not good, and less with the offered menu. At midday I had really enjoyed the meal, in spite of being very spicy. Relatively early, the waiter had passed by to take the supper order, but I, without worrying at all, refused, since I had supposed there would be a Dining Wagon opened the whole night, or at least till very late, where I could appeal to if needed to get some food.

About 8 o'clock in the evening, I began to feel hungry. Later I could communicate with the waiter, who stated that everywhere was closed and locked, and there was nothing of nothing, up to the following day.

Usually, when we made a tour with Giovanna, we always took fruits, fresh or dried, or something else to eat. This time, with the urgency of the last moment preparations, we hadn't carried anything at all, not even a sweet pack.

My friend had ordered her meal in time, and it was a long while she had eaten it away, so she was absolutely self-satisfied, writing something down on her travelling diary; but I had a long night ahead, and the hunger was growing more and more insistent.

Up to that moment, we had only interchanged some smiles with our new journey mates; I noticed that the three had brought the meal from their places, and, in silence, were beginning to eat, very concentrated in what they were doing and as if they were carrying out a sacred rite, in the typical attitude of Eastern people.

As soon as they heard my questions to the waiter, the three offered me their meals, so earnestly and insistently, that my stomach didn't admit a rejection : so I accepted an apple and a chapati.

88. Routine on Rails

The train passengers who didn't take bed linen (our companions had everything), for few rupees could ask for a complete set, which would be worn the whole trip and consisted of : pillow and pillow case, sheets, towel and blankets.

The first night, my companion wanted to sleep in the upper berth, and the second, it was me who slept there. As the air-conditioning was working at full day and night, the carriage was a little cool; therefore, and in spite of going to bed with our clothes on, it was necessary to use the blankets.

In a moment, I realized that it had slipped to the floor. Half asleep and rather lazy, I was thinking what to do, since, on the one hand, I was cold and, on the other, I didn't want to awaken myself completely going down to pick the blanket up.

All of a sudden I felt that one of the boys, who obviously was awake and realized what was happening, got up, picked it up from the floor, and with great kindness, very quietly, may be thinking I was asleep, wrapped me up again. Thank you very much!

Usually, at home, I used to get up early, even more in India, and the two nights on the train were endless. The carriages with the drawn curtains looked all the same from the corridor; from time to time a Hindu coming back from the bathroom, mistook the wagon, and his black head appeared in ours, looking for his place; then his white teeth smiled apologizing with the "sorry", said quite low not to wake anybody up.

My wishes to have "mates" were also increasing, but with such a lot of belongings I didn't even remember where I had put the equipment, and if it wasn't in hand it was a good fuss; thus I was obliged to repress my desires until the arrival at our destination, where, surely, I would take revenge.

From very early in the morning, all kinds of specimen of the different races who live in India, with or without turbans, began to circulate along the corridor, bound for the bathrooms. I observed there were of two sorts : for Eastern, the turkish type, with the hole on the floor, and for Westerners, with toilet. One could note that the last was not frequently used, since there were even cobwebs, and I guess that during that journey, it was only used by Gio and me.

Outside the bathrooms, there were little basins with a tap and a mirror. Sometimes I saw the Hindus take out a little box with a white powder, maybe salt, rub with their forefingers the teeth and gums, and later rinse them with clean water.

In front of these mirrors and also from very early, women redid their plaits, the Hindus retouched the spot on their forehead, Muslims arranged their typical caps and the Sikhs wrapped their long hair up in a Chignon rolled up over their heads and then, tidily and carefully placed their turbans again.

Speaking of turbans, in New Delhi, a taxi driver who worked for our hotel, had promised to let me film the "ceremony" of the turban usage, but later we had a discussion about the taxi tariff, I got angry and didn't fetch him at the place agreed.

During the two days that our train trip lasted, we carried out lively conversations with our three companions, about all the imagined subjects. They ascertained on our age, occupation, family, religion, life philosophy, etc. Also asked our opinion about their country and what we thought of some deeds, political as well as religious or of any other kind.

As I had already told in preceding chapters, it was not strange that on such occasions, persons from other carriages approached to ours; they sat down just to listen with full attention, without taking part in anything, and when our chat was over, sometimes after hours, so silently as they had arrived, retreated.

89. "Music", Again

I have already talked about the "instrument" I had got at the Mysore Zoo surroundings, at the end of our tour with Ramachandra. On the train, I had left it in hand, inside my bag, with the intention of practicing, in order to see if I could take any harmonic sound out, but the truth is that afterwards, I didn't dare torture my companions' ears.

When arranging other things in the bag, I took the "jewel" in my hands to observe it, and one of the boys asked for it. As he knew a lot of music, he began playing it wonderfully, and since then we varied joyfully the long trip with merry melodies. (Ramachandra was missing to liven up with "Music, Music"!).

On one of the train stops, we got out to take some pictures

with our travel mates, with whom we were integrating more each time, and constituted a sort of family. We had already taken some inside the carriage, and as soon as we arrived at New Delhi, were going to develop them, for the boys to be able to carry their copies.

Outside the train, the heat was hellish and there were sickening smells. At each stop we could see the sellers who, on the platforms, offered some rice to the passengers, from a big pan prepared for the occasion. We quickly came back to the air conditioning of the interior; besides, we didn't like to leave our luggage alone either.

The scenery of the centre and North India was rather boring, not at all comparable with the fascinating South. It looked more like the extensive Argentine plains, with predominance of wheat cultivation, always in a rustic way.

From the whole train trip, the best to be rescued was the friendship with our wagon companions, who promised to visit us at the New Delhi Hotel. At last, on the third day, we were approaching our destination, and the only worry was to think that, at getting off, new quarrels with the coolies about baggage affairs would be waiting for me.

But, in accordance with my philosophy, at every moment I solve my problems with one of the *Niyamas* (ethical precepts) of the Ashtanga Yoga by Patanjali, the Ishvara Pranidhana, that means to surrender oneself to the Divine Will. Thus, I calmed down and told myself "Thy Will be Done", and from there on, there was already nothing to be afraid of.

✱

13

THE CAPITAL OF INDIA

90. We Lodged, at Last!

On our third day in the Karnataka Express, in the afternoon, we finally arrived at our destination, leaving our journey companions with whom we had started a nice friendship. Just as they had promised, later on and at several opportunities, they visited us in our hotel, where we had lively chats and took advantage, consulting them about some matters we needed to do.

The Terminal Train Station of New Delhi, looked very dirty, crowded and without any attraction, with the most heterogeneous human tide walking on its platforms. This time, the discussion with the coolies had another style, since we had been conveniently instructed about what was the usual tip to carriers.

In what we had to show resolution was with the taxi driver, who was taking us to the hotel. He insisted on driving us to another one place that, according to his words, was better and cheaper; I also, with rather firmness, earnestly ordered him to take us at the hotel I had pointed to (probably taxi drivers get a tip from hotels if they get customers). O.K.

My friend and I had decided to lodge where the Tandoori Restaurant Sikh, from Bangalore, had advised. Besides, our train companions knew it and corroborated the information.

Among discussions, we reached the chosen hotel. We observed it was a modern building, of about twenty storeys, which was located very near the Commercial Area and Janpath Road, the wide avenue where most of the Tibetan Market Bazaars are.

This hotel was very useful to our needs, although I must recognize that considering it was built only few years before, it looked rather ruined. With Giovanna, we had to change several rooms up to be able to find the one that fulfilled all the living conditions : in fact, the one where the roof fan worked, surely had water problems, or the lights were lacking, or the mattresses were in bad state, etc. We changed five rooms until we found the one which satisfied us, and in it, we asked for new mattresses. In this way at last we lodged at ease.

After settling down, we took a bath and rested for a while. Our "mates" had never been so tasteful! Then, we set off to the spectacular offices of our Air Line, to confirm the return flight. With my friend, we had wondered about the possibility of changing the tickets date, to remain in India 10 days more.

We were kindly and efficiently attended, and luckily, we could get everything according to our wishes, thus we could have a little more time to stay at this hallucinating country, and carry out at ease the planned visits, with time to spare besides.

91. The Tibetan Market

Calm and happy after we were able to delay the returning flight, we walked through the hotel surroundings; later, we went towards Janpath Road, in order to "snoop" a little about the Tibetan Market Bazaars.

For several blocks we entered every shop that attracted our attention, and again, "bargaining" was up to date. There was really everything, and we could get true "bargains" in clothes as well as in stones, masks, etc. We found beautiful goods of fine handicraft. Besides, it was possible to get articles from all over the country, and, in general, at rather better prices, but also there, the absolute lack of space in our already packed bags, restrained us.

In that area, the bazaars were mostly in hands of Tibetan Chinese, like Doma, who was later my fondest friend, a very wise old woman; she knew a lot about the idiosyncrasy and behaviour of the people of the different races that share the Capital of the Country. Doma always received me friendly and her sensible advice was very useful indeed.

There were also bazaars kept by Muslims, specially from Kashmir, as our friend Sajad, and Sikhs with great turbans, native of Punjab.

Just in one of these bazaars, where silver and semi-precious stones were on sale, I came in to ask the price of a *bracelet.* A stout Sikh man, with a showy turban finished off with a stone brooch, and a not less prominent belly, diligently attended to me, and proposed to exchange the jewel (which price seemed very high to me), for my camera.

As all Indians used to do, he wanted to know my data, from origin, age, occupation, to marital status, journey aim, religion, etc. Later, he asked if I liked his country; when I answered it seemed really fantastic to me, he wanted to know why I didn't stay there for ever. He couldn't believe that in my homeland I had to work, a Goddess like me!

I imagined that the question would be over, answering back that apart from the work, I had a husband waiting for me. Without turning a hair, and as if that was not an excuse enough either, the Sikh argued :

— And for ONLY ONE husband you think of going back ?

I suppose that as some of them have several wives, he wondered that number one was really a very little amount...

92. Frustrated Meeting with a Yogi

On the second day in New Delhi, I returned from the Reception Office, surely because of another problem in the room, when I heard somebody calling me in Spanish. The possibility to be known there was so remote, it was so far of the imagination that, surprised and without believing it, I went to approach the person who spoke to me; at the same time I tried to locate him from somewhere; my mental file quickly looked for, until I managed to recognize a Hindu Ayurvedic Doctor, established in Argentina, who at certain occasions I had taken some Ayurveda Seminars with, in Buenos Aires, during my Yoga Master Courses.

The truth is that I also found it hard to identify him, since in Argentina and every time he gave classes, he was dressed in Eastern clothes, while in his own country he wore Western garments : trousers and shirt. Then, I remained thinking of this paradox.

He told me that he had travelled to India with the Integral Yoga Group, led by who had been my teacher in Argentina, but he had stayed in India to make some matters and visit his family. We talked for a moment, and he agreed to come back later to accompany us to meet Sri Dass, the President of the Great White Fraternity and Spiritual World Yoga Governor, whom my friend Gio and I wanted to meet.

Doctor Madariya commented us on the extraordinary seer powers that came to Sri Dass by lashes. As our aim had always been to visit holy persons with special faculties, we were very pleased that somebody whom we knew, would introduce us to this Yogi.

Unluckily, we came out and moved quite away from the hotel, and it was impossible to return at the appointed time. We consulted later in Reception about our friend, being informed he had set off from the hotel.

We were sorry for this mischance and that with it, the possibility to meet Sri Dass faded away, and the worst of all was that we also blamed ourselves since it had been because of us.

A long time later, I met Dr. Madariya in Buenos Aires and could offer him my apologies for the delay, which had been the cause of the misconception in New Delhi. He assured me that after the appointment day, he had appeared several times at the hotel to meet us, but consulting Reception for the room we were staying at, the clerk watched in the computer and informed him that we had also set off. What a pity...!

I imagine the confusion came about, perhaps, by the fact that we had changed rooms so many times, that we were not registered on that number any more. All right, and as Muslims says, "It is Allah's Hand"...

93. The New and the Old Delhi

Near our hotel, on Janpath Road, we consulted several Tourist Agencies. Then, we booked two seats at the one that inspired us more trust, for a city tour, that is to say, a run along the interest spots through the city, comprising New Delhi, and also the old, called only Delhi.

In fact, it is a question of two completely different cities : New Delhi is a modern city, with long and wide tree lined avenues, shaded in all its length by huge trees, which flank beautiful gardens and great buildings of several storeys like our hotel. It looks quite clean and with a more or less ordered traffic.

Its commercial area is a large circular space called Connaught Place, with squares, gardens and bowers, walking and shopping places, in which all the avenues converge as the rays of a wheel. At this spot the majority of the cinemas are, crowded at any time.

Walking through this centre, a varied sort of people can be found : clerks, students, tourists from the whole world, hippies, massagists who offer their services, curious persons, etc.

And as a contrast, the Old Delhi, which was moved to be India's Capital from Agra, by the Emperor Shah Jahan in the 17th Century. He settled down in the Red Fort, built for that aim, and established in that place "The Peacock's Throne". It was just there where Queen Victoria of England was proclaimed Indian Empress in 1877.

The Old Delhi!... A human tide : a noisy, exhausting, dirty and a risky city (even for the Indians themselves), where the racket of the life cannot be avoided feeling at each step.

There, it is usual to see the buses, within which there is no place even for a pin, with people hanging from doors, and many times settled on the roof.

The typical rickshaws zigzagging among the dense traffic, bicycles twisting in the crowd, motorcycles, persons on foot, two wheel carts pulled by tame oxen, policemen walking through people and brandishing long sticks...

To move about its commercial street, Chandni Chowk, with the old bazaars, travelling sellers, food stalls of fruit juices, taken out with prehistoric presses, is a complete hallucinating experience.

Also mixed with this human tide, there are thieves, swindlers, tale tellers, false astrologers and seers, with the most sophisticated abilities to perform their "work".

Sometimes and for long distances, we had to walk so tight among people, that we had to force our way through with shoulders and elbows. Not even speak about crossing the street!

94. Time for Beauty

When we came back to the hotel, in the evening, we observed a little poster with an arrow that pointed out : "Beauty Saloon — Hair-dresser — 1st Floor". The truth is that until then, we hadn't had time enough to dedicate to "beautify" ourselves, so that, encouraged by the chart, we went upstairs to know the place, from the ground floor where the Reception Office was. We intended to ask if they made waxing or plucking, which was what both of us needed.

A young and charming Hindu lady, neatly dressed in a showy silk saree, attended to us, and in a kind manner in her precarious English, she questioned what we wanted. In varied ways, we tried to make her understand that we wished to remove our face unwanted hair, and she answered back that, in fact, that service (of beauty) was performed there.

My friend Giovanna always waited for me to take all decisions, for instance to ask any new dish of food, or for any other step we might do. But this time and opposed to her habits, she went forward while stating :

— "Yyyyo voy primero" (I go first), — and, very arrogantly, she settled on the arm-chair in front of the mirror, while I observed all the activities of the Hindu.

First, the beautician took a long thread out of a drawer, from a shelf she had in hand, on the right side of the mirror. She wrapped up one of her thin fingers, and with a magician's ability, she carried out very quick movements, while trying to pluck some hair each time, with a grace and speed that one couldn't believe!

My mind was as if I were hypnotized by such skill and maneuver, and was not able even to analyze the situation. Besides, I found this never seen method so funny, that I burst out laughing, before the alarmed Hindu who didn't know what was happening and my stupefied friend, who just went on repeating : "Oh no, no", while withdrawing her face to take herself away from the hair hunting.

When I could calm myself down and articulate a word, I tried to explain the best I could that we didn't wish that method, called "bleaching", but the wax system.

Just when she heard "wax", she understood and made the preparations for the new method, which seemed was only used on legs and arms, but not on the face. At last, we achieved to be waxed both moderately well, and, pleased with the results, could retire to our room.

At night, we remembered the affair in our room, and laughed so much that we cried, while recreating the unimaginable gestures of the Hindu performing her work.

95. Sajad's "Friendly" Relatives

Our friend Sajad, the Muslim boy who attended a bazaar in Puttaparthi, had given me a card with the address of some members of his family, who had a shop in the commercial area near Chandni Chowk, in the Old Delhi.

Card in hand, we tried to look for them; we started asking around, and according to the indications, we were going into alleys narrower each time, dirtier and more twisted, always crowded with people, which set off from the populous main street.

In the way, we only ran across few Muslim women, entirely dressed in black and with the veil, also black, covering their faces, in accordance with their Islamic tradition.

Always asking, and asking again, we crossed courtyards, went up and down staircases, to find out that by the other side, another narrow side-street set off.

The slums were each time of worse appearance; the area seemed and felt sinister. We saw coarse food stalls, of desserts, of bread and biscuits, all full of flies, kept by bearded Muslims who observed us from the blackness of their eyes, with grim sights, not friendly at all.

Evidently in that zone, the majority was of this race, belonging to Islam. I knew through my "son" Sajad that, his people, frown upon women walking alone in the street, and that was the reason of the strong hostility that was guessed in their gestures and attitudes.

At last, we reached the place and, just as well!, because my friend was very frightened and wanted to go back. I heard her complaining and protesting while walking after me :

— Let's go away from here! We are going to be robbed and raped; we are going to be killed and nobody will even find out about it.

I recognized that the "set-design" was rather sinister, as to think about hidden crimes. I would say it was more adapted to the shooting of suspense and horror films, than making social relations.

The place was really that one, since to confirm our doubts they showed us a card, exactly like the one Sajad had given us, but the communication with his relatives was nearly impossible, since nobody there spoke English.

Lying about on the floor, over a carpet, there were two teenagers of an incredible beauty, fair-haired and light eyed Muslims, who were roaring with laughter for the unusual situation of not understanding our language. I remembered Sajad remarks, in the sense that in Kashmir there were people with light skin, hair and eyes, for what I supposed they would be some of his cousins.

Another very kind young boy, accompanied us from a room near to the shop. He seemed to understand some English, and stated he was our friend's brother, even though Sajad had told us he had only two sisters.

When, from my land, I commented Sajad this misunderstanding, he answered that I didn't realize anything, because if a person has good clothes and thriving business, everybody is his brother!

Then, an elder man, of about 55 years old and very grave countenance, I would better say with an unfriendly aspect, appeared on stage. While looking at us, I wonder he asked the others "what the hell we were looking for in that place". Even though I didn't understand his language, I observed the suspicious manner in which he faced the situation.

I tried to make him know we were Sajad's very close friends, but this statement (I don't know if he interpreted it either), didn't show to impress him at all, and the meeting was just there over.

I asked the boy who had declared to be our friend's brother, to accompany us up to the main street, since with so many pathless places, so entangled, as we had trodden through, we were afraid of not finding the way out. He, smiling widely and seemingly pleased, repeated "O.K., O.K.", shaking his head sidewards, but didn't move from there!

Very disappointed, we tried to look for the way out by ourselves. At the limit of our misfortune, while we were walking along one of those winding alleys, the wheel of a cart pulled by a tame cow, passed over Gio's foot. Between her ear-splitting shouts and my outbursts of laughter by the comic situation, we made a great fuss and attracted again the angry and flashing glances of the Muslims, who did neither understand nor approve such a scandal, specially done by women, and demonstrated their attitude sternly frowning.

Happily, we could go out safe and sound to Chandni Chowk, the main street...and wonder of coming back to that zone on our return from the Himalayas, since, in spite of all the inconveniences, we observed that the prices there were even better than those of New Delhi's.

That night also, when remembering Sajad relatives' incidents, we laughed so much that if it was not for the thickness of the walls that rather muffled the noises, we had been thrown to the street, for the uproar!

96. City Tour : History, Religion and...Business

On undertaking the contracted tour through the city, we set off very early in the morning. A small bus picked up all the passengers, in the broad majority Easterns, who showed to be very pleased with their fair companions, and at every moment, offered us gestures of friendship and full smiles.

Our first visit was to the Red Fort, called this way precisely for its building in red sandstone, very common in all India. First, we went through, after crossing the great entrance gate, a domed gallery, full of antique dealer shops, which, besides silk, stones, perfumes, etc., sold some precious reproductions of Tantric paintings.

We walked visiting the Audience Room (High Court), the place where the emperor received the famous visitors; we crossed extensive gardens, the private apartments, the monumental bathrooms, all in white marble, the exquisite Harem places, etc. The walls and floors of the bathrooms, were inlaid with precious and semi-precious stones, shaping very beautiful figures.

We visited the private mosque, galleries, balconies, etc. Very valuable candle holders and handicraft mirrors adorned the great halls, a whole fascinating world, which, I imagine, how would have dazzled and filled with admiration the European visitors.

Nearby, the famous Jama Masjid, the greatest mosque of the whole India. I was amazed by the harmonious arcades, the soft beauty of its domes, the roomy galleries emptied of shrines and pictures, since, according to Mohamed, The Prophet, "nothing must intervene between the Man and his God Allah".

In the evening, the spectacle in the Jama Masjid was really great : thousands and thousands of Muslim males, dressed in white, gathered in the large courtyard inside the enclosure, for fervently praying to their God, in the typical posture : sitting on the heels with the body on the ground and both arms stretching forwards (this asana is justly called "The Muslim Posture" in Yoga).

Jama Masjid, the monumental mosque of the Islam, was also built by Emperor Shah Jahan, close to the Red Fort, with a very high minaret from the top of which and through the look-out, the view of the two Delhis is extra-ordinary. The very important Chandni Chowk commercial way, set off nearby, which, crowded with people and all sort of vehicles, was seen from above like a busy ant hill.

At the alleys behind the mosque, by its surroundings, and around the Red Fort, we could look over (and bargain over) among the typical and always full up bazaars, which displayed everything one can imagine. They grouped together according to specialities : ivory, silver, perfumes, silk, ancient pieces, confectioner's shop, sweet stores, natural fruit juices and spice sellers, tailors, etc.

97. Ruins, Memorials, Palaces...

Our tour went on : we visited Kutab Minar ruins, erected in the 12th Century and from which its spectacular minaret is still standing, with fine Arabian inscriptions, the highest Delhi tower, with a height of about 75 mts. and 380 steps. Inside the courtyard, where only the ruins of what were splendid buildings have remained, an iron pillar is famous; there, people leaned on trying to join their hands at the back, with what, and according to an ancient legend, their wishes would be fulfilled.

The bus went methodically on its run. Just a glance at the India Gate, the great arcade raised in memory of the Indian soldiers killed during the First World War, fighting with the British. It is spoken of about 90,000 dead persons, but maybe this figure is lacking some zeros. Who would worry about counting the humble Indians, who had always been cannon flesh of all the powers that subdued their territory, stole their fabulous riches and left this glorious country at the most awful of the miseries!

In New Delhi again, we stopped to visit Humayun's Tomb, placed in the middle of a large garden. This precious shrine was built by his widow's command in the 15th Century. Constructed in white and red stone, crowned by a great Moorish Style dome. It is said that the architecture model of this mausoleum was later adopted in the famous Taj Mahal.

We admired the memorials of Indira Gandhi and her sons, one of them killed in a flight accident, and the other in a bomb blast, and she herself was assassinated by the Sikh body-guard who belonged to her personal custody. Roomy parks covered with green grass, with extensive blots of flowers, grouped together by colours : white, lilac, yellow, pink... From time to time, great stone blocks straighten in the wide park, with varied inscriptions standing out the virtues of these martyrs.

Only from outside, we could see the spectacular Rashtrapati Bhawan or Presidential Palace, where the Indian *Flag* proudly waved, and the Parliament House, the greatest circular building of the world, which holds both Chambers, the High and the Low.

The Presidential Palace was formerly the British viceroy's residence, and became what today is after the Indian Independence in 1947. Our guide remarked that, in fact, the Indian President didn't live there, in order to give a better image of simplicity, and, if this is really true, it seems admirable to me.

Around the commercial area Connaught Place, where we had lunch, we visited Jantar Mantar, one of the observatories built by the *astronomer* Maharaja Jai Singh, to observe the star movements.

Monumental in shape and coloring, the modern Birla Temple, with its numerous domes of different heights and varied colours, of recent building in this century. Every day at evening fall, the "puja" to the deity is celebrated there.

In the interior, a nice Krishna picture, in a room covered with mirrors, including the ceiling, reproduces the God's image hundred times, and the devotees bend up to touch the ground with their heads, in lovingly reverence.

98. Lotus Temple : the Paradigm of a New Religion

We moved away a little to visit the Lotus Temple, a lotus-shaped spectacular building, raised in pure white marble, with extensive avenues edged by flowers. The same ornamentation is seen along the several-flight of steps that lead to this great architectural construction, considered the next Taj Mahal.

On walking through its interior, completely empty of images, with only some benches for meditating or praying, a little booklet with the history of this religious independent movement : "Baha 'I Faith", was delivered to me.

I was thus informed that it was founded about 150 years ago, by a young Persian man known as Bab, who was persecuted and martyred for his ideas, considered heretic by the orthodox religions of that time.

His followers were also persecuted and murdered, but in spite of it, this religion could spread beyond Persia and the Otoman Empire to the Caucasus, Turkey, India, Burma, Egypt and the Sudan. Today it comprises more than 1820 different ethnic groups over 360 countries, territories and islands, representing a true crusade of the human race.

Their Holy Books and other literature have been translated into more than 740 languages and its doctrine seem really extraordinary to me. Some of its principles are :

The Oneness of the whole Mankind.

The independent investigation of Truth, and not the blind acceptance imposed by dogmas.

The common foundation of all religions.

The essential harmony of Science and Religion.

The equality of Men and Women, on their rights in society.

The elimination of prejudices of all kinds.

The Universal Peace, etc.

As my own life philosophy and religion are just based on these principles, I think it is suitable to enumerate the ones I consider really important.

99. The Light of India

At the evening fall and as a worthy brooch to our run through the two Delhis, in which much of his History, Religion and Politics had paraded before our eyes and our hearts, we made the last visit of the city tour : the house where Mahatma Gandhi lived his latest 144 days, and the spot he had his "appointment with death".

I am a fervent admirer, I would say a "fanatic" if the word doesn't displease me, of the ideals of this "Mahatma" or Great Soul, and as a Yoga teacher, I also took the precept of "Ahimsa" or Non Violence as mine, with whose principle, together with "Satya's", this "Light of India" fought up to get the Independence of his beloved country.

With reverence I visited the gardens where he gave his "darshans" to his countrymen, without distinction of races. With deliberate slowness, I walked through the places where he stepped, and felt his sweet presence in my heart.

Later, I cried kneeling in the exact spot where he was murdered, and from where, with the last breath of his weak life, he blessed his executioner.

My eyes, still veiled by tears, read Albert Einstein's words, engraved on a big stone in his garden, referred to this incomparable Indian leader, known and honoured by his fellow citizens as "Mahatma", "The Saint".

> "A victorious fighter, who has always scorned the use of force; a man of wisdom and humility, armed with resolve and inflexible consistency, who has devoted all his strength to the uplifting of his people and the betterment of their lot; a man who has confronted the brutality of Europe with the dignity of the simple Human Being, and thus at all times risen superior. Generation to come, it may be, will scarce believe

> that such a one as this, ever in flesh and blood, walked upon this earth".

And I cannot help remembering, J.H. Holmes' words either :

> "When I think of Gandhi, I think of Jesus. He lives his life, he speaks his words, he *suffers*, strives and will some day noble die, for his Kingdom upon Earth"[1]

Dear Father, today you will be sitting, talking with the Heavenly Father, or perhaps, in your usual *Maunas* or word fast, since with Him, certainly they are not needed.

Did your killer know by chance, that when the ideals are defended even with one's own life, is it because they really have a valuable worth and pierce deeply into the human heart ?

There you were, trustful and helpless, like immortal beings ! How would I have wished to meet you, feel your hand over my head when giving me a blessing, look into your gentle eyes, listen your wise advice!

What a lot of intelligence, what a lot of wisdom, what a kindness, what a love! I think it is not much to say You are the "Light of India"; for me, You are the "Light of the Whole Human Racc".

✷

1. M.S. Deshpande : "Light of India or Message of Mahatmaji" (Chapter XXV — In his Heart Homage — "The Greatest Man" — Page 262 — India — 3rd Edition 1978, by Navajivan Publishing House, Ahmedabad-380 014.

14

THE MONUMENT TO LOVE

100. Bound for Agra

Every person who has sometime travelled to India, usually receives the same question from people :

— Did you visit the Taj Mahal?

As we were in Delhi, relatively near Agra (about 250 kms.), it was almost a must to make this visit to one of the places where the fruit of love, gave the world one of the most beautiful monuments known by man up to the present : the perfect Taj Mahal, one of the earthly wonders.

My friend and I had loitered for more than four days, travelling through both Delhis and their surroundings, as a rest from the long train journey to the South. We came again to our known Tourist Office on Janpath Road and contracted an Agra Tour for very early the following day.

In fact, the bus picked us up from our hotel around six o'clock in the morning, and after gathering other persons from several agencies, we set off to the main road and headed for Agra.

Every time we went on a tour, we observed the behaviour was the same : each agency integrated the passengers they get, and thus the trip was cheaper, since the bus was always full (sometimes exceedingly).

It occurred to me that the buses were designed for the small Hindu bodies; for us, both rather stout, the seats were quite tight, above all with not much room for the legs, considering that we travelled more than five running hours, and the same on the return.

Besides that inconvenience, or maybe as its consequence, I didn't keep in my memory anything about the journey, therefore, I reckon that there was nothing of interest.

Our guide, a Nepalese established in India, constantly gave me his affection and knowledge : he explained me that during hundreds of years, Agra had been the Capital of the Mongol Empire, together with Delhi, but that afterwards, it was established definitively in the latter.

101. The Perfect Taj Mahal

At present, Agra has about a million inhabitants, and the first impression we received was that it was a big, ugly, dirty and poor city, where it seemed impossible to be something important.

But, walking through the surroundings, we began changing our opinion : large parks and well cared gardens started to appear, to serve as a frame at one of the most famous monuments of India, such a perfect mausoleum that the human word can scarcely tell about.

Only love may conceive such an authentic masterpiece : that perfection of lines, the pure whiteness of marble, the harmony in shapes and colours of the precious and semi-precious stones, inlaid with skill and grace on their walls : coral, agate, jade, lapislazuli, ruby, emerald, etc. I repeat, all the infinite range of figures and shades that draw symmetric edgings of flowers in tidy and beautiful garlands, the spectacular birds, and the slimness of the four minarets, that surround it as silent guardians, the delicacy and charm of the perfect domes...

There is not a spot where one can direct the sight and not find or not discover more than beauty and harmony, as if this arrogant monument sprang from the infinite space and it were placed there by angelical beings : from afar or from nearby, always that slightness impression, as a butterfly that had just settled over the most precious flower.

The Taj Mahal irradiates such a purity and perfection, that one has the certainty that it will never need not even a retouching, that it cannot exist the most remote possibility to add or take anything away.

A large access avenue, edged by neatly pruned trees, led us towards this wonder; in the center of it, a wide water channel, which, in the evening, the sun inflames with its shining gold. From the blazing water mirror, it reflects and emerges quivering this majestic Taj Mahal.

To say this shrine was built in the 17th Century (1648) by, at that time, Emperor Shah Jahan, as an immortal tribute to the memory of his wife Moumtaz Mahal, the beloved, the chosen of the Harem, is a very well known story. The sovereign himself designed the plans, and more than twenty thousand workers, including Turkish artists, laboured at this monument, during 20 long years.

And before the presence of this love miracle, a story read at my adolescence, in the Secondary School, came to my memory, which remains recorded in a spot of my mind. I am not sure even if it was about this mausoleum : the tale was about a powerful monarch who wanted to build something extraordinarily beautiful evoking his beloved dead wife.

It was said, likewise, that the monarch had summoned as many artists as he could find out, and redid his original plan a lot of times : he took out, added, demolished, changed materials and decoration, without seeming to him beautiful, perfect and worthy enough for his beloved.

After many indecisions, advances and backward movements, he had achieved at last, the ideal design that satisfied him; the noblest and most luxurious materials, the most exquisite stones, completing the work at his absolute pleasure.

But on placing the coffin in the central pavilion, which contained his beloved wife's physical remains, the contrast between the pure beauty of the shrine and the gloomy ugliness of death was so extraordinary, that he couldn't avoid shouting :

— Take this thing away!

I wish it were not this story Shah Jahan and his wife's one, since there is a romantic halo in the Taj Mahal, that visitors stay enraptured, without daring speak in a loud voice. I hope that the fact those coffins (later it was placed the monarch's too) are in the basement, is just a coincidence.

When one visits places like this, and such love after death

stories are remembered, one would wish to be able to inspire that kind of deep feelings, resigning to a Taj Mahal built in the purest of the heart.

Some years later, this sovereign was made prisoner by his own son, in the Red Fort of Agra, and his sole happiness and intimate pleasure was to look with longing from his captive chamber, at the dear Taj Mahal. The single contemplation of the monument calmed down his anguish and eased his loneliness : the perfect domes, the slim and slender minarets, the whole impeccable beauty of the shrine, fruit of his unforgettable love, served as a solace to his broken and desolate heart.

102. After the Red Turban

The Red Fort of Agra is the replica of the Delhi's, and it is located very near the Taj Mahal. Built in the same style and with the same red sandstone : solid walls all around, which contrasted with the delicate pavilions inside, of pure white marble.

Graceful arcades and balconies, supported by pillars skilfully carved on stone, with a splendid view to Taj Mahal. The Jamuna River stretched softly at its feet, to offer irrigation to that zone of the North. The whole palace is surrounded by extensive and well cared gardens, with trees and flowers in perfect avenues.

On its outskirts and fenced in the same way by splendid gardens, we visited Fathepur Sikri or "The Victory City". This palace was raised on a hill by King *Akbar*, as gratitude to the saint who forecast his son's birth.

Later, the city was abandoned for not fulfilling the minimum healthy conditions, since at that time, the water supply was very difficult. At present, only a modest little town at the palace feet remains. Everything was silence while we walked through the deserted courtyards and the ancient halls emptied of audiences.

King Akbar's tomb is situated close to the palace. The place is called Sikandra, and the Shrine is in a square garden surrounded with walls. Its style is similar to Taj Mahal's, which, I think, has inspired and for many years, all the monuments of its age.

Raising a very long staircase, the Fathepur Sikri has its access by the rather dirty and abandoned Bulland Gate. Inside it, there are several bazaars, besides a little band of musicians who are waiting for the visitors to offer them lovely "concerts", to get in this way some rupees.

By that area there are a lot of stores and bazaars, where marble goods with inlaid semi-precious stones, manufactured with the same handicraft technique as the Taj Mahal, are specially sold. Also carpets, leather goods with little applied mirrors, black velvet handbags with embroidered stones and pearls, jewels, perfumes, silks, etc.

This time, my friend and I were the only Westerners of the tour, and, as usual, the other people smiled and pampered us on the bus. If any time I delayed for taking a photo or buying something, they were waiting in good mood, or somebody went to fetch me; the day always got short.

When I got lost, what happened quite often, I used as a guide, the impressive red turban of a Sikh gentleman from our group, who felt very proud when I revealed him this fact, and always tried to keep himself even more in sight.

With so many monuments to visit, some of them rather far from the others and as I had said before, the time was scarce, and we could start the return just in the evening.

Again the red disc of Surya (sun) began descending in the horizon, inflaming the clouds with winding reddish tongues. The day's emotions and experiences found their place in my heart; stories of loves above death; of the greatness and also of the littleness of the Human Being. The days of glory and splendour, followed by the humiliation of the defeat, of those who once were powerful; also the unbreakable faith in the immortal Human Values.

And after this balance, I bring again to the memory Paul Brunton's reflections :

> "A benevolent and beautiful power is hidden behind the cruel appearance of life. Minutes that shame our every day hours. They leave from the dark emptiness like a meteor, to light up a fugitive path of hope, and at once disappear from our conscience."[1]

---

1. Brunton, Paul, "The Secret India" — 10th Ed. (Page 161 on his "The Sacred Fire Hill" — Chapter IX-Bs. As. Edit. Kier – 1992).

103. Krishna's House

Just about 55 kms. from Agra, there was still a place to be visited : Mathura, the home town of Krishna, God's aspect more known and revered in all India. Unfortunately we arrived at nightfall; the first lights began shining when we walked through a great courtyard, where we had to be submitted to a police survey. Always the same problems between Hindus and Muslims for religious affairs, for which the beloved Mahatma Gandhi fought until immolating himself.

About this, my opinion is that, perhaps, somebody strengthens those differences for his own convenience. During my several months of stay, all along and across India, I talked over these matters with a lot of persons, of different ages and also from distinct social classes; I was pleasantly surprised by the fact that nobody was in agreement with these religious struggles. Even more, for most of them they seemed just stupid, in the conviction that there is a single God to all religions, no matter the shape nor the name, and moreover, this God has always been, that is to say, he existed before the formation of religions.

However, the conflicts go on arousing. To me, the whole affair let me reflect : is it possible that such incidents are being generated by some murderers, "jackals that the jackal would reject", as the great Pablo Neruda says, fellows payed by those who profit from wars?

I am absolutely ignorant about the internal facts of that country which could cause such confrontations, and truly I pride myself on all my Indian friends, Hindus as well as Muslims or of any other race. But according to the gathered opinions and my own observations, I dare say that behind all the fights, there is a sinister black hand, which doesn't belong neither to Muslims nor to Hindus.

Inside the large temple courtyard, always the bazaars and stalls offering flower garlands and fruits for the "puja", delicious sweets and very fresh yoghurts, recently prepared and very good, which were served in rustic pottery cups to be taken away as souvenirs.

In one of the pavilions we visited, annexed to the main temple, we observed that the walls as well as the ceiling, were covered with mosaics on which dates and names of persons were written, for the Gods to dispense their blessing. I also left my collaboration in the name of the person who most needed to receive that help in my family. With such names and the dates of the visit, the Brahmins painted a mosaic, to be later placed also in that holy enclosure.

Because of the late hour, we couldn't walk through the Ghats or staircases over the Yamuna River (the place where Lord Krishna rested), which are used in the ceremonies of the corpse cremation. It was a pity!

Our guide commented that large white shell tortoises usually used to swim in that river and approach the faithful in search of food, but we could not see this curiosity either, because it was too late. It also remained us to go for a sail on a barge by the river and visit the archaeological Museum.

At last we came into the Govinda's Temple at *Vrindaban* (as the whole complex is called), which dates from the 16th Century. Inside, all the temples are quite modern, since the former ones were completely destroyed by the Muslims, the guide commented with absolute indifference.

In the interior of this temple, the vibrations were very powerful. A crowd was worshiping their God and singing at the frantic beating of timbrels or tampuras. The expressions in all the countenances were of ecstasy, and showed devotion at the highest voltage. One can't even image what it would be like during Krishna's feast !

The Brahmins, with their ochre robes, offered something to drink to the devotees, who took it with great reverence (somebody commented us that that liquid offered to drink, was the water already used to wash deity's pictures). Then, they performed the "arati" ritual, or fire offering, with the "pujas" that the devotees had done by means of those same priests : the symbolic sacred delivery consisted as usual of half a coconut, flowers, incense, or well some rupees.

The piercing scent of incense and camphor, the symbolism of the fervent rites, the music raising its strength, the vehement Hindu's singing; it was very difficult to withdraw oneself from that spiritual atmosphere, of deep religious faith that caught us up all : men, women, children, with the same love, thanking the Lord at any name or shape; it doesn't matter to call Him Krishna, Allah, Budha, Jesus or any other !

15

RAJASTHAN (DELHI-JAIPUR-DELHI)

104. Som Pal's Future Wife

When we arrived at our hotel after the Agra tour, it was more than two o'clock in the early morning. We felt very tired but happy, after the experiences lived in that long and beneficial day.

The Reception clerks, who always inquired into all our plans, of course, were worried by the delay and wanted to know all the details of the journey.

In the following morning, we enjoyed a little rest from the intense and tiring trip of the day before. We slept until later, had our "mates" inside the room and developed a good fellowship with the floor attendants. During the few elapsed days, we had already become friends, specially with young Som Pal, who made the room cleaning up with special care.

Every moment he showed himself humble and diligent, and didn't forget a single detail in trying to fulfil our needs. While doing the cleaning up, he liked delaying in our room to talk, always with great respect, and he seemed happy that we dispensed him our friendship.

So, we were not surprised when that morning he told us that he had received a letter from his parents with a picture of a girl from his village, with the possibility of arranging the marriage soon.

He left the photo in the room, at our consideration, and we could observe that the girl in question didn't look older than 13 or 14 years of age. He was just 21, and that seemed to be the age considered appropriate to fix up the *wedding*.

While the three of us (my friend, he and I) were looking at the photo, Som Pal, who spoke just a little English but managed himself, remarked, following the girl's image with his forefinger :

— She will not be a heroin (the cinema actresses are so called), but has nice eyes, good body, beautiful arms, and if my parents agree and the "Mamas" (we) as well, everything is O.K.

Som Pal was already starting to make future plans; he would go to Agra for the Honeymoon-trip, using for that circumstance a bag I had given him as a present.

During a following conversation with Vyjendhar and Sukbhir, the other two elder floor keepers, I made the remark that, in my opinion, Som Pal was still rather young to get married. The three young men, really seemed close friends and confidents, and it is usual in India for young people to respect elders' opinions to the letter.

Vyjendhar, the oldest of the three and who spoke English better, answered me :

—Som Pal is already a man, Mama.

Besides, he remarked that if the boy didn't obey his parents decisions as it is the habit there, Som Pal would have serious problems with his family, and that kind of conflicts was not any Hindu's ideal.

—We also, — he said, referring to Sukbhir and himself, — according to our own parent's agreement, had carried out our marriage being as young as Som Pal.

At that moment, they were only 30 and 35 years old, respectively, and had already teenager children, specially Vyjendhar.

Today the wedding had come about and Som Pal doesn't live alone in his modest room any more : he has somebody who is waiting for him with the supper ready, in the evenings.

105. Shopping and Fried Potatoes

On that free and quiet day in New Delhi, we went for an indolent walk along Janpath Road, where we already had some acquaintances who greeted us when passing, and approached the Commercial Area of Connaught Place.

In a little kiosk over the square, I glanced at some Yoga books; I asked the cost of one by Swami Sivananda that interested me, but it seemed rather excessive. Later, I found it in other shops, but unluckily, it was still more expensive.

Two days later I came back to that area; I thought that with such movement of people, the seller wouldn't remember me, and perhaps, the price he had given me was to bargain, and I hadn't insisted enough. I seriously took the book in my hands and asked again with the known "How much?", at what the seller, without turning a hair, answered with the same formality :

—. The same as two days ago.

This time I had to purchase it, even though I recognize that with a little shame!

By that area of Connaught Place, there are a large number of shops, bazaars and tables with goods on offer, specially clothes and the most varied articles. Also many stalls where fruit juices and food were sold.

Every time we walked by with Giovanna, we saw a little kiosk in the open air, where small pieces of potatoes were cooked on a plate put over a heater. The gesture of sprinkling some oil drops over the potatoes was usual, what was performed by wetting the tips of the fingers and shaking them later over the meal.

We observed that they were served to the customers, in some little straw or reed bowls; a very refined powder similar to ash (maybe a spice) was spattered over; next a pinch of salt and a lot of lemon juice.

One could also order another variant, which was served on a tray of the same material but a little larger, and consisted of fried potatoes, mixed with little pieces of fruits, and with a different seasoning. For that variation, sugar was used instead of salt.

The stall in question was attended by some very young boys (we later knew they were three brothers), one of them owned, annexed to his brother's place, a modest press, with which the most exquisite natural fruit juices were prepared : pineapples, oranges, bananas, pomegranates, melons, water melons, papayas and others. typical of the zone.

The fruits were heaped up over a rustic table and shelves, in a very special way, combining the colours perfectly, and they seemed like aligned domes of different shapes and shades.

Several times we had observed how one of the Hindus filled, with his blackish fingers, those bowls and trays. After seasoning, he covered them with one of his hands, putting the other beneath to shake them well and for the potatoes or fruits to receive the flavoring. At this view, we said :

— What a revolting thing!

That day, the fried potatoes scent was tempting...and we were hungry. Forgetting our apprehension, we came close to the stall and asked for both, potato bowls and juices. It is obvious to say they seemed delicious to us; we talked with the boys, who were really pleasant and took some pictures, including them, of course.

On another occasion we were in that zone, and gave them some copies of the photos as a present, and they were so happy that it was unbelievable. Besides, and from that moment on, they refused to collect for the food and drink, since we went several times, and had to insist on leaving the rupees in their pockets, because it was not right to take advantage of their hospitality.

In New Delhi, we could give a little rest to our stomach from the spices. Apart from the boys of the fried potatoes, who at our request served them with only salt and lemon juice, we had discovered another place, where to eat very well without spending much money; it was a nook on a secondary alley, where very fresh Chinese dishes were prepared. In this way, we varied a little from the rice and hot stew menu.

At this "Chinese Restaurant", as a poster at the front said, sometimes we also ate rice, but with greens, mushrooms, fried eggs in thin threads, very tiny pieces of chicken, etc., seasoned with sweet-and-sour sauces, typical of that "cuisine".

The mentioned restaurant consisted of a small veranda opened to the street, with quite rustic wooden tables and benches, and another little room inside, with the same furniture. A narrow and steep spiral staircase by which we could hardly climb, led to another dining-room, equipped just like the others.

From the first time we went to that place, the same waiter always attended to us, named Kalendar, who, as Ganesha in Puttaparthi, remained standing beside our table smiling all the time, and on many occasions, his boss called his attention for disregarding other customers.

A lot of foreigners frequented the Chinese Restaurant, surely for its cheap prices and good food. There we knew some North Americans, Frenchs, Germans, a young very beautiful Moroccan lady who was travelling alone, etc., mostly very young people.

Kalendar got on well with us and became very sad when we announced him that we were going to set off; he wanted me to explain him thoroughly the steps he needed to follow to leave his country, and finished asking me to bring him to Argentina with me !

106. Towards the Rajput's Land

In the afternoon on our free day, we approached the Tourist Agency on Janpath Road again, of which we were already customers. We looked over the short trips that were offered, and decided to make another day tour to Rajasthan, or Rajas (Kings) country, at the Southwest of Delhi.

It is known also by the name of Rajputana or "Rajput's Land", name given to its famous warriors, who are considered the cavalry symbols and direct descendant of the epic heroes of the *Mahabharata* and *Ramayana*, two of the sacred Hinduism Books.

I had read in the tourist guide book, that this not much favoured by nature region, was inhabited by a surly and proud population, that coincided with the arid, deserted and wild region where they live.

As in preceding circumstances, again in the early morning, before six, we were picked up from our hotel and also, as they usually do, gathered the other passengers from the different tourist agencies.

At this opportunity, the bus was really crowded, and not to lose any customer, they filled even the box that all tourist buses have in front, separated from the other passengers by a glass and wooden panel, which was usually occupied only by the chauffeur with an assistant boy and the tour guide.

We were also adjusted in this compartment, together with four German young ladies who travelled in couples. One of these pairs, only talked to each other and didn't pay attention to anything or anybody else. The other two girls were very pleasant. For the absolute lack of space, two Hindus were situated in the same way, inside the cabin, one middle aged and the other very young, who were very polite to us, like the rest of the Eastern passengers.

My seat was against the front windscreen of the bus, without room to move in any way. When the sun began warming up, my position became rather uncomfortable, since the oppressive heat was more intensely felt through the glass.

When it was full day, we started seeing how the scenery changed, becoming more and more deserted. From afar, the mountain chains were distinguished, eastwards as well as northwards and westwards, which accompanied us during the whole run.

Animals were also adapted to the zone : camels, goats, sheep, were seen quietly grazing withered stunted shrubbery, under the shepherd's vigilant eye. These shepherds covered their heads with the typical turbans, tied down on singular shapes, of very brilliant colours, dominating the red, and long tails at the wind.

In fact, around this area, dried and prickly thicket, typical of desert regions, of species demanding very little humidity, were seen. We crossed several villages and little towns, and the landscape was always more or less the same.

In that Rajasthan area, people go on faithful to their tradition on their attire : women with long and wide red skirts, from which several petticoats were glimpsed. In the upper part, tight corset waistcoats fitted the body, down to the waist. A large shawl covered their heads, shoulders and backs, usually of transparent cloth, with handicraft big golden spots embroidered, painted or with little selenite mirrors appliqué.

The women's wrists overloaded of wide bracelets, the same as the upper forearms and also the ankles; the ears with long earrings, and, as it is usual in almost the whole India, a very bejeweled nose.

In a few circumstances and when their English allowed them, they showed a very good disposition for talking to foreigners. The same excellent disposal was made evident by the men, who wore the typical dothi gathered up between the legs, forming like a wide "Bombache", or very well becoming trousers, baggy model (as we call them in the West), very wide at the hips, with the looseness given by several and deep folds, that set off from the waist, and very narrow at the ankles. At the torso, they mostly wore a white jacket with high collar, military style, tied at the waist with a wide belt or sash. Always the spectacular turbans, gathered up in different ways and also with long and showy tails.

The majority of the males used great and dense moustaches with the ends upwards, as from many centuries ago, being this typical figure popularized in the ancient tales and paintings about their feats. I asked the reason of this preference in most men, and they explained that the moustache was their male "chauvinist" symbol. O.K.!

Through the long run, that lasted more than six hours, we crossed wooden carved carts, decorated and painted, with compact wheels, pulled by tame oxen, with long and very bent horns. The same were usually colored in stripes, painted silver, golden, or of any other picturesque shape. A great cloak of strident colours, also painted or embroidered, protected the beasts.

The more we penetrated the region, the greater number of camels were seen. These noble animals are the ones which specially adapt to this zone, and they gave the impression of being very tame and docile. Many times I observed along quite intense traffic roads, carts pulled by these dromedaries that circulated at their step rate, with the peasant driver lying as long as he was, inside them! There is no doubt that the loyal animal knew its destination. Perhaps to travel from one village to the other lasted half a day, as if they were on foot; but as I have already commented and with my friend Giovanna's words : "We are in India, Dellia", and in India, time doesn't really exist.

Our objective was to know the famous city of Jaipur, which has inspired so many poets and travellers, and for almost 300 years, has been the Rajasthan Capital.

Many kilometres before arriving, we could see on the mountains that flanked the road at its whole length, the fortress that still exists in the region, like silent and eternal witness of the ceaseless fights of which this zone of Rajasthan was the scenery.

Nowadays, the Rajput's feats are told like heroic legends, but between the centuries 7th and 16th, they filled that period's chronicles, until its forced pacification with the British invasion.

107. The Amber Palace : Inside and Outside

About ten kilometres before Jaipur, we stopped to visit Amber and its fabulous palace. The road already began climbing the mountain, and we were moving among rocky peaks. In the last stretch, we got off our bus, to go up a paved ramp that climbed up to the palace.

The ascent could be done riding on elephant, walking or well by some jeeps, as those waiting for our group. Personally, I would have preferred swinging myself on one of the huge elephants, which with their baldachins lovely adorned in shining colours, were very attractive. But the whole group got into the jeeps and I could not lose sight of it; so, in spite of my wishes, I had to do the same.

First, we visited Goddess Kali's temple, with profusion of carved marble columns, where, according to our guide, long ago, human victims were sacrificed. A giant image of Ganesha led the entrance, the smiling God with elephant head and plump belly, whose protection, as I have already remarked, is very common in all India.

The palace decoration is mostly based on coloured crystals and little selenite mirrors, exquisitely inlaid on walls and ceilings, shaping very nice figures.

In one of the rooms adorned this way, our guide closed all the openings up to remain in complete darkness, then he lit a match and with this brightness, thousands of the blaze reflections shone in the obscurity; it gave the impression of being moving in a whirlwind, twinkling as myriad of firefly that lighted their magic flash in the night darkness. Although it lasted just some instants, the spectacle was astonishing.

In the private audience hall, the lovely worked alabaster pillars stood out, and from the balconies we could observe the totally geometric fantastic gardens, with a pool in the middle.

Along the cornice and due to the city walls, the horizon was very limited : one could just distinguish from afar, the great Jal Mahal, a palace in the middle of the waters. But if just for a moment we would have closed our eyes, may be it would have been possible to visualize the clouds of dust of the camel caravans crossing the desert with their precious load, brought from the Far

East or Arabia (Saudi) and then, it would have been difficult for us to differentiate the reality from the fantasy...

Let us leave the dreams and come back again to the jeep and to our bus, not after tasting an exquisite "kulfy" offered by a travelling seller, a handicraft ice-cream typical of India, absolutely white and with a savour of milk and sugar.

108. The Beautiful City of the "Pink Cameo"

On the uncomfortable bus we went on travelling towards our final destination : Jaipur, the city built by the order of the Maharaja Jai Singh II at the beginning of the 17th Century. The sovereign left Amber, the former capital and established at the new, constructed with European plans and Hindu architecture norms.

In accordance with his astrologers (he himself was an Astrology and Astronomy passionate), the city was orientated towards the North-northeast, "where the Gods dwell". Just like all that zone, Jaipur is also surrounded by a continue city wall with seven fortified door ways, always consequence of the never-ending fights of the Rajput in that singular region.

Most of the buildings had their fronts pink, color that prevails in all the city, and for this reason a known poet called it "the city of the pink cameo". This colour, I think, is due to the use of red sandstone in many of the buildings.

Besides, our guide related that on occasion of one of the British princes' visit to that city, all the facades were painted of pink in his honour, by what it was compared to the decorations of "The One Thousand and One Nights".

Broad avenues, which cross in perpendicular way, limit the different caste and sub-caste areas, and several gates give access to the diverse commercial zones, like tapestry and jewel bazaars, flower market, etc.

From any angle the imposing pink facade of the City Palace stood out; later we saw that the upper floors were only frontispiece empty at the back, such as the sets of Hollywood films.

Our journey was quite hurried, since we were short of time; we visited the museum, a sector of the palace, and, once in the main avenue, the so called Winds Palace, from whose balconies the women of the Maharaja's Court looked at the festivals and processions, remarked our guide in his awful English.

Near the palace, Jantar Mantar, the spectacular observatory with giant stone instruments, replica of the one built in New Delhi. From them, Jai Singh II studied the stars, and measured the distances from earth. It seems, in accordance with experts, that those ancient apparatus have a precision not achieved yet by the most modern instruments nowadays.

Just in front of the palace there were a lot of bazaars where I tried tc approach to look over, but our driver hurried me up to go on with the run since, according to him, parking in the surroundings was impossible, and besides, we had not enough time. I'm sure that was not the reason, but, the same as in my own country, tours always have a commercial aspect.

In fact, after following the journey and transposing one of the gates, we were led to the so called "Emporiums", where the prices were quite higher than downtown's, and I have no doubt drivers had their commission there.

In that place I could observe the handicraft printing of cloth, with figures cut out in a kind of wooden blocks, which were wet in a painting receptacle. Next, they were rested neatly on the cloth, and in this way the stamp was made.

Some days later in New Delhi, I got some blocks of that kind, on Janpath Road, at Doma's Bazaar, my dear Tibetan friend. Returning home, I made some experiments and printed as many rags as fell into my hands.

Once inside the Emporium, the haste of our driver finished; people could take all the time to do their shopping quietly, of the varied goods of that zone, with what we were rather delayed.

Before setting off back to Delhi, we visited another Birla Temple, which looked very nice, with a tidy and extensive park around. All the complex showed impeccable, with their ochre and dark green buildings, and it gave the impression to have been recently refurbished.

I could read on a plate located near the temple, that this sanctuary, as well as others which are real masterpieces, are being restored with the funds contributed by a benefactor, Hindu in birth and blood, named Birla, one of the greatest industrialist of India.

There, of course, the Hindus made their "puja" and we took some photos. From outside the temple, a moving "bhajans" music was heard, which completed the adequate background of the holy place.

From the Birla Temple, we would reinitiate our return journey. Unluckily, the setting off was quite delayed, since a woman of the group had taken a rickshaw from the Emporium, to arrange some matters downtown, and after waiting for her around two long hours, we had to leave without her.

The discontent for the delay was general, and angry protests were heard, specially by Muslim persons, who being during the fast days of Ramazan, found themselves without a bite, since the early morning. The truth is that everybody felt displeased by the lateness, thinking on the long way we had ahead to come back to Delhi.

Fortunately, the four German girls stayed at Jaipur. The couple with whom we chatted, had thought of remaining there more time, to visit Agra later, and come back to Delhi in 4 or 5 days.

With the Germans' absence, we would have a little more space in the driver's enclosure, so the return journey was something more pleasant. We could use the seat to doze a little, what made the trip shorter, which anyway became rather quicker than the going, for the night traffic on the road wasn't so heavy.

Anyway, the bus left us at the hotel door at about three o'clock in the early morning, with the great worry of the Reception Clerks, who were anxiously waiting for us, and didn't stop with their amazement exclamations at telling them the journey vicissitudes.

✷

16

BOUND FOR THE HIMALAYAS

109. Making the Way at Going

The following morning of our trip to Jaipur and after a refreshing rest at the New Delhi hotel, we reordered the monstruous bags that we would leave in guard at the hotel deposit. We tried to put the indispensable things into a little bag, to take to our next destination : Rishikesh or the "Rishes (sages) Land", a village placed at the first spurs of Himalayas Mountains, and by the Holy Ganges River.

As I have commented before, our goal was to visit "The Divine Life Society" Ashram, founded by Swami Sivananda, which is considered one of the most prestigious of India. We had already written from our country with the due anticipation to ask for lodging; later, we confirmed our imminent arrival through a friend of Giovanna's who would visit it before us.

After considering the different possibilities to carry out the journey, either by train, bus or taxi, we decided to contract this last one, which arrangements were once more made in our friend Agency in Janpath Road.

Very early the following morning, after leaving everything in order in the hotel, we set off as always, full of faith and optimism towards what would be the last step of our fantastic voyage through the legendary India.

The taxi driver didn't stand out precisely for his friendship (a pity to be so far from Ramachandra). Before setting off, he passed by his home and picked one of his children up, to accompany him, specially on the return, in such a way that along the run, he limited himself to chat with the boy.

We looked absent-mindedly how the scenery was slipping, in a rather cool morning in the middle of March. It only attracted our attention to see how Indians made a creation from the most simple things; for instance, we observed heaps of straw or pasture, arranged in a circular way as if they were domes, which ended in a very thin tip above, crowned by a tie like a sort of bun.

We also saw great piles of bricks, forming furnaces similar to huge palaces, with the holes like moorish windows, and everything perfectly tidy. At the road sides, on several opportunities we found out something like slender towers and, when we approached, we checked they were kinds of cakes, made with cow excrement and straw. The "cakes" were heaped up by the edges to get dry, shaping this "watchtower". Once completely dry, people commented us, they would be used as a sort of fuel (nothing is wasted)...

Likewise, we saw some receptacles, similar to little houses, which were placed there to be used by the snakes, which, as I have said before, are considered sacred beings in India, mystery and supreme wisdom symbols.

So, a little bored and sleepy for the early getting up, or perhaps, already rather melancholy before the voyage end that was approaching, we went on making our way to The Himalayas, with a halt at middle morning to have breakfast.

We stopped at a very attractive restaurant, surrounded everywhere by flowers, and with the tables and benches placed in the open air, among the trees, under single dome shaped roofs. I specially remember the great amount of dahlias of very bright colours, and of a huge size like sunflowers, even though this comparison may seem exaggerated.

All the region of the high Ganges Valley, and its tributary, the Yamuna, with the luxuriant greenness of the surrounding forests, is, really, magnificent.

Besides, in those regions of the Himalayas slopes, great Yogis and Holy Men made their retirement from the world, in search of realization, and they sanctified with their feet, that sacred land.

The weather there is also very pleasant, as we could check it all the time we stayed in the Ashram : rather cool at night, then along the morning, the sun increases its strength up to midday, to drop the temperature again in the evening.

110. "The Lord's Door"

Around midday, we arrived at Haridwar, at about 500 mts. high, place where the Ganges leaves the mountains to go to fertilize, for more than 2000 kms., the plain it travels through towards the East, down to its mouth at the Bengal Gulf.

Haridwar means "The Door of The Lord", and it is one of the seven sacred Indian cities; according to the chronicles, its name is due to be the starting point to the most famous pilgrimage spots on the Himalayas, as Gangotri (the Ganges source), Kedarnath, Badrinath, etc.

Unluckily, these sacred spots are situated at a great height, and they cannot be visited up to the month of May, because of the lot of snow on the road; we were told that the best period to know them is from May to October.

Our "friendly" driver left us at the city entrance. We had to cross over a long bridge above the river, crowded with beggars, sadhus with their ochre robe, and also very tame cows, monkeys and other animals.

We arrived at the main street, full of bazaars selling the most varied articles. We visited some temples and ghats, that is to say, the staircases where the corpses are cremated. The ashes and rests are, later, thrown to the sacred river, since the belief is that when they are dropped into that holy place, their souls go straight to Heaven.

The City of Haridwar is very famous, since there, every 12 years, they realize the *Kumba Mela*, religious feasts where a lot of gurus, Spiritual Masters, Holy Men, sadhus or renouncing ascetic meet.

These fairs attract hundreds of thousands of pilgrims, who, from all over the world, make an appointment for bathing in the confluence of the Ganges and the Yamuna, at the same day and at the same time, as a sacred rite of purification.

The chronicle tells that in 1987 more than ten millions and a half pilgrims assisted at Prayag. I must clarify that these holy festivals, take place in four sacred cities (Prayag, Haridwar, Ujjain and Nasik) in turns, that is to say, in one of them every three years, and between the 15th of January and the 15th of February. This cycle of twelve years, corresponds more or less, to the entrance of the Planet Jupiter in Taurus.

According to the Mythology, the Universe before existing as it is known, was a milk ocean, from which the Gods decided to extract the ambrosia or quintessence, to take its energies. As their strength was not enough, they needed to call the asuras (demons) to help them to beat, grasping each one of an end of the rope. But when the amrita was ready, the demons stole a jar. The Gods chased them for twelve days, but every three, a drop fell down on the earth over each one of those cities.

So, even though each one of them is concerned to organize such meeting every twelve years, and taking into account they are done in four different cities, in fact, the celebrations are carried out each three years. The last Kumbha Mela in Haridwar was in 1986 and almost five millions of pilgrims participated, so that the next will be in the year 1998.

After walking through the main street, we visited some temples over the mountain. We made the climb on air-seat and from above, enjoyed the wonderful spectacle of the whole city and the encircling rivers.

There, in Haridwar, the sage Kapila lived, very well known in the Yoga world as the Preclassic *Samkhya* School's founder, one of the six Hindu systems of thought, whose philosophy and teachings took shape in the first post-Christian centuries.

In that city, like in all sacred cities, its inhabitants are absolutely vegetarian, and nobody eats nothing that is not vegetable; eggs, meat, fish, are definitively forbidden, the same as cigarette and alcohol.

111. Ishvara Pranidhana, Swami Krishnananda

After the quick run through Haridwar, we came back to our taxi, to go on the kilometres that were left for the arrival at Rishikesh, place we reached at around two o'clock in the afternoon.

We saw the taxi off and appeared at the Reception. A young and very grave Swami with the renouncer ochre robe and the shaven head, attended to us. After the greetings and finding out our background, he pointed us to leave the luggage there and go to the Ganges to purify ourselves.

He told us that after that, we had to attend the Meditation Room at 5 o'clock in the afternoon, which was presided by Swami Krishnananda, who would decide our stay there (or not...). This monk was temporarily in charge of the Ashram, in the absence of Swami Cidananda, the Director of it, who had been my friend Giovanna's Master, initiated her in Mantra Yoga, and was her first Instructor in Asana Yoga, but at that moment, unluckily, he was on a journey.

We left the Reception, and according to the Swami's advise, walked towards the Ganges; we went the steps or ghats down the river and sat on its bank, where we put our feet in the water; we also washed our faces and hands in the holy river, and I drank some water sips.

Before the appointed time, we came back to the Ashram building and settled down in the Meditation Room. An heterogeneous group from the whole world, Eastern and Western, were already gathering there too.

After a few minutes, an interior door opened and Swami Krishnananda appeared, dressed with the ochre robe and a cloak of the same colour that covered his head and shoulders. He came accompanied by his bed-side doctor, a white Western lady, dressed impeccably with a saree, who seemed to be also his disciple; she overwhelmed him with loving care and looked at him with real devotion.

The aged Swami coughed from time to time and gave the impression of not being in good health conditions. He sat down cross-legged on an arm-chair, in the lotus posture and stayed for more than an hour in perfect stillness, the same as everybody there.

The truth is that neither when coming in nor when leaving, he even wandered his sight towards our sector, and we thought he had not even noticed our presence.

A little disappointed, we went back to the Reception, where we found out we already had his approval to be admitted. As always, "Ishvara Pranidhana" or "Thy Will be done".

Feeling very happy, we filled in some forms and delivered our passports to be checked. Once all the formalities were fulfilled, a young boy was ordered to accompany us uphill, to the building where we would lodge, to take our luggage up.

We climbed long staircases, really tiring (I counted nearly 300 steps). On that building, situated at the highest part of a hill, the foreign visitors were lodged, specially white Westerners.

There, the person who would be our attendant during all the time we would stay as the Divine Life's guests, was waiting for us also : an extremely thin and tall young boy, of wide smile, who during our short stay, did his best to care for us, with absolute dedication and humbleness.

Giovanna and I were very pleased for what, for a time, would be our home, and were sure that the personal experiences which, during the whole voyage, had lightened our hearts, would not be lacking there either.

✷

17

AT THE RISHIS' LAND (RISHIKESH)

112. We Entered "The Divine Life"

Rishikesh was the last step of the journey to India. After three months of travelling through the country, enjoying wonderful and unforgettable experiences each day, of course, the nostalgia already began insinuating, on perceiving in our hearts that the end was close.

With these feelings of sweet melancholia, the days as "The Divine Life Society's" guests were sliding away. That Institution, together with the Ashram and the Yoga Academy, were founded at 1935 by H.H. Sri Swami Sivananda there, in Rishikesh (or Rishis'Land), on the first spurs of the Himalayas and at the banks of the Holy Ganges River, or Ganga, as it is called by Hindus.

Swami Sivananda, great Yogi and Hindu Sage (1887–1963), Professional Doctor, resigned his career and all his wealth very young, to follow the spiritual path and devoted his life to the Service of Humanity and the *Vedanta's* study.

His strength and energy were prodigious, publishing more than 300 books, booklets and journals. The Divine Life Society is dedicated to the ideals of truth, purity, non-violence and self-realization. His prescriptions for the spiritual life are summed up in six simple commands : "SERVE–LOVE–GIVE–PURIFY–MEDITATE AND REALIZE".

At Rishikesh, he trained many exceptional disciples in Yoga and Vedanta, among them Swami Vishnu Devananda, whom he sent to spread the practice of Yoga in the West.

The majority of the most renowned Yoga Masters from India and the whole world, belong to his famous school, in charge of which, as I have said before, Swami Cidananda, another of his disciples, was.

And, in that ancient and very respected Ashram of Rishikesh, Giovanna and I had the luck to be admitted. We were aware of how fortunate we had been, since we knew that many times, persons of international fame, whether in Literature, Philosophy or any other branch of knowledge, had to wait for a long while at hotels nearby, without getting the admission.

Daily, we shared with my "Sister of Adventures" in the faraway India, nearly the same sweet routine : in the morning, meditation at 4.30; Yoga practice at 6, from 7 o'clock, the breakfast, later singing of Bhajans (devotional tunes), Vedanta Philosophy Courses and going hiking by the surroundings up to midday. The afternoon programme was more or less the same.

Lunch and supper always consisted of rice and very hot sauces of greens and pulses. They were cooked by the monks of the Ashram, and after being put into the temple to offer the meal to the Lord (as it is done in every ashram), it was served in the dining room on a piece of banana leaf neatly cut out.

As it is the modality, we took the food sitting down on the floor, and only using the right hand, and shared it with the other persons, Eastern and Western, who were also doing their experiences of life in community.

Sometimes, we only asked for plain rice in the kitchen and ate it in our room, seasoned with dehydrated grated cheese, that we had taken from Argentina. On other occasions, we wanted to give a break to our stomach and went to the other side of the Ganges to eat. We crossed through a slim bridge hanging over the river, that the Government built as a present for that Society, when it celebrated the 50 years of Service to Mankind.

113. The Bridge of Ahimsa (Non-violence)

Along that bridge, the beggars usually lined up to ask for something to eat (with the universal hunger gesture). They whispered with a quivering voice a "Mataji" (Dear Mother), with the humility of their little half-closed eyes, while taking both hands joined over their mouth or their heart.

Below, in the river, a lot of big fish milled about to receive the little pieces of chapati or other food the beggars threw to them, sharing the meal that a moved pilgrim gave them by charity.

Every time I was present at this daily scene, my heart was filled with a tender joy and I could not avoid making the comparison : in the West, people kill fish as a sport, without needing them to subsist. In the East, the Ahimsa or Non Violence is carried to such an extreme, that the persons prefer starvation to death, before opposing this command that for them, is the natural law of life. And it is not necessary to say who would win the confrontation.

As I have told before, the aim to cross the bridge was that on the other side, there was a small village with some bazaars and a restaurant with a showy billboard of "Hindu and Chinese Food". There, beside the super hot local food, almost uneatable for us, some variations of noodles fried on ghee, were also prepared, which, as I have already remarked, is a Chinese dish of sweet-and-sour taste.

I have told before how rewarding it was for us, the fact of being admitted into this Yogic Community. Inside the Ashram, we had access to absolutely everything : house, food, Yoga courses, Philosophy, Sanskrit Language, Music Courses, etc. When we came into "The Divine Life", a little booklet was delivered to us, with the Ashram's activities, with the suggestion to participate on them, what we did really pleased. I am sure that if some people think of entering an ashram just to save money and make free tourism, the second day of stay they receive the invitation to go away.

The Society publishes books in their own printing house and also prepares Ayurvedic Medicine, that is sold in their Pharmacy, and with these resources the Community keeps going, besides the voluntary contributions they receive from their country and abroad, and what visitors can leave them when setting off.

114. Ashram Life

The Divine Life has a section of its buildings on the Ganges : Reception, Printing House, Bookshop, Hospital, Ayurvedic Pharmacy, etc., and the other sector at the front, over the hills, where the monks and candidate rooms, the housing of the families that work there, the Yoga, Music, Sanskrit Academies, the Philosophy classrooms, Temple, Meditation Room, etc., are.

Just on the hill section, at the highest part, the three storey building for foreign guests is located, white Westerner mainly : some like us, that could only pay a short visit, and others, established there for a rather long time, as a young British man, named Alexander, whose room was close to ours, and on one occasion asked us to teach him all the secrets of how to prepare our "mate".

That young man, told us he had decided to stay living there with his Master Cidananda, for personal matters, and he had been lodged at Rishikesh for more than two years, in complete world retirement. There were also Japanese, French, Australian, Italian, German, Finnish, Central, North and South American persons, etc., in short, people from all over the world and with the most varied occupations : artists, philosophers, writers, doctors, psychologists, Teachers of Yoga, of Languages, of History, etc.

The apartment assigned to Giovanna and me within that building, was very comfortable, nothing lacking nor spare; the private bathroom with the well known bucket and jug to pour the water over oneself, and a broad bedroom that opened in the front part, to a sunny and beautiful garden.

From there, we could admire a magnificent scenery; the buildings and domes of the Ashram, the Holy Ganges at the other side of the road, and the first hills of The Himalayas, which on those latitudes, were still covered with a thick forest.

We also had another room, next to the bedroom and with its entrance on the central hall of the building, in which there was a long granite board with a basin, and we could use it according to our needs, as kitchen or laundry.

I have already commented that the young man who attended our edifice, was always alert to our smallest needs, to solve all the problems. Many times when we arrived at the room he wasn't seen anywhere, but if I put the key in the hole and the door wasn't immediately opened, just in seconds he appeared for helping. The same if a drainpipe clogged, or if we required warm water to have a bath; he at once brought a great bucket over and over again.

The last day of our stay at Rishikesh, we took the things we were not going to need any more from our luggage, and offered them to our attendant. He accepted, receiving them very pleased : instant coffee, powdered milk, stocks, dehydrated noodles, argentine grated cheese, towels, steel and plastic receptacles, clothes, etc.; everything was going to end up in his noble and humble hands.

Later, we were already in bed, reading, when we heard somebody softly knocking on our door. What a surprise to see it was the attendant, who took for us rice and pulses inside a small viand for the trip, surely his own supper for that night! Giovanna is right : "No son divino lo Hindúe, Dellia?" (Aren't the Hindus divine, Dellia?).

115. "Namaste, Namaste"

At Rishikesh, it was very easy to keep oneself fit, since several times a day we climbed up and down, hundreds of steps and steep slopes, for going from our place to the Dining-Room, Meditation Hall, Temple, Library, Academies, Samadhi Shrine and the other spots where the different activities of the Ashram took place, and then coming back.

Within there, tame cows were walking through peacefully. Sometimes they stood obstructing the staircase, or any other way, and we had to push them, to make them move on and let us pass. Besides, the monkeys shouting, which the place was full of, and were heard yelling over the trees, added up to the barking dogs that harassed them from the ground.

While climbing and getting down, we always saw a lot of monkeys that made their way along the staircase banisters. From there, once, they caught me offguard, and stole from my hands a bag of oranges that I had bought outside. The fruits were quickly scattered steps down, and right away several monkeys picked them up and vanished in no time at all. Later, they glanced at me from the trees, while finishing off my oranges, as if they were laughing at me! Besides the amusement, this taught me to be more careful from then on and not to take food in sight in the future.

Very near our building, another similar one was being constructed. Very humble Hindus were working on it, and every day, when passing by, I received their respectful greeting : *Namaste, Namaste*, joining both hands over their chests.

Twice a day, at about six in the morning and at 4 in the afternoon, I set off towards the Forest Academy, to take my Yoga classes, which were very important for me, since I had the opportunity to receive this millenary science from its own and genuine source. During my studies in Argentina, I had utilized mostly Swami Sivananda and other Himalayic Masters' texts, and it seemed to me incredible to be physically among his disciples.

I climbed a steep slope that surrounded one of the hills, to arrive at the Yoga room, situated in a rather distant building, which stood out by its reddish colour. Then, I lied among the few persons, most of them Westerners, besides some Japanese, who were generally at their places in the penumbral room, with enough anticipation.

The sessions were very similar one to the other; they always started with the Surya Namaskar (Sun Salutation) for a brief warming up, and went on with the most classical asanas or postures, up to reach the Relaxation and final Meditation.

The classes developed without any kind of music, unlike what we use in our Yoga Centers in Argentina. I understand that the motivations and the inner climate that music springs up, when it is harmonic and fits for its aim, fulfil a therapy function; it pierces the subtle centers of the body and quietens it down deeply, what is known as music therapy.

At the Forest Academy, during the short time I was lucky to assist, the sweet and tuneful voice of the Swami in charge of the classes, gave the instructions to perform the different asanas, as well as the *pranayama* or breathing control, singing them very gently and quietly. With this musical singing, the special atmosphere that those practices required, was created, with which no other motivation was necessary. Besides, the Master never left the classes without thanking the people present for their attendance and blessing everybody.

One morning, before setting off to my classes (which I didn't miss for anything in the world), I had to stop at the building entrance as it was raining and the Academy was rather distant. Some Western ladies lodged in our same building and who also attended the Yoga classes, swiftly passed next to me with large umbrellas, without even realizing that they could share them with me. But the modest bricklayers of the close work in construction did realize, and one of them, without a word, handed me a broad piece of nylon with which, surely, he had protected himself to go to his work that rainy morning. Thank you!

116. "Why do you want a Mantra?"

In this way, our valuable stay at Rishikesh was passing, with some little and sometimes laughing incidents that varied the routine. The days went on calmly, full of peace, of a sweet placidness, with the inner joy to walk those holy spots, on which for thousands of years the sages, saints, rishis or Yogis travelled, leaving their holy aura. We felt those subtle presences in our hearts, that although invisible to the physical eye, filled with a sacred atmosphere even the air we were breathing.

I've already remarked that in those moments and due to Swami Cidananda's absence, Swami Krishnananda was in charge of the ashram. This venerable old man, great Jnana Yogi (from the knowledge and wisdom) and author of several books on Vedanta Philosophy, apart from a wonderful study on the *Bhagavad Gita*, even though of weak health, also made his very powerful vibrations felt, when we shared with him, day after day, the afternoon meditations.

Each day, when with Gio we set out for the Meditation Room, my friend insisted me to ask the Master for a Mantra, specially for me. To receive a Mantra from a guru is as a kind of initiation, since those sacred syllables are only worth if they had been given by a realized spiritual Master, who, in such case, adds his own energy.

It was rather a long time since Giovanna had hers, which had been given precisely by the absent Swami Cidananda. On repeated occasions my friend remarked that, in the circumstance she received it from her Master, the emotional strike had been so great, that she fell on the ground unconscious.

As Swami Krishnananda always looked so grave, almost surly, and he had never spoken to anybody in the Meditation Hall, I didn't dare walk to the front to request it.

Even though I don't consider myself a shy person, this Master Krishnananda did restrain me, and although I fervently wanted to have my own mantra, I postponed my request day after day, as far as the last day of our stay there.

In fact, it was my friend who, let us say luckily, almost pushed me (or not almost) to dare do it; then, I wrote the petition on a sheet torn out of my diary, and with the heart getting out of my breast, I moved forward to deliver it; I also carried some of his books, in order to ask for a dedication.

The Master received my note, and after reading it, raised his eyes and glanced at me, with a look that seemed to me reproachful, while in an unkind tone (always in my opinion), asked me again and again :

— Why do you want a mantra? Why do you want a mantra?

Giovanna always used to remark that when Hindus speak, they throw the words to the speaker as if they were barking, and at that opportunity, I had to agree with her.

I was ashamed to death, exposed to the inquisitive looks of everybody present there. I felt my legs trembling and a burning heat rose in waves up to my face. Surely I violently blushed up to the roots of my hair. With a voice scarcely audible, I don't even know where I took the courage from, I dared myself answer him :

— As a personal gift, Master. (I used the word *Swamiji*)

Swami Krishnananda stared direct and deeply into my eyes. Then, pointing to a bracelet in my wrist, asked me again :

— Why do you want a Mantra, if you already have one?

In fact, during the first days of our friendship, Sajad had given me as a present, a nice bronze bracelet of very little commercial value but really beautiful, with an inscription engraved of Sanskrit hieroglyphics. I had never taken the trouble to find out its meaning. Surely, my "son" had explained it to me, but in those moments I neither cared nor registered it in my mind.

Precisely, it was that same mantra Swami Krishnananda gave me as a present, which he later repeated again with the appropriate pronunciation...

I sighed relieved when his countenance softened, becoming really friendly. He not only signed, but also dedicated for me all the books I had taken. Besides, on announcing him we were going to leave, he put his holy hand over my head and offered me the most wonderful blessing!

117. The Face of Ecstasy

While we were staying at Rishikesh, every night Giovanna and I went together to the Samadhi Shrine, the place where the physical remains of the Institution founder, Swami Sivananda, lied, to join the bhajans singing. It was exactly in that spot, where we had the gift to be witnesses of a moving deed.

Inside that sacred enclosure and about 7.00 to 7.30 in the evening, time it started to darken, people, guests of the ashram, were going to take their places where they please, sitting respectfully cross-legged or as they were more comfortable (never stretching the legs towards the Masters or their pictures), with straight backs and meditative attitude.

Some of them, enjoying bhajans in absolute silence and concentration, and others, who knew the lyrics of those devotional tunes, joined them with their voices and share the "chanting". They were accompanied by a group of *musicians*, formed by some young swamis and candidates, who beated the rhythm with tampuras and other percussion instruments : in this way, the music rose in strength and intensity, up to reach an almost frantic "climax".

As we had lived in the ashram for several days, nearly every day we met the same persons at the Samadhi. Thereby, of course, a mutual liking had been established with some Hindu women, whom we could not talk with, since they didn't speak English, but anyway we exchanged smiles and affection gestures. On many occasions, they invited me with signs to sit down at their sides, and I accepted very pleased.

One of those nights, on taking our places in the pavilion, we observed the presence of an old man, who looked very venerable, with long hair and beard, absolutely white. His disciple had brought him close to Swami Sivananda's shrine to pay a visit and pray there, and later, he was moved on wheelchair up to the place where the singing was.

It was touching to see how his chela looked after him, really with reverence. He constantly adjusted his Master's clothes and lovingly cared for him with all kinds of caresses, since, apparently, the old man was completely paralytic.

The wheelchair was placed almost in front of me : I could observe his honorable countenance from very near; the half-closed eyes while enjoying the music and a just outlined smile of deep bliss. In my imagination, and even though I had never seen the illumination of any person, a face with that expression was the nearest to my idea of ecstasy.

From time to time, the old man opened his eyes halfway and, in a whisper that only his disciple could understand, asked for other bhajans, which were sang like the angels by a Western lady who was in the room and whom, perhaps, he knew.

The lady sang once and again as a soloist, since on raising her voice so masterly, all the others had kept quiet. That female voice transmitted so much sweetness and strength, so much love, so much spirituality, that a very special atmosphere was going to wrap everybody up.

Even though I didn't understand the meaning of all the words, the same I got carried away to the highest summits, at such an extraordinary exaltation that, once more, I experienced a complete harmony with everything created; from the deepest and purest of my feelings, I thank the Creator, for letting me enjoy these wonderful personal experiences.

An intense bliss lifted up in bubbles, from my soul, to burst on the surface of the skin, while the silent gratitude flowed by the intimate rejoicing at those single moments that life, sometimes, offers us, and that I had the luck to share in that holy and revered spot of Rishikesh, at that misterious land of India.

The "climax" prolonged for quite a long time, even though very few actually knew what was happening. At last, everything was over at the Samadhi Shrine and we left the place in silent spiritual absorption. A heavy rain started to fall, and this contributed also to keep an unreal atmosphere, as if we were in another dimension.

Among the phantasmagoric shadows of the trees, faded by the rain, a diligent swami emerged, and accompanied us upwards, to the house, with a powerful flashlight, since the storm had cut off the line that was giving electric current to the narrow alleys, uphill, towards our building.

On thanking him for the trouble he had taken for us, he answered that he had to do it, since many times the rain brought snakes and scorpions! from the near woody mountain, to the street-side.

Giovanna and I remained amazed and dumb. We tried even not to touch the ground with our feet when walking, and each step we did, we wanted to pierce the soil with the eyes fully opened.

When we could articulate a sound, I asked him for the particular person who had created such outstanding atmosphere in the Samadhi Shrine. What a surprise when we were informed he was no less than Swami Vishnu Devananda, one of the favourite disciples of Swami Sivananda, the founder of that Center.

In 1957, his Master had sent him to America, saying :

> "Go, people are waiting. Many souls from the East are reincarnating now in the West. Go and reawaken the consciousness hidden in their memories and bring them back to the path of Yoga"[1]

Swami Vishnu Devananda arrived at San Francisco in 1957 and travelled for several years throughout the United States and the world, lecturing on the millenary science of Yoga. Later, he established an international network of Sivananda Yoga Centers and became one of the foremost exponents of Raja and Hatha Yoga in the whole world. His great personal quality and dynamism, made him also dedicate to the cause of peace and Universal Brotherhood.

Thousands of students were inspired in his numerous ashrams, and many more changed their philosophy of life through his writings. On them, he synthesized the ancient wisdom of Yoga into five basic principles, to provide the foundations of a long and healthy life :

(1) Proper Relaxation,

(2) Proper Exercise,

(3) Proper breathing,

(4) A Proper Diet,

(5) Positive Thinking and Meditation.

1. Lucy Lidell with Narayani and Giri Rabinovitch, "The Book of Yoga" (in his : "Foreword by Swami Vishnu Devananda") — London (England), 1991, page 7 (The Sivananda Yoga Centre).

At those moments, S. Vishnu Devananda, very old and disabled, had asked to be brought from Canada, where he was residing, to the beloved India, to leave his physical body joined to his loved Master of Rishikesh. Later, and always according to his express will, he would be carried upward, to the Himalayas, to the cave excavated on the rock where he used to meditate in his youth.

Every night in India, my friend and I chatted or read up to rather late. We always commented our points of view on the day events or the plans for the next. That such a special night, both of us were in silence, as if each one would keep into the heart and for herself, that wonderful experience, to be brought back again to the mind in the solitude of the bedroom, in the darkness, as another valuable gift of God.

I felt my heart go on beating with an unusual violence and found it hard to induce the sleep : images and sounds came over and over to my mind and intermingled, as if in a kaleidoscope. Then, a large sensation of peace and calmness made me sleep little by little.

Without realizing it, other images sprang into my-unconscious : I could see in complete sharpness, the great shape of Swami Sivananda, all of light, that was sweetly stretching his hands towards his loved and favourite disciple, whom he had rebaptized Vishnu Devananda. And I also visualized the latter, who advanced radiant of bliss towards his Master, with his young body in plenitude and a holy smile in his deep eyes, while the divine bhajans music recreated that delightful and perfect Heavenly Scene.

OM, SHANTI, SHANTI, OM!

*

18

THE RETURN HOME

118. Nostalgia, from the Heart

If I could become aware of the person who had arrived in Bombay three months before, surely I would not associate her with whom was going to leave from the modern Indhira Gandhi Airport, in New Delhi; but the truth was that there we were Gio and me, feeling in our hearts that the voyage to India was coming to an end.

We had already despatched our luggage and there was time enough before the plane's departure. Without enthusiasm even to have a look at the free shops of the Airport, we very silently sat down in a bar where, certainly, each one of us mentally checked all what had happened up to the present.

In the taxi that took us to the Airport, Som Pal had accompanied us, the young Hindu who was in charge of our room cleaning up in the hotel. I constantly told him and his workmates on the floor, Vyjendhar and Sukbhir, that they were "Three Golden Negroes", for their kindness, dedication and absolute humbleness. During all the way, Som Pal, who I don't know when, had grasped one of my hands, squeezed it strongly between his, with his dark eyes watering.

So many and different scenes paraded in my mind : I sharply remembered the wonderful events that had happened since our arrival; faces and more faces sprung over and over, changing the pictures dizzily : the holy persons we had visited, the fascinating experiences we had; our friends, Hindus as well as Muslims, who always gave us their warm affection, and made us feel absolutely cared and protected : the love of Sajad, Assif, Tanveer and the other boys from Puttaparthi, the humble dedication of Ramachandra, my "son's" despair on the farewell, the friendship of Som Pal and his companions...

All and each one of the landscapes travelled through, stored up in the memory, of the personal experiences that overflowed the heart, the fragrances, the musical background at the different sceneries, and always that sense of "already lived, already seen, already experienced"...

At that moment, it became very difficult just to think of coming back to my house, home, to face the thousand and one worries of daily life. Because I asked myself : "Which is really my home, where is my place?". One single and terrible fear seized by breast and it was that the magic would finish and the life reality burst in.

To tell the truth, I was invaded by very contradictory feelings, as if what I had lived in India, my whole experience there, would have a determined purpose. Which would really be God's plans for me, in the future? How would I manage to endure, in my land, that inner climate, when people had mostly other kinds of interests and urgencies? Would it be possible to trap and retain that sacred climate of spirituality which had installed in my soul, that made me feel so well and what I didn't want to resign to, even for a moment? How would it be possible to retake the familiar life and the fulfilment of my duties, while I was already innerly tearing by so deep nostalgia?

Like a sleepwalker I boarded, together with my friend, the plane that would carry us to London. I remember neither the flight, the arrival, the Customs steps, nor the cold day we spent travelling through that great city, before embarking to Argentina.

It only comes to my mind the moment we were sitting at London's Airport. We were whiling away the time in a bar, waiting for the departure, when my friend pointed me out a group of persons, among which some Indian ladies stood out. They were gracefully wearing their elegant sarees, which, as always, showed with a great distinction, and gave the image of slipping among the crowd.

One of the groups settled near our table and I would have

liked to extend a little more my contact with India, to meddle in the conversation for enjoying their closeness; but on sharpening my hearing I could only recognize some "Accha, Accha" (Yes, Yes), in their sweet *Hindi* language.

119. Comparisons...and Contrasts

With the English accuracy, we set off again bound for Buenos Aires. On this flight the Eastern passengers ran out; just white westerners who didn't seem attractive to me any more; after seeing only dark-skinned persons for such a long time, I found my countrymen pale and lifeless, as if they were sick, without neither shine in their eyes nor warmth on their countenances.

In our same enclosure, a group of young Argentine-sportsmen were travelling, of a junior rugby team, whose chats let us know that they had just won in France. The inner climate I had lived in the East, contrasted with the bad manners, of disrespect to others and the typical "Argentine adroitness" of the boys.

Just embarked, one of them placed before the television camera and imitated the gestures of the Survival Programme, which in a little sector of the set, was given for deaf and dumb persons. Later and repeatedly in the trip, they threw a ball to one another, that at several opportunities, run up against the head of off-guard passengers. Also, they called one another shouting, and seemed to have all the same name (b——)[1]

Around them, the plane became a dump : all the trays, napkins, packing, wrapping, bottling, etc., delivered on board, ended up on the floor. I thought : why does it bother me so much if that is the usual behaviour of many of my countrymen, specially when they travel abroad? But the truth after observing the conduct of the "poor Eastern negroes", of extreme respect to his fellow men, to see my people in such attitude made me feel very ashamed. Who do we believe we are?

I could not less than shelter myself again in the nostalgia. My mind brought at lashes the memories of other flights carried out through the interior of India : an atmosphere of peace and silence; only the classical music of the ragas, and the scent of perfumed

1. boludo = dirty word in Spanish.

incenses. Beautiful air-stewardesses who slided silently along the corridors, and let us hear only the silk creaking of their sarees. The only thing that denoted their presence was the trail of their sweet Eastern perfumes which remained floating; and, at performing their duties, it was impossible to take oneself away from the magic of their white and warm smiles and the tenderness of their diligent affection gestures. It still seemed to me that I felt the whisper of their words!

I could just control my indignation to such a lack of consideration, maybe unconscious, when, on nearly arriving at my land, a beautiful, young and very fairhaired stewardess, seemed to read my thoughts : she gently put her white hand over my shoulder, and with a mischievous wink in her ingenuous blue eyes, whispered in my ear as if it were a caress :

— Sai Ram[2]

Smiling, she moved away along the passage... The pronounced words kept on repeating inside me as if it were a prayer, or the Mantra that Swami had given to me at The Himalayas.

I thanked her for that present from my heart. I also regretted the displeasure that the behaviour of my compatriots produced me. Perhaps, at any other circumstance, I also boasted of such "adroitness". And if it were not so, who do I believe I am to judge others?

✷

2. Formula to invoke Sri Satya Sai Baba.

EPILOGUE

The great Eastern sage Krishnamurthi asks himself if "human beings are capable of changing, radically and fundamentally; if we are able to look at the world in a new way, with different eyes, with a distinct heart, not full of antagonism, of racial pre-judgement any more, but with a very clear mind, new, fresh, young, innocent, relieved from its charge, to know what to love and to live in peace mean".

I sincerely believe that it would result impossible for anybody to make a voyage like mine, which was a journey inside and outside, and be indifferent to what has been experienced. As the Hindus say, India is a land to feel more than to see.

I know, I am absolutely sure, that the transformation Krishnamurthi speaks about has already began on me, and that I shall be able to live peacefully and with a great love towards the whole world. I also have the full conviction that, for this, I am going to need a lot of strength, a lot of energy, and therefore, I can't dissipate them in inner conflicts nor conditionings of any kind.

My holy intuition has the absolute certainty that I shall come back to India very soon, and that I'll do it over and over again, whenever I need to recharge my batteries. Many people will ask me : Why? What for?, and I'll answer the same way as Sajad : "To feel better".

It is exceedingly hard to put in plain words, almost unrealizable to express with my poor words, that indescribable nostalgia, that warm "feeling" (as it is now called), that imperative need of going back to the places where I was so happy, to meet again the persons I feel so close to my heart... Maybe, it can be better defined with the lyrics of an old and melancholy tune :

"ONE ALWAYS COMES BACK TO THE OLD PLACES WHERE HE LOVED LIFE..."

OM, SHANTI, SHANTI, OM !

*

GLOSSARY

Ablution	: Action of purifying by means of water. The "ablution" is found in all the Eastern Cults, in some religions as The Jewish (Judaic), Hinduism, Islam, etc.
Acharya	: Master, Spiritual Preceptor. It is used after the name (Ex. Shankaracharya). In Yoga, this title designates whom had attained all the study levels, up to reach the Mastery (Yoga Master). Feminine from Yogacharya : "Yogacharini".
Ahimsa	: Great compassive doctrine (teaching), that is stressed by the Hinduism, Buddhism, Taoism, Sufism, etc. In the Raja Yoga of Patanjali, it is the first of the Yamas, first anga or division (Ethic Restrictions). It means "no killing", no harming, no using violence. In the positive sense, it is LOVE towards all beings, of all the species : human, animal, vegetal, including the environment. It is one of the highest doctrines that leads to spiritual goals. It was the fundamental creed of Gandhi (together with Satya) who, coming from a Jain family, revered Ahimsa as the root-virtue (Jainism, a sect of Hinduism, was founded and widely spread in the 6th Century by Mahavira the "Great Hero"), a contemporary of Buddha.
Akbar (1542–1605)	: "Akbar the Great", famous moghul emperor, who consolidated one of the most

extensive Indian empires. Owner of a great administrative skill, as well as a benevolent nature, and an interest in the Indian Culture and Religion, he was profoundly loved by his subjects.

Amrita : "nectar of the Gods, of Immortality". When it is participated by mortal beings, it awards them with the longevity of hundred of thousands of years, enjoyed by the higher or superior gods. It is said to be produced by yogic practice when, through *pranayama*, it tends to the semen evaporation, and then this great strength rises to come back as "amrita" or nectar.

Ananda : Heavenly Bliss (blessedness); free and full happiness delight, ecstasy, the essential origin of pleasure.

Attachment : selfish and possessive love. One of the "Four Noble Truth" of the Buddhism, refers to it as the main reason of human suffering.

Arati : fire offering; ritual that is carried out to the deities by means of the priests. With this ceremony, it is understood that the evil is burnt and consumed by the fire of wisdom.

Asana : Yoga bodily posture. The word comes from: "A" = towards, to go towards, and "SANA"= health. But in Yoga, health is understood as a perfect stillness state, not disturbed by lust, envy, hatred, jealousy, pride, etc. That is to say Holistic Health (in the three aspects: physical, mental and spiritual). Asana is the third "anga" or division in the Classic Yoga by Patanjali. Each of these "postures" affects different parts of the body, organ, glan, system or energy centre, and has names of animals, plants, nature elements or deities. In spite of being specific bodily positions, they have nothing in common with the traditional gymnastic systems.

Ashram : Yogic Community, a kind of monastery, placed generally at spots separated from the big cities, where disciples usually live, and devotees visit during some time, to be close to their Masters, to carry out the "Sadhana" or psycho-physical-spiritual practice. When gurus are alive, they are the ones who personally guide the teaching, and if they are dead, it is done through their disciples. The Vedic Sages or *Rishis* divide a man's life span into four parts or steps : the first 25 years are devoted to study and preparation; the next 25 years, to family life. After enjoying this step, he must live in an ashram in the forest or in a remote place, where he devotes to meditation and teaching students. In the last years, that is to say the fourth step, he has to renounce to the world and dedicate his life to the Service of Humanity.

Astronomy : In the 3rd Millennium B.C., Hindus were very advanced in this science, which was of great value to decide the favorable dates to carry out certain events. In the Vedas, important astronomic treaties of great scientific value can be found, the same as in the "Kanshitaki Brahman", where the rishis or prophets shaped their wisdom. It is said : "The wise man wins his stars", referring to the reach of these influences, adding : "The fool ones only obey them". No doubt it alludes to the capacity of the human being to manage and check his own destiny, in spite of the adverse influences.

Avatar : (or avatara) : descent, a divine incarnation. "After death, realized beings can choose to incarnate into the physical plane in order to serve Humanity. Ordinary mortals are merely reborn to continue their growth process and do not have the choice of remaining beyond" (Swami Rama, in his "Path of Fire and Light", Vol. II).

Ayurveda : From the Sanskrit "Ayus"= life, and "Veda"= knowledge. Ancient science of life, considered the traditional Medicine of India, with a deeper spiritual base. The old texts say : "Ayurveda is for immortality". Dr. Deepak Chopra upholds that "Ayurveda foments longevity without limits, from the belief that life is immortal". According to Dr. Domar Singh Madariya, from Argentine Ayurvedic Centre of Buenos Aires: "Ayurveda is Mother Medicine, from which all modern medical systems of the world were born. Its history goes back to more than 5000 years, being transmitted from Master to disciple, until arrival of the writing age, period in which two famous doctors, Charak, a clinical and philosopher, and Sushruta, a great surgeon, gave to the world the first treaties of this Medicine. To serve the Lord in the shape of all His Suffering Beings, is the Ayurveda goal, for that reason, its doctors have to be priests inside their spirits, apart from being shrewd psychologist and experienced clinics. For Ayurveda, life is a holistic whole : body, mind, energy and spirit, and the cause of the illness could be in any of the four aspects. The symptoms are not attacked, but the root of the illness, for its definite healing, with natural medicine, neither toxic nor synthetic".

Baba : Hindustani-urdu word, that means "father". Usually, it is used after the name, as courtesy, and not only related to the real father, but also to persons considered outstanding, worth of respect and love. It is an affectionate term for a Holy Man. Also, the negative aspect of Nature. (Babu, related with Baba, means Sir, as a way of addressing a man).

Bhagavad Gita : Fundamental book and Hindu Philosophy source, which contains the essence of Upanishads. Literally : "Singing to the Lord", or the Heavenly Tune; Sanskrit poem considered as the Hindu's *Bible*. It is part of the *Mahabharata*, and has a lot of translations, studies and commentaries by prominent Indian masters. It is about the dialogue that Lord Krishna, one of the most known and revered Gods of India, holds with his disciple Arjuna, before the Kurushetra battle, on how to fulfil the sacred duties of life. This book is considered a Yoga text, since its main teaching is the means to get the liberation.

Bhagavan : Sir, Lord, venerable, saint, holy.

Bhajans : Singing of God's praise. Devotional tunes to a deity, or the Guru or Spiritual Master's praise.

Bindu : Red dot on the forehead, usually of sandal paste, that in spiritual environment symbolizes the "Third Eye" or "Spiritual Eye" opening, in the interior of Ajna Chakra, where the two "nadis" or energy channels end and join together : positive and negative (Ida and Pingala), beginning there the way towards Sahasrara, the 1000 petal lotus, which is opened at Samadhi. The "Bindu" is the Symbol of the Hindu Race and it also represents the married woman, who has transcended sexual life. Nowadays, women, specially the young ones, use it as coquetry.

Bracelet : "Pure metals or its combination, the precious stones or semi-precious, give off an astral light that serves for checking the adverse force of some planets, with their subtle electric and magnetic radiations". For a real protection, they must be used in contact with the skin. For instance, the mixture of silver and lead is recognized by its virtues as liver protector; those made of gold, silver and copper are also valued.

Brindavan (or Vrindavan) : Krishna's house place, in Mathura, called the Jerusalem of India. It is said that there, Lord Krishna "unfolded his glories for the benefit of Mankind". This name is also used as a synonym of "Gardens".

Burials : Even though the Hindus' funeral custom requires the cremation of their corpses, there are occasional exceptions with swamis or other monks or spiritual masters, who are buried, usually in mausoleums or "shrines". Such attitude is because these bodies are symbolically considered to have undergone cremation in the fire of wisdom, at the time of taking the monastic vows.

Body : "Signifies a soul encasement, whether gross or subtle. The senses use the physical body, to dream and visualize the astral body is used; and in the deep sleepiness, thinking and meditation, the causal body is used. The activating power of unfulfilled desires is the root of all man's slavery".

Castes : There are four main castes, besides the sub-castes. (1) Brahmins, the priests cast, spiritually inspired; (2) Kshatriyas : warriors and of governing talents; (3) Vaisyas : business people and (4) Sudras : the ones who serve society through labour. The origin of the caste system, as well as the Justice, comes from the "Writings or Laws of Manu". This great Hindu legislator is worldly respected and his rules are not only for the Hindu Society, but for the kings and the whole world. The *Mahabharata* declares : "Only character and conduct can decide", that is to say that "inclusion in one of these four castes depended originally not on man's birth, but on his natural capacities, as demonstrated by the goal in life he elected to achieve". This goal could be : (1) "Karma", desire, life as identified with the senses (Sudra stage); (2) "Artha": gain, fulfilling but controlling the desires (Vaisya stage); (3) "Dharma": self discipline, the life of responsibility and right action (Shatriya Stage) and (4) "Moksha", liberation, the life of spirituality and religious teaching (Brahmin Stage). The four castes render service to Humanity by : (1) body; (2) mind; (3) will power and (4) Spirit. Profound Western thinkers like Nietzche have admired the Indian Caste System, by considering it as preventive or check against license, or the so-called liberty or liberality, that has preserved the purity of the race through millenniums. The Guru will be able rightly to determine a man's caste or evolutionary status. When this system is criticized, generally by persons who don't know the Hindu idiosyncrasy, they defend themselves by assuring that "to a certain extent, all races and nations observe in practice, if not in theory, the features of caste".

Ceremonies : Singing of ancient hymns, with flowers, water and fire offerings, symbol of the body elements and their liberation in the Infinite Source.

Conscience (Divine) : Superior state, in which "the inspiration, the or Super-conscience genius and the moral values are produced". It is the quality that mystics refer to, specially Sri Aurobindo.

Chaitannya : Of divine nature.

Cows : The cow and its protection was a passion of Gandhi, being obvious to him that the ancient rishis would have selected the cow to worship. According to him : "The cow in India was the giver of plenty; not only did she give milk, but she also made agriculture possible. It is a poem of pity, such a gentle animal. She is the second mother to millions of mankind. Protection of the cow, means protection of the whole dumb creation of God. The appeal of the lower order of creation is all the more forceful, because it is speechless". The first daily ritual in India, the offering of food to the animal kingdom, symbolizes man's readiness to succour the weak, as he in turn is comforted by countless solicitudes of higher unseen beings. The evolutionary barriers of incommunicability among Nature, animals, man and astral angels is thus overcome by offices of silent man".

Chakras : "Wheel or circle". According to Kundalini Yoga, it refers to life energy or consciousness centers, located within the spine, the tickling of which raises and is perceived as an electric overwhelming sensation, when the prana or vital energy flows. This sensation can be felt during the Yogic practice, specially in the deep Relaxation and during Meditation.

Chanting : The moment when the devotees meet for the devotional singing.

Chapatis : Indian bread, round and flat, made with wheat flour and water, without yeast, which is usually cooked on an iron plate, placed over a flame heater. Finally it is passed through the flame, to get some little burnt lumps, procedure that seems to make them more digestible.

Chela : Name applied to a disciple, who usually lives in an ashram with his guru or Spiritual Master. This one is concerned with the intellectual and spiritual education of his protected, receiving on the other hand the young disciple's devotion of his life. "Chela derives from "to serve".

Chinars : Western banana tree; tropical plant very common in India, specially in the South.

Darshan : "Divine sight or vision''. Blessing received by devotees, just at the sole presence of the Spiritual Masters, and which flows from them. In the Ashram Prashanti Nilayam, in Puttaparthi, this name is given to the moment when, daily and twice a day, Sai Baba leaves the temple or Mandhir and walks through his faithful.

Dharma : Sanskrit word, that means "Law", understood as the natural righteousness. The Scriptures define "Dharma" as "the Natural Universal Laws, the observance of which enables man to save himself from degradation and suffering".

Dhobi : Laundryman; male person whose task is to wash clothes, work that is usually performed in the river, striking the clothes against the rocks.

Disciples (Western) : From distant times already, there were in India some Western disciples, famous for their noble birth, like Miss Madeleine Slade, called "Mirabai" or "Mira Behn" by her Master, who, daughter of a known English Admiral, became Gandhi's disciple for more than 20 years. Later, she founded her own ashram near the Himalayas, in order to give hygiene help and agriculture teaching to the humble villagers. Another distinguished Western Disciple, was Miss Margaret Woodrow Wilson, the eldest daughter of the President of the United States. She established at Pondicherry, following the spiritual path at the feet of Sri Aurobindo Ghosh, the illuminated Master of Integral Yoga.

Durga : Goddess Durga, "The Inaccessible", one of the aspects of the Shakti or Divine Mother, who symbolizes the personification of the creative force. An important Indian feast, where cult and offering are paid to this Goddess, is the "Durga Puja".

Education : According to Rabindranath Tagore, "The education must not limit itself to develop the intellect, but also the body, the will power and the feelings, able to solve the complex problems of existence, and thus, peace and good will may reign on earth. A school based on common sense and free from mysticism".

Fakir : Literally "poor". It is specially applied to Muslim Yogins, who make poverty vows. They acquire fame by exhibiting their skill in difficult acrobatic Yoga postures, which require a complete power of the physical body and great mental concentration

Flag : (of India) : It was designed by Mahatma Gandhi in 1921. Its colours are saffron, white and green, with three equal horizontal stripes. The "chakra" or spinning wheel in the centre, dark blue, is used in humble homes to spin the fleece of "khaddar" or home-cotton. According to Gandhi, the "chakra" symbolizes energy and reminds us that during the former prosperity ages of Indian History, hand-spin and other domestic professions were prominent.

Gandhi : Complete name Mohandas Karamchand Gandhi. Politician Saint, statesman, who victoriously faced thousands of social, legal and political battles. His followers called him "Mahatma" or Great Soul, even though he never referred to himself with that nickname. Of small body (only 45 kgs.), reduced even more during his long fasting periods, and with a clever shining in his eyes, showing sincerity and discernment. He usually dressed just with a loincloth, as a symbol of unity with the trampled masses who can't provide themselves with other clothing. He had a great influence in the fight for India's Independence, using as creed just the Ahimsa or Non Violence and Satya or the Truth.

Gayatri : Sacred mantra to the Divine Mother.

Ghee : Clarified butter, the essential ingredient in the Hindu diet during the practice of the strong pranayamas.

Fat Persons : As Indians are mostly of slim structure, a reasonable fatness is their ideal, and it is considered something beautiful. There is even a saying about it : "to be happy it is necessary to be fat".

Finger Eating : According to a known Hindu master, about this custom of India : "the Lord has given us the fruits of the good earth. We like to see our food, to smell it, to taste it. The Hindus like also to touch it. One doesn't mind "hearing it" either, if no one else is present at the meal!".

Guru : Literally "the one who dispels the darkness of ignorance" and reveals the path to divinity to his students, carrying them from obscurity to light. It is the name given to Spiritual Masters. "Gurudeva", from the same family, is the name that disciples give to their teachers with great respect and reverence, meaning "The Divine Master", the bright Being.

Guru Nanak : (1469–1538) the founder of Sikh Religion, born in Punjab, near Lahore. He devoted his life to consolidate this doctrine, giving a lot of lectures and sermons. The main topic of his creed was the opposition to the caste system and the division between Hindus and Muslims.

Ham-sa : "I am He", a reference to the Universal Spirit. It is the prayer constantly and unconsciously repeated by every being, during the incoming and outgoing of the breath.

Hanuman : "That of strong jaws". Powerful chief of monkeys, owner of an extraordinary strength. He was the perfect servant of Lord Rama, son of Arjuna and Vayu, the God of the wind. The execution of his feats are told in the epic poem *Ramayana*, by Tulsides.

Hatha Yoga : The realization of the Being, through a severe physical body discipline, awakening its sensitiveness to transform it in a "divine body", "rainbow body" or "body radiant of glory". The term "Hatha" means strength, power, faculty. It is also the joining of : "HA"= sun and "THA"= moon, as the electro-magnetic fusion of the positive and negative forces within the human being. The principal tools for this transmutation of the coarse physical body are asana and pranayama. Even though it refers to the physical body, it must not be thought as a kind of gymnastics. All the paths and Yoga Methods, without exception at all, search for the man's emancipation and his realization.

Himalayas : They are considered sacred mountains, as every natural phenomena. According to Nicolas Roerich, Leon Tolstoy's friend, writer and philosopher who lived many years in India, near these mountains : "From its peaks come revelation. Inside the caves and over its summits live the

	rishis. Over the snow covering Himalayan peaks, a golden shining is glimpsed, more brilliant that the stars and than the fantastic twinkle of the lightning".
Hindi	: Hindu-aryan language, common in the whole North of India, derived from Sanskrit roots. It is the official tongue at colleges, being its main dialect the Hindustani, and also the Urdu spoken by Muslims.
Hinduism	: The majority religion of India, practised by more than 80 per cent of the population. It derives from the impersonal Vedic Scriptures, which apart from teaching devotional practices, it regulates all important social customs, etc., to bring these actions into harmony with the divine law. Its Gods are : Brahma, Vishnu and Shiva, the Three that constitute the One, with many names, according to their diverse manifestations.
Intuition	: Sanskrit "Agama", inner protection, soul guidance. Intuitive knowledge, means that it springs straightly from the soul's perception. It is the sixth sense that perceives the sensations by any channel of the body.
Ishvara (or Ishwara)	: From ISH = to rule, guide, govern. Lord God, regent of the Universe, inspiring model of the Yogi. The triple manifestation of Creator, Preserver and Destroyer. "Dynamic aspect of Brahma, the highest Guru, source of all knowledge and Wisdom". (Walter Gardini). According to the Indian Scriptures, the One, the Deity, is designated with 108 names, each one of them representing his different philosophical aspects.
IShvara Pranidhana	: The last of the five Niyamas, obligations, rules or disciplines for the self-purification. It means to surrender oneself to the divine

will, devoting our whole deeds and will to the Lord.

Japa : Repetition of the Mantra or divine name, like the Rosary of Christians. The Japa Mala is used for such aim, a kind of rosary with 108 beads, which is usually made of seeds of "rubraska", sandalwood, crystal balls, etc., each one of them is passed with certain fingers, while repeating the invocation.

Kailasa : In accordance with the Mythology, it is Lord Shiva's dwelling, over one of the peaks of the Himalayas.

Kali : Goddess Kali is the divine symbol in its female aspect. Eternal Mother of Nature, of terrifying aspect; she is pictured as a four-armed woman, being the four arms, the symbol of her cardinal attributes: two beneficent, of kindness, and two maleficent or destructive, showing thus the essential duality that takes place in the whole creation.

Karma : Law of cause and effect, by which each action generates a reaction, that is again the cause of new actions. It is one of the Laws in the Hinduism Doctrine, also found in other religions. Definitely, it would be the good or bad result of the deeds registered in this life or before, on previous incarnations. "All human wish must find satisfaction. The desire constitutes the chain that fastens man to the reincarnation wheel".

Kashmir : Northern Indian state, considered one of the most beautiful places on earth, the same as their inhabitants.

Krishna : "The Brown, who irresistibly attract". The eighth incarnation of God Vishnu, whose descent to the world came about to lighten man from sin and evil. The history of his life and spiritual teachings, are told in the *Bhagavad Gita.*

Kumbha Mela : Religious fairs, realized in India from immemorial times (they were already mentioned in the *Mahabharata*), with spiritual aims. Besides world-wide pilgrims on the spiritual search and Hindu devotees, thousand of fakirs, sadhus, yogis, swamis and all kinds of ascetic hermits gather there, leaving for the moment their hidden retirements to, on this feast, concede their blessing to the crowd. Many devotees state that there, in the Ganges River, "it is the opportunity to feel the pulse of the nation and the spiritual ardour" in the purification symbols. "Solemn rituals of worship are performed, devotional offerings are strewn at the feet of silent sannyasis; naked sadhus who wave gold and silver sceptre, flags and pennants that show their origin and the group to which they belong, their bodies besmeared with ashes and the spiritual eye (the third eye) painted by a single spot of sandalwood paste on their forehead, with the hair braided and massed in coils on the top of their heads, and the long white beards, curled and tied in a knot. Shaven headed swamis with the ochre robe, each one carrying a bamboo staff and begging bowl, and the rubraska necklace in their necks. All the faces beamed with inner peace."

Lotus : Beautiful and scented flower, which grows in the mud, usually of white colour (there are also pink and red ones). It is an ancient divine symbol in India, and represents the spiritual search of the human being, up to reach the expansion of the soul. Its growth from the mud suggests that even though man's origins are dark, there is always the chance to rise in search of the light and become a pure flower, that expands its beauty and perfume.

Maharaja : Title given to some Hindu princes. From "maha" = big, large, great, and "raja" = royal, prince. "At the South of India, the Maharaja assumes every year a hereditary obligation to expiate the sins originated by wars. For fifty-six days, annually, he visits the temple thrice daily, to hear Vedic Hymns and recitations; the expiation ceremony ends with the "Lakshadipam" or illumination of the temple by a hundred thousand lights."

Mahabharata : Together with Ramayana, they are the epic poems, the sacred Hindus' books, real treasures of History, Mythology and Philosophy of that country.

Maharishi : From "maha" = great, and "rishi" = grand spiritual seer. This name is given to the great illuminated, enlightened sages or prophets.

Mahasamadhi : Term used for the Final Meditation, when a spiritual master "knows beforehand when the final hour is about to strike for the physical body and merges himself in the Cosmic Aum (OM). It is also called Great Samadhi. Thrice revolving the body, then, facing the North, are parts of a Vedic rite used by them".

Máma (or Mother) : It is usual in India to call Máma (mother) to women, when it is considered that their age is older than the speaker's. "Máam" is an other meaning for Madam, used by a servant to his lady (mistress), or by a shop-keeper to their woman customers.

Mantra : From "Man" = to think, and "tra" = instrument, tool, that is to say, the Instrument of Thought. It signifies "the ideal, inaudible sounds which represent one aspect of Creation", and they are mostly used during religious ceremonies, being "potent vibratory chant, which when vocalized as syllables constitutes a universal terminology. The infinite powers of sound are derived from "Aum", the "word" or creative hum of the Cosmic Motor". According to Swami Rama, from the Himalayas, "Mantra is a set of syllables, sounds or words, received from the teacher during the initiation, for meditation and spiritual advancement.

Marriage : It was, and it is still nowadays, a custom in India, that the parents of any religion, choose their son's wife within the same caste, group or sub-caste. There is a belief that marriage among persons of different groups or religions, weakens the race, being their offspring compared to a barren hybrid kind like the mule, which is incapable to propagate its species, with what it would reach the extermination of these artificial types. Generally, the sons and daughters accept their parents' choice pleased; if it were not so, they would become discasted, persons of the lowest rank in the social scale, whom no group offers protection. Besides, it seems that with this behaviour of the family election, the percentage of happy and successful marriage is very high.

Mataji : "The Holy Mother". In North India, it is used to name adult women, as a sign of humility and respect.

Materialize : Yogic power that consists of transforming the energy into matter, that is to say, to create from nothing from spiritual hidden levels. These powers are shown by some self-realized Masters, who possess complete Oneness with the Creator.

Mauna : Spiritual silence. Time for inner and exterior

silence, in which it is not expressed a single word. Mahatma Gandhi observed it every Monday of the year, the same as many of his followers. (The person who practices it receives the name of "Muni")

Mecca : The birthplace of Mahoma (570 A.D.), the Islam Prophet. It is considered the "Holy City of the Muslims", one of whose five duties in life is to carry out a pilgrimage to this city. The Muslims, all over the world, focus their little carpet facing the Kaaba, the famous shrine placed there, the Prophet's Sanctuary, to perform the *Namaz*.

Meditation : Or Dhyana, the seventh anga or division on the Ashtanga Yoga by Patanjali. This technique is preceded by the retraction of Senses (Pratyahara) and deep concentration (Dharana), having to dominate the body anxiety before, by means of relaxation. There are several techniques of Meditation, through which the Masters teach how to solve the problems of life. A Persian proverb says : "Seek the Truth in the Meditation, not in the Sacred Books. Look at the sky to find out the moon, not in the pool."

Miracle : "Effortless command over Nature. When the Self is in communication with the Superior Power, Nature obeys man's will". There is also a saying about it: "The man who can't wonder and worship is but a pair of spectacles behind which there is no eye".

Namaste : A mixture of greetings and welcome, used specially in North India, joining hands with the palms together, over the heart.

NAMAZ : The principal prayer among Muslims, repeated five times a day, knelt on the little carpet for this purpose, facing the Mecca.

Niyamas : The second of the eight steps of Classic Yoga by Patanjali. They are five rules of self-discipline to harmonize the relation of the yogi with the Transcendental Reality (or Truth). They are: Sausha or Purity; (2) Santosha or Contentment; (3) Tapas or Austerity; (4) Svadhyaya or Self Study, and (5) Ishvara Pranidhana, or the Surrender of Oneself to the Divine Will.

Om : The most sacred syllable, the first sound of the Almighty. From it, all the others emerge, either of language or music. In the Upanishads, this sacred syllable appears as a mystic sound, and it is considered as the base, the inner essence, of all the other sacred mantras. "Meditation on Om is of great vibratory power and it satisfies all the needs, reveals the truth and leads to liberation". It is the first letter in the Sanskrit Alphabet and the symbol of the Hinduist Religion. The old seers found out the relation between the sound of nature and man. By means of OM, the control over natural manifestations can be acquired, through certain mantras and devotional songs. Om is considered as the manifestation of the Holy Ghost; Masters say that the whole Universe fits inside the OM.

Padha Namaskar : Gesture of humbleness; rite consisting of touching the Holy Masters' feet, either with the forehead, hands or lips.

Paramahansa : From "Param" = the highest, & "Hansa"= swan, Brahma's vehicle, the Supreme Spirit, the First Person in the Hindu Trinity. Han-Sa is also a natural mantra related with the incoming and outgoing of the breath through the nostrils.

Patanjali : Great sage whom the Raja Yoga is awarded, also called Classic Yoga, Patanjala

Yoga and Ashtanga Yoga (The Yoga of the 8 steps). It is one of the most diffused Yoga Systems in the whole world, and was compiled in the so called "Yoga Sutras" (or Aphorism of Yoga), being the last aim, "the control of the mind fluctuation" as a means to reach Samadhi. There is no agreement about the exact period in which this wise man lived, including period of probability between the Centuries second to third B.C. up to second or third A.D.

Paths or Tracks : The four ancient paths of Yoga by means of which the last goal or Samadhi is achieved, are : Bakti, or devotion to a deity, or to the Guru; Jnana : knowledge of the Scriptures and self-knowledge; Karma : or unselfish work, without waiting for its fruits, and RAJA YOGA or the "checking of the whirlwind of the mind".

Prana : Creative intelligent strength, bio-electricity or cosmic universal energy. It is the most subtle shape of biological energy, present in all the physical and mental deeds. It flows from the spirit or pure consciousness, to penetrate of cleverness and conscience all the aspects of life. It is also defined as vital force or life energy. It is the "Chi" of the Chinese and the "Ki" of the Japanese.

Pranayama : The science that studies the checking and conscience of the vital energy or Prana, through breathing. It is the fourth anga or division in the Raja Yoga of Patanjali and one of the most important techniques of Hatha Yoga.

Prasad : Blessed or divine Gift. It refers generally to food, which is usually offered to God first.

Pronam : "Holy name". It is the Hindu word of greeting, with the hands joined over the heart, raising them up to the forehead. It is a gesture of homage and could correspond to the hand shaking of the Westerners.

Rabindranath Tagore : Exquisite Bengal poet, founder of the famous school "Santiniketan" or Port of Peace, at Boldir. His concepts over children and education are mentioned in this work. After the 60 years of age, he made an incursion on Painting, and he took this new art with great enthusiasm.

Ragas : The most known ancient and important classic Hindu music. Its melodic fixed scales are basically six, which are subdivided into 126 derived ones, called "ragins" (or wives) and "putras" (or sons). Each raga consists of a minimum of five notes, a main one or "vadi" (the king), a secondary one or "samavadi" (the first minister), "anuvadi notes" (assistants) and a discording note "vavadi" (the enemy). Each one of the basic ragas is corresponded to certain time of the day, season of the year and deity, who concedes its attribute, always summoning or evoking Universal Love, Compassion, value, calmness, etc. There is also an association of each one of the musical notes, with a colour and with a bird or beast shout. On the basis of such fixed notes, the Hindu musicians use their exquisite sensibility to create an infinite number of improvisations : it is not used to read the music, but the fixed structure is delicately broached up to the limits of its originality. The main eagerness of musicians is to unite the artist with the Cosmic Tune or Universe Sound, not looking for the brightness of the performance but giving preference to his personal harmony.

Rama : One of God's names; central personage of the epic poem "Ramayana", considered the seventh incarnation of Vishnu. Lord Rama and his wife Sita, are considered as models of "Dharma", the perfect spouses. Their Guru is the sage Vasishta, whose teachings are compiled in the Vasishta Yoga.

Ramadan : Fasting time of Muslim, that consists of abstaining along a whole month, from eating, drinking and having sexual relations during the day up to sunset. It is also recommended to refrain, during meals, from all vain speech, and from any reading except the *Koran*. All along this period, a lot of prayers and visits to the mosque are achieved, to pray and sing Allah's glories, culminating with a great feast.

Ramakrishna : (Paramahansa) (1836-1886). A great Bengal Saint, who worshipped the Lord in the shape of Kali, the Divine Mother. He was the spiritual Master or Guru of Swami Vivekananda, and the founder of the Ramakrishna Order of Swamis or monks.

Refuse Food : The Indian hospitality is one of the features that characterize them, known in the whole world. To refuse an eating invitation is considered an absolute rudeness and lack of respect.

Religions : In India, there is a great tolerance in religious matters, and it is very usual to find, together with the Hindu Gods, other religions' prophets, as Lord Budha, Jesus, Zoroastrus, Mahavira, etc. Gandhi perfectly defined this aspect, when he declared : "I believe the *Bible*, the *Koran* and the *Zend-Avesta* (the sacred Scripture given to Persia by Zoroaster about 1000 B.C.), to be as divinely inspired as the Vedas... Hinduism is not an exclusive religion. In it there is room for the worship of all the prophets of the world. Hinduism tells each man to adore God, according to his own faith or *dharma*, and so it lives in peace with all religions."

Rickshaw : A kind of covered motor scooter, of three wheels, which is the cheapest and most practical way used in India and other Eastern countries for the transport of passenger.

Rishis "Illuminated sages", usually with Yogic powers or Siddhis. The saint, Seers, authors of the Vedas and the Upanishads are designated with this name. It would be equivalent to other religions' prophets.

Rites (or Rituals) : "Beside the first Indian rite that consists in the food offering to the animal reign, there are other two : to the ancestors ("Pitriyajna"), whose wisdom lights up man nowadays, and the food offering to the poor and the foreigner ("Nri Yajna"), symbol of man's responsibilities and duties to his contemporary mates". About this last rite, there is a very common saying in India which is particularly true : "The Guest is God".

Sadhana : "Spiritual Path that conveys to God". In the yogic practice, it refers to the physical, mental and spiritual exercises to reach illumination.

Sadhus : Renouncing ascetic, who are found usually along the roads, walking completely absorbed, with his crooks (a stick with a bent end) and the Kamandalu, a chipped bowl to beg rice. They are also commonly found near the temples, ashrams and pilgrimage places, practising the "Sadhana" or spiritual discipline. The other Hindus generally respect, revere... and feed them.

Sai : Feminine aspect of the Universe.

Samadhi	:	The last yogic step and final goal of all the methods, ancient and modern, of Yoga. In the Raja Yoga by Patanjali, it is the eighth and last division. At this step, the individual Soul joins with the Infinite Spirit. Literally, it means: "lead together". Samadhi is determined as a state of deep ecstasy, in which one becomes aware of the identity of the spirit. It would be equivalent to the Nirvana of Buddhism.
Samadhi Shrine	:	The sepulcher of a Yogi's body, used as a place of worship and spiritual exercise, since it is considered that it becomes impregnated with the spiritual power of the one who lies there.
Samkhya	:	One of the six school of thought in the Indian Philosophy, of Pre-Classic lineage. The others are : Nyaya, Vaisheshika, Yoga, Mimansa (Purva) and Vedanta or Uttar Mimansa. Samkhya teaches the emancipation by means of the knowledge of 25 principles or aphorisms.
Sanathan Dharma	:	Literally "eternal religion", name given to the Vedic Teachings. The Greeks were the ones who in the beginning called it Hinduism, to designate the people on the banks of the Indus River, as Indoos or Hindus.
Sanskrit		The most ancient Indo-European tongue and the language of the Yogic Scriptures. Its alphabet of 50 scripts is considered of a mathematical and psychological perfection, owning a very abundant literature on philosophy and spirituality. It was not the language of the common people, but of the priestly caste (Brahmins) and the hymn composers. "Who knows my Grammar, knows God", said Panini, the great philologist of ancient India.

Sanyasin : Or renouncer, person whose only objective is the spiritual realization. Usually they wear the ochre robe and shaven head.

Sari or Saree : Costume worn by Indian women, since ancient times, which falls down along the body according to an established model, about turns, pleats, positions, etc.

Sarva Dharma : Stupa or column, containing the badges of the main religions, as a symbol of oneness. Inside Prashanti Nilayam, Sai Baba's Ashram in Puttaparthi, it has a predominant place, meaning that man may realize God following any of these paths

Sat-Sanga : From "Sat" = Being, hence Essence, Reality, and "Sanga" = association; the meetings where any spiritual experience is shared is designated with this name. "Fellowship with the Truth".

Satya : "The Truth", one of the five Yamas or Ethical Rules from Ashtanga Yoga by Patanjali, which was taken by Mahatma Gandhi as a banner, together with "Ahimsa" or Non-violence. The Scripture declares : "Who tells the truth, will have the power to materialize its words, since the commands that are pronounced with the heart, will become real in life".

Satyagraha : The eleven vows to be observed in a spirit of humility by Gandhi's followers, in a movement that shook up to the roots, the British domination : (1) Non-violence, (2) Truth, (3) Non stealing, (4) Celibacy, (5) Non-possession, (6) Body labour, (7) Control of the palate, (8) Fearlessness, (9) Equal respect for all religions, (10) Swadeshi (use of home manufactures) and (11) Freedom to the Untouchables.

Shanti : Peace; it must be repeated thrice, for the three entity : body, mind and soul. It also means "Sweet Presence" or stillness of the mind.

Shiva : "The God", the Third Person in the Trilogy of Hinduism. Lord or Sir Shiva, is designated in the Scriptures as the "King of Yogis". In the Mythology, Shiva is the Lord of Renouncers, who appears in front of devotees under different aspects or manifestations, just as Mahadeva ("The Great God"), the long-haired Ascetic, Nataraya, the Cosmic Dancer, etc. Shiva is represented by several ways, but the characteristics which distinguish him are : the tiger skin seat, several cobras around his neck and shoulders, the long and matted hair tied up in a shock at the top of his head, the crescent moon, the holy river Ganga (Ganges) falling down from his head and flowing by his side, the trident as a power symbol, the sacred bull as his carrier, the beggar bowl, the vertical third eye, etc. When he is represented riding over his bull Nandi, his whole body is covered with ashes, and symbolizes the yogi who has burnt all his bad wishes, purifying in the ritual fire. In fact, Shiva represents the whole cyclical process of Creation, up to Destruction and Renovation or Regeneration. The best known aspect, even to Westerners, is as Nataraya (or Nataraja), God of the Cosmic Dance, trampling the dwarf Avidya, that represents Ignorance, surrounded with the cremation fires

Shivaratri or Mahashivaratri : Feast in honour of Shiva, in which the devotees sing sacred hymns at the temples all night long.

Siddhis : Great powers possessed by the wise Yoga Teachers, called Rishis or Seers. Such attributes let them, for instance, see, hear, taste, smell and feel the Oneness of Creation, without using the sense organs.

Sikh : Member of a military community from Punjab, established in the 16th Century. Also the religious group who follows Guru Nanak's Teaching, who are outstanding for wearing great turbans. It is considered the Indian fighting group, even though they declare to be people lovers of peace, who only fight to banish injustice.

Snake (Cobra) : In India it is the symbol of mystery and wisdom. In the Kundalini Yoga, the serpent represents the energy slept at the base of the spine, coiled up thrice and a half, and with the tail closing the mouth. This energy is awakened by means of Yoga practice, Pranayama or breathing control, the Bandhas or keys, etc. In the human body, the spine represents the Life Tree, and the energy rolled up at the base of the spine excites the sexual nerves. According to the Bible, God forbade Adam and Eve to enjoy the fruits of the tree, referring to sensations, being the apple the centre or "the midst", the symbol of sex. Here, also, the polarity is "Adam" as reason and Eve as feelings. "The divine man first made by God, had its consciousness outered in the omnipotent single eye in the forehead : all the creative powers of his will, focused at that spot, were lost when he began to cultivate his physical nature".

Sri : Sir, Lord, saint, pure. It is usually placed in front of the Great Hindu Master's names, as a title of deep respect.

Suffering : Mental, physical and spiritual, which are showed like illness, psychological disorders, complexes and spiritual ignorance.

Swami : Monastic order of India. It literally means "He who is one with his Self". This title is similar to "reverend" of other religions. Usually, at completing a certain step of the training as a monk, the disciple receives a new name from his guru, which in some way symbolizes his virtue, or well, any outstanding feature of his personality. The ending "ananda" is added to this name, what means "supreme bliss", or "to attain the supreme blessing through the divine state", being precisely this "divine union" the goal of Yoga. The new swamis take vows of poverty, chastity and obedience to his Master or Spiritual Authority, being his ideal the selfless service to all Mankind, or Karma Yoga. They keep the precept of Human Brotherhood besides, and renunciate to personal ambitions and ties with the world.

The initiation ceremony is called "Bibidisa" and also "Fire Ceremony", with symbolical funeral rites, "which represents the dead physical body of the disciple, cremated in the flame of wisdom". After being rebaptized, the newly made Swami is then given a chant, such as "This Atma is Brahma" (This Soul is Spirit), and the new swamis answer : "Ham-Sah" (I am He).

Swamiji : Suffix "Ji" is used in India in the personal dealing with Masters and other adult persons, as a sign of respect, love and worship. "Mataji" "Gandhiji", "Guruji", "Swamiji", etc., are commonly heard.

Tampuras : Musical beating instrument, used to accompany religious singing.

Thali : Tray where the typical Indian dish is served : rice in the center and bowls with stew around it, made with greens and pulses, and seasoned with many spices.

The Third Eye : Only Eye or "Spiritual Eye". It is also called "The Eastern Star", "The Inner

Eye", "Shiva's Eye", "The Intuition One", etc. It is situated in the forehead, in the frown, and it is Ajna Chakra, the clairvoyance. In deep Meditation it becomes omniscient, that is to say, of the complete or Infinite Knowledge.

Upanishads : Also called "Vedanta" or the end of Vedas. "These are sacred spiritual treatises which weren't written by one author nor belong to one particular period. They are spread over several hundreds of years and issued from many authors. In fact, they are the sermons given by the Spiritual Teachers to the students who approached them to learn Brahma Vidya, the knowledge of Brahma. They are dialogues between the teachers and the taught. There are above 200 Upanishads, but only those commented upon by Sri Shankaracharya, are regarded as authentic. These are eleven. The Upanishads contain the essence of Vedas. The Vedanta Philosophy is mainly based on them. Every verse of these Scriptures contains lofty, sublime and original thoughts, which are the revelations of self-realized sages and the Rishes" (First Steps to Higher Yoga, by Sri Yogeshwar and Paramahans-Yoga Niketan Trust-Bharat-India).

Vedanta : "End of Vedas". One of the six orthodox school of Indian Philosophy, founded by Badarayana. It arose by the discussions over Upanishads about the Nature of the Being, and a part of these books were systematized by Shankaracharya (see "Upanishads").

Vedas : Literally "knowledge". They are the four sacred more ancient books of India, distributed in about 100 volumes. They are considered of divine inspiration : *Rig Veda*, *Sama Veda*, *Yajur Veda* and *Atharva Veda*.

To refer to this scriptures, Emerson said : "It is sublime as heat and night, and a breathless ocean. It contains every religious sentiment, all the grand ethics which visit in turn each noble poetic mind (...) Eternal necessity, eternal compensation, unfathomable power, unbroken silence (...) This is her creed. Peace, and purity and absolute abandonment..."

Vibhuti : Sacred ashes, that Sai Baba from Puttaparthi, and other Masters, often materialize for their devotees. They symbolize the last reality that remains when the slag of the ego is burnt by the fire of illumination.

✠

Note : This Glossary was made, partly, in accordance with my knowledge as Yoga Master, and the rest, with the information gathered in the Libraries of some Ashrams that I have visited. Also, consulting some Masters and people in general, as well as from my personal experiences. Likewise, I transcribe (between quotation marks) some definition, or part of them, taken from the book "Autobiography of a Yogi", by Paramahansa Yogananda, published in India by Jaico Publishing House — 121, Mahatma Gandhi Road, Fort, Bombay-400 023, an authorized publication of Yogoda Satsanga Society of India — Self Realization Fellowship — Tenth Impression 1992. I constantly use this work as a teaching source, for considering it the most reliable book about this subject, and which most influenced me in the knowledge and admiration of India, this wonderful country, its customs and its people. Thank you very much !